SELF-LEARNING MANAGEMENT SERIES

VIBRANT
PUBLISHERS

MACHINE LEARNING ESSENTIALS

YOU ALWAYS WANTED TO KNOW

A Beginner's Guide to Machine Learning with
Hands-on Coding and Real-World Applications

DHAIRYA PARIKH

MACHINE LEARNING ESSENTIALS YOU ALWAYS WANTED TO KNOW

First Edition

Published by Vibrant Publishers LLC, USA, www.vibrantpublishers.com

Paperback ISBN 13: 978-1-63651-377-5
Ebook ISBN 13: 978-1-63651-378-2
Hardback ISBN 13: 978-1-63651-379-9

Library of Congress Control Number: 2025930696

This publication is designed to provide accurate and authoritative information regarding the subject matter covered. The Author have made every effort in the preparation of this book to ensure the accuracy of the information. However, information in this book is sold without warranty, either expressed or implied. The Authors or the Publisher will not be liable for any damages caused or alleged to be caused either directly or indirectly by this book.

All trademarks and registered trademarks mentioned in this publication are the property of their respective owners, including but not limited to Python. These trademarks are used for editorial and educational purposes only, without intent to infringe upon any trademark rights. This publication is independent and has not been authorized, endorsed, or approved by any trademark owner.

Vibrant Publishers' books are available at special quantity discounts for sales promotions, or for use in corporate training programs. For more information, please write to bulkorders@vibrantpublishers.com

Please email feedback/corrections (technical, grammatical, or spelling) to spellerrors@vibrantpublishers.com

Vibrant Publishes in a variety of print and electronic formats and by print-on-demand. Some material included with standard print versions of this book may not be included in e-books or in print-on-demand. To access the complete catalog of Vibrant Publishers, visit www.vibrantpublishers.com

Exclusive Online Resources for You

As our valued reader, your purchase of this book includes access to exclusive online resources designed to enhance your learning experience. These resources can be downloaded from our website, www.vibrantpublishers.com, and are created to help you apply Machine Learning concepts effectively.

Online resources for this book include the following:

1. **Chapter-wise glossary** for quick revision and improved retention

2. **Guided video tutorials** for Python installation on any computer (Chapter 2)

3. **Link to access dataset** for hands-on coding practice (Chapter 3)

Why these online resources are valuable:

- **Simplified learning:** The resources break down complex machine learning topics into manageable, easy-to-understand components.

- **Step-by-step practice:** Working with real datasets and guided tutorials supports gradual skill-building and confidence in writing code.

- **Real-World Application:** Designed to bridge theory and practice, these tools reflect how machine learning is used in professional settings.

How to access your online resources:

1. **Visit the website:** Go to www.vibrantpublishers.com

2. **Find your book:** Navigate to the book's product page via the "Shop" menu or by searching for the book title in the search bar.

3. **Request the resources:** Scroll down to the "Request Sample Book/Online Resource" section.

4. **Enter your details:** Enter your preferred email ID and select "Online Resource" as the resource type. Lastly, select "user type" and submit the request.

5. **Check your inbox:** The resources will be delivered directly to your email.

Alternatively, for quick access: simply scan the QR code below to go directly to the product page and request the online resources by filling in the required details.

bit.ly/mlvp-slm

Happy learning!

SELF-LEARNING MANAGEMENT SERIES

TITLE	PAPERBACK* ISBN

BUSINESS AND ENTREPRENEURSHIP

BUSINESS COMMUNICATION ESSENTIALS	9781636511634
BUSINESS ETHICS ESSENTIALS	9781636513324
BUSINESS LAW ESSENTIALS	9781636511702
BUSINESS PLAN ESSENTIALS	9781636511214
BUSINESS STRATEGY ESSENTIALS	9781949395778
ENTREPRENEURSHIP ESSENTIALS	9781636511603
INTERNATIONAL BUSINESS ESSENTIALS	9781636513294
PRINCIPLES OF MANAGEMENT ESSENTIALS	9781636511542

COMPUTER SCIENCE AND TECHNOLOGY

BLOCKCHAIN ESSENTIALS	9781636513003
MACHINE LEARNING ESSENTIALS	9781636513775
PYTHON ESSENTIALS	9781636512938

DATA SCIENCE FOR BUSINESS

BUSINESS INTELLIGENCE ESSENTIALS	9781636513362
DATA ANALYTICS ESSENTIALS	9781636511184

FINANCIAL LITERACY AND ECONOMICS

COST ACCOUNTING & MANAGEMENT ESSENTIALS	9781636511030
FINANCIAL ACCOUNTING ESSENTIALS	9781636510972
FINANCIAL MANAGEMENT ESSENTIALS	9781636511009
MACROECONOMICS ESSENTIALS	9781636511818
MICROECONOMICS ESSENTIALS	9781636511153
PERSONAL FINANCE ESSENTIALS	9781636511849
PRINCIPLES OF ECONOMICS ESSENTIALS	9781636512334

*Also available in Hardback & Ebook formats

SELF-LEARNING MANAGEMENT SERIES

TITLE	PAPERBACK* ISBN

HR, DIVERSITY, AND ORGANIZATIONAL SUCCESS

TITLE	PAPERBACK* ISBN
DIVERSITY, EQUITY, AND INCLUSION ESSENTIALS	9781636512976
DIVERSITY IN THE WORKPLACE ESSENTIALS	9781636511122
HR ANALYTICS ESSENTIALS	9781636510347
HUMAN RESOURCE MANAGEMENT ESSENTIALS	9781949395839
ORGANIZATIONAL BEHAVIOR ESSENTIALS	9781636512303
ORGANIZATIONAL DEVELOPMENT ESSENTIALS	9781636511481

LEADERSHIP AND PERSONAL DEVELOPMENT

TITLE	PAPERBACK* ISBN
DECISION MAKING ESSENTIALS	9781636510026
INDIA'S ROAD TO TRANSFORMATION: WHY LEADERSHIP MATTERS	9781636512273
LEADERSHIP ESSENTIALS	9781636510316
TIME MANAGEMENT ESSENTIALS	9781636511665

MODERN MARKETING AND SALES

TITLE	PAPERBACK* ISBN
CONSUMER BEHAVIOR ESSENTIALS	9781636513263
DIGITAL MARKETING ESSENTIALS	9781949395747
MARKETING MANAGEMENT ESSENTIALS	9781636511788
MARKET RESEARCH ESSENTIALS	9781636513744
SALES MANAGEMENT ESSENTIALS	9781636510743
SERVICES MARKETING ESSENTIALS	9781636511733
SOCIAL MEDIA MARKETING ESSENTIALS	9781636512181

*Also available in Hardback & Ebook formats

SELF-LEARNING MANAGEMENT SERIES

TITLE	PAPERBACK* ISBN

OPERATIONS MANAGEMENT

AGILE ESSENTIALS	9781636510057
OPERATIONS & SUPPLY CHAIN MANAGEMENT ESSENTIALS	9781949395242
PROJECT MANAGEMENT ESSENTIALS	9781636510712
STAKEHOLDER ENGAGEMENT ESSENTIALS	9781636511511

CURRENT AFFAIRS

DIGITAL SHOCK	9781636513805

*Also available in Hardback & Ebook formats

About the Author

Dhairya Parikh is a skilled data engineer with more than three years of hands-on experience in the technical consulting industry. He has a proven track record of helping clients across diverse sectors leverage data to drive strategic insights, optimize processes, and overcome complex challenges. Dhairya's journey in data science led him to pursue a master's degree at the University of Waterloo, where he specialized in Machine Learning and Artificial Intelligence. This academic foundation, paired with his industry expertise, equips him with a unique perspective on both the theory and practical applications of cutting-edge AI and ML technologies.

Beyond his work in consulting, Dhairya is also an accomplished technical writer and author. His book delves into core concepts of Machine Learning, providing accessible insights and practical guidance for readers at all levels. Additionally, he has contributed extensively to the field through various blogs and articles, covering topics ranging from Machine Learning fundamentals to the latest trends in the Internet of Things. His writing consistently reflects his commitment to making complex ideas understandable and actionable for a broad audience.

An avid project developer, Dhairya has created several innovative projects that have earned industry recognition and awards. His work demonstrates a keen ability to blend technical skills with creativity, and he's particularly passionate about projects that drive tangible impact. As he continues to build on his expertise, Dhairya remains dedicated to advancing knowledge in data engineering and AI, both as a practitioner and as a thought leader.

What Experts Say About This Book!

Machine Learning Essentials You Always Wanted to Know offers a clear, friendly, and practical introduction to machine learning. The book is structured like a guided learning journey—from understanding what machine learning is, to seeing how it's applied in real life, to writing hands-on Python code. It's beginner-friendly, yet technical enough to build a strong foundation. The historical timeline, real-world examples (like Netflix recommendations and Google Maps), and helpful visuals make the concepts relatable and easy to remember.

**– Julia Appelskog, Book Trade Professional,
Productive Planet**

Machine Learning Essentials You Always Wanted to Know is a solid introduction to AI and ML, especially for beginners who already have a bit of "coding or technical background." What I liked most is how it keeps the curiosity alive throughout. It doesn't go too deep into every topic, but it gives a good, broad overview, which I think is perfect for someone just starting out. The visualizations are really helpful and make the concepts easier to grasp. The overall tone stays engaging and encourages you to explore more. It's very beginner-friendly and keeps you wanting to learn more!

**– Akshat Baheti, Data Scientist,
TD Bank**

This page is intentionally left blank

Table of Contents

1 Machine Learning: A Gentle Introduction   1

    1.1   What is Machine Learning?   2
    1.2   Machine Learning: A Historical Overview   5
    1.3   Where is Machine Learning used in Daily Life?   8
    1.4   Overview of a Typical ML System   9
    Chapter Summary   12
    Glossary   13
    Quiz   14

2 Mastering the Fundamentals of Machine Learning   17

    2.1   Types of Data in Machine Learning   18
    2.2   Math and Machine Learning   21
    2.3   Introducing Python and Other Essential Tools   27
    Chapter Summary   37
    Glossary   39
    Quiz   40

3 Supervised Learning: Starting with the Basics   43

    3.1   A Refresher on Supervised Learning   44
    3.2   Linear Regression: The Starting Point   45
    3.3   Logistic Regression: The Fundamental Classifier   56
    3.4   Evaluation Metrics in Supervised Learning   64
    Chapter Summary   71
    Glossary   72
    Quiz   73

4 Going Beyond the Basics: Exploring Non-Linear Models   77

    4.1   Decision Trees: Unraveling the Tree Structure   78
    4.2   K-Nearest Neighbors: Finding Friends in Data   98
    4.3   Support Vector Machines: The Magic of Margins   107
    Chapter Summary   117
    Glossary   118
    Quiz   119

5 Ensemble Techniques: Improving Prediction Power   123

5.1   Bagging: Harnessing the Power of Multiple Models   124

5.2   Boosting: Learning from Mistakes   137

5.3   Advanced Ensemble Models: Introduction to Random Forests and LightGBM   147

Chapter Summary   154

Glossary   155

Quiz   156

6 Unsupervised Learning: Finding Patterns in Data   159

6.1   Clustering Basics: K-Means and Other Clustering Techniques   160

6.2   Dimensionality Reduction Techniques: PCA and t-SNE   176

6.3   Association Rules: Market Basket Analysis   191

Chapter Summary   195

Glossary   196

Quiz   197

7 A Gentle Introduction to Neural Networks and Deep Learning   201

7.1   Neural Networks - Building Blocks of Deep Learning   202

7.2   Convolutional Neural Networks: A Smarter Approach for Image Data   211

7.3   Recurrent Neural Networks: Sequences and Predictions   217

Chapter Summary   226

Glossary   228

Quiz   229

8 Machine Learning in Real-World Scenarios   233

8.1   Exploring Machine Learning Use Cases across Domains   234

8.2   How to Develop a Machine Learning Application   244

8.3   Ethics in Machine Learning   250

8.4   The Future of Machine Learning   256

Preface

With the recent "Artificial Intelligence" buzz, everyone wants to get into the field of machine learning. Well, I was one of those people, so I chose to leave my job as a Data Engineer and got back to studying ML at one of the best universities in the world, the University of Waterloo. However, after learning so much about it for a year, I can fairly say that it is a complicated subject.

Well, I thought let's do something about it! So, six months and many hours later, here is my view on how I would start learning Machine Learning again if given the chance. This book has all the bells and whistles: the theoretical content for all the fundamental Machine Learning concepts, and also the practical implementations which will allow you to apply your theoretical knowledge to understand how things work.

I will describe the book in a single sentence: "We will break into what Machine Learning is, what it does, and how it works, one step at a time." So, get excited! You are about to enter a world that will just seem magical until you look under the hood and find that it's just crunching a lot of numbers, although at a much higher scale.

Introduction to the Book

In today's world, where technology is advancing rapidly, machine learning is becoming more important in shaping how we live and work. From the recommendations you see on your favorite streaming service to self-driving cars, machine learning is at the heart of it all. But what exactly is machine learning, and why should you care about it?

Machine learning is a branch of artificial intelligence (AI) that gives computers the ability to learn from data and improve their performance without being explicitly programmed. It allows machines to identify patterns, make decisions, and even predict future trends—all by learning from experience, much like how humans do.

As we explore this exciting field in the pages ahead, you will discover how machine learning is transforming industries, from healthcare and finance to entertainment and transportation. This book will guide you through the fundamental concepts, methods, and real-world applications of machine learning, offering you a clear understanding of how it works and why it matters.

By the end of this book, you will be able to answer the following questions:

- What is machine learning, and how does it differ from traditional programming?
- What are the key types of machine learning and when is each one used?
- How do algorithms, data, and models come together to make machine learning possible?
- What are the challenges and limitations of machine learning, and how can we overcome them?
- How to get started with coding Machine Learning models?

So, let's dive into the fascinating world of machine learning and unlock its potential together!

Who Can Benefit From This Book?

You should consider picking up this book if:

- You are a student eager to dive into the world of machine learning and pursue a career in this rapidly growing field.
- You are an experienced professional seeking a career shift and want to explore the exciting opportunities in Artificial Intelligence.
- You are curious about AI, no matter your background or profession, and want to explore this fascinating field as this book serves as an excellent starting point for your journey!

How to Use This Book?

This book is designed for both beginners and professionals with some experience in machine learning. It is organized into various categories within the field (such as types of models, architectures, etc.). For those new to the subject, it is highly recommended to follow the chapters in sequence to build a solid foundation.

However, if you are seeking specific information and already have some familiarity with the field, you can approach the book more flexibly:

- For example, if you're interested in Supervised Learning (a major focus of this book) and are comfortable with the basics, you may skip the first two chapters and proceed directly to Chapters 3-5.

- Conversely, if you're seeking a gentle introduction to machine learning without delving too deeply into complex topics, Chapters 1 and 2 will provide a solid overview of the field and help you assess whether it aligns with your interests.

- For readers with a strong background in machine learning who are eager to explore advanced topics, such as Deep Learning, Chapters 7 and 8 will serve as a suitable starting point.

Chapter 1

Machine Learning: A Gentle Introduction

KEY LEARNING OBJECTIVES

- Have a clear understanding of what the term machine learning means.
- Attain knowledge of some notable discoveries in this field over the last several decades.
- Figure out which applications you currently work with using machine learning.
- Explain the essential components of a machine learning-based system.

This chapter will introduce you to the world of *Machine Learning* and *Artificial Intelligence*. The chapter starts with a very simple explanation of what machine learning is. Then, we delve a bit deeper into the history of this field, exploring some critical discoveries over the past century that significantly impacted its evolution. After this, we look at the real-world applications of this versatile technology, followed by a simplified overview of a basic system that utilizes machine learning at its core.

So, without waiting any further, let's start our journey!

1.1 What is Machine Learning?

"Machine Learning" may sound intimidating initially, but its core principles are easy to grasp. If we simply break down the term into its words, i.e., "Machine" and "Learning," the simplest definition is a machine that can learn something. Interestingly, that is how the term was first coined in 1959 by Arthur Samuel to define the world's first machine that could play checkers and learn from the games it played.

But, if we accept the explanation, wouldn't it make machines sentient? It learns in a much different way than you would expect. To make things even simpler, let me present the following analogy (refer to Figure 1.1):

"Machine Learning Models are essentially Data Labeling Machines."

Figure 1.1   Machine learning models as data labeling machines

| Data + Labels | Creating the Data Labeller | Finished Data Labelling Machine |

ML Model Training

Simply speaking, it is a machine that looks at some information (which can be anything: a photo, a paragraph, or audio), compares it with examples of the same type it has seen before, and tells what to label this piece of content. Doesn't sound so attractive now? That is why the catchy term "Machine Learning" was coined to catch people's attention.

The next question you might have is if things are that simple, why does one need to know some level of mathematics to get into this field? Where does the math fit into this equation? The comparison that the machine makes with the previous examples is somewhat complicated and this is the process where the majority of mathematical calculations are involved. We will reflect on this in much more detail later in the book.

How does a Machine Learn?

| Figure 1.2 | Types of machine learning paradigms |

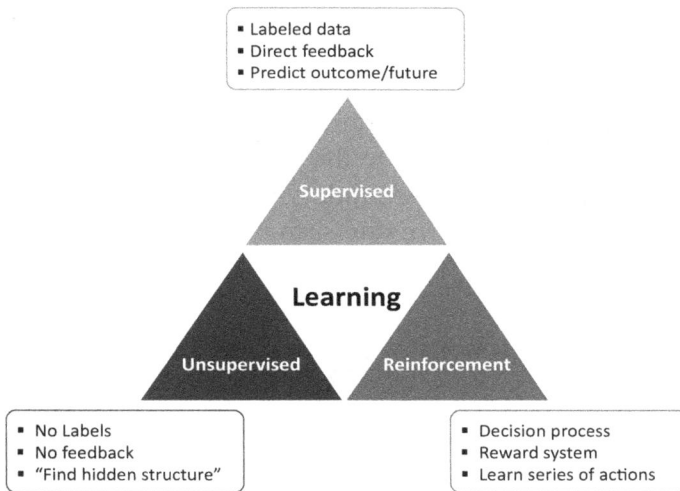

Source: Dhairya Parikh, "Learning Paradigms in Machine Learning." DataDrivenInvestor. Medium, June 15, 2020. https://medium.datadriveninvestor.com/ learning-paradigms-in-machine-learning-146ebf8b5943.

Another interesting aspect to consider is how the machine learning (ML) model learns. As you would expect, there is more than one way to learn something. The same goes for this: there are numerous ways for a machine to understand when some information is given to it. Its approach pattern for some particular content is defined as a "learning paradigm." ML researchers defined three main paradigms (see Fig. 1.2).

Figure 1.3   **A visual representation of supervised learning**

SUPERVISED LEARNING

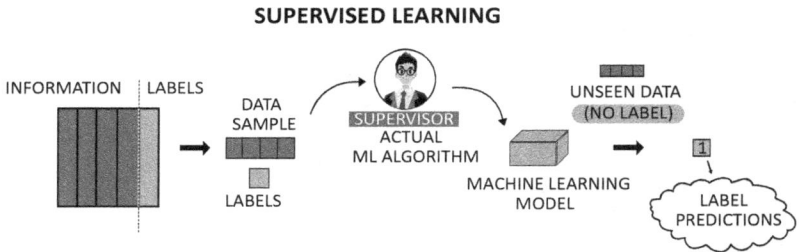

1. **Supervised Learning (Fig 1.3):** The essential aspect of this form of learning is that the information is presented to the computer or machine as *input-output pairs*: the information as input and its label as output. The system "trains" itself to learn what kind of outputs particular input types give. The term "train" refers to the method used by the computer to understand. We will cover various techniques that utilize this form of learning later in this chapter.

Figure 1.4   **A visual representation of unsupervised learning**

UNSUPERVISED LEARNING

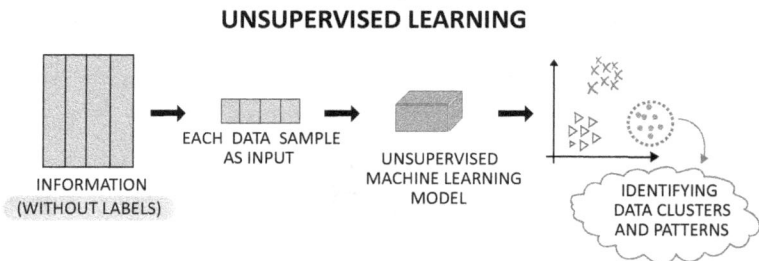

2. **Unsupervised Learning (Fig 1.4):** Consider a scenario where it is not possible to simply label the data. What if you would like to identify patterns within the data instead? The machine is given only the information without any results and is tasked with finding a mold (pattern) that fits the provided information. For instance, given a set of news articles, what if we categorize them into different

sections for our website? This is a problem that this learning paradigm can be used to solve.

Figure 1.5 **A visual representation of reinforcement learning**

REINFORECEMENT LEARNING

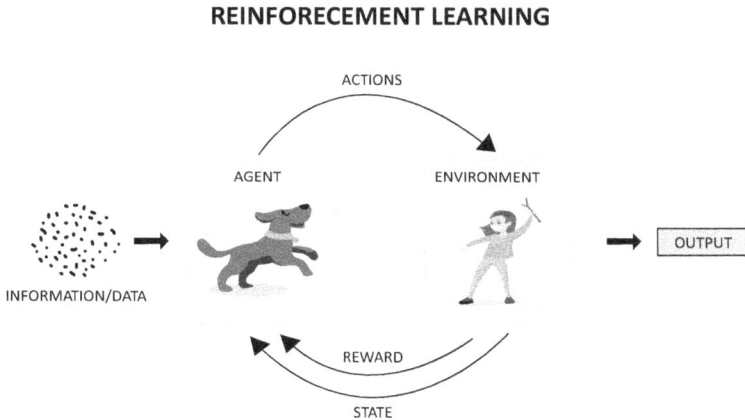

3. **Reinforcement Learning (Fig 1.5):** This learning method allows machines to automatically figure out the ideal behavior for some given condition (or information) to maximize its performance. An excellent analogy to understand this technique is "training a dog." This learning paradigm is like a dog trainer, which teaches the dog how to respond to specific signs, like a whistle, clap, or anything else. The dog is rewarded with an incentive like a bone or a biscuit for every correct response by the trainer.

Now that you know what machine learning is, let's delve into its history and explore how it has evolved over the last eight decades.

1.2 Machine Learning: A Historical Overview

Let's take a journey of some of the most pivotal moments that led to various notable developments in this field. Figure 1.6 gives you a visual chart that shows how things evolved in this exciting field of technology.

| Figure 1.6 | A peek into machine learning history |

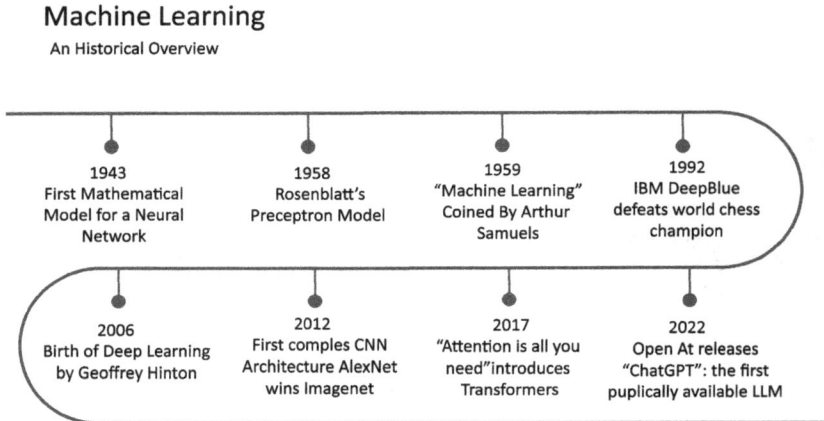

Machine Learning
An Historical Overview

1943	1958	1959	1992
First Mathematical Model for a Neural Network	Rosenblatt's Preceptron Model	"Machine Learning" Coined By Arthur Samuels	IBM DeepBlue defeats world chess champion

2006	2012	2017	2022
Birth of Deep Learning by Geoffrey Hinton	First comples CNN Architecture AlexNet wins Imagenet	"Attention is all you need"introduces Transformers	Open At releases "ChatGPT": the first puplically available LLM

1.2.1 Laying the foundations

We have always been fascinated by how a human brain works, which was the motivation for the foundation of the field of artificial intelligence. Machine learning, although sometimes used interchangeably with it, is a subfield of AI. As discussed, it all started in 1943 when Walter Pitts and Warren McCulloch presented the first mathematical model of a Neural Network. After that, the term *"Artificial Intelligence"* was coined by John McCarthy, Marvin Minsky, Nathaniel Rochester, and Claude Shannon in their workshop proposal in 1956, which was often regarded as the founding event of this field. Then, in 1958, Rosenblatt introduced the Perceptron, the first foundational model of a single-layer neural network (again, to mimic the workings of a human brain!). The term "Machine Learning" was coined by Samuel the following year in his seminal paper describing how his computer outplayed a human. After a few years, the nearest neighbor algorithm was created in 1967, allowing computers to recognize things like patterns. The coming years saw increased research and development of various multilayered network architectures.

1.2.2 The phase of ground breaking development

Fast forward to 1990, when there was significant development in computing hardware, there was a shift in the ML domain where the models relied more on a data-driven approach rather than a knowledge-based setting. The first major press event was in 1992 when IBM's Deep Blue defeated the reigning world chess champion, Garry Kasparov. This motivated companies to spend considerable resources on ML development. Then, in 1998, Yann LeCun and team released the ever-popular MNIST (Modified National Institute of Standards and Technology) dataset, which anyone working in recognition or classification methods in ML would have worked on at least once. After that came the golden year of 2006 when Geoffrey Hinton coined the term Deep Learning. Fei-Fei Lee started the AI boom by starting her work on the Imagenet data repository, and Netflix launched its first competition, where people from all around the world competed to create a state-of-the-art machine learning model that beat Netflix's proprietary recommendation software. Then, in 2012, Geoffrey Hinton, Ilya Sutskever, and Alex Krizhevsky introduced a CNN architecture called AlexNet, which won the Imagenet challenge by a whopping 10% difference in the error rate with the next best performing model. This acted as a significant catalyst for deep learning research. Then, in 2014, Ian Goodfellow and their team invented GANs (Generative Adversarial Networks), which enabled computers to generate new data (this was the foundation for LLMs).

1.2.3 2015–2025: The decade of deep learning

The subsequent considerable development was in 2017 when Google researchers introduced the concept of Transformers in one of the most famous ML papers, "Attention is all you need." Then,

OpenAI released GPT-1 in 2018, the first step in creating LLMs like ChatGPT. After that, in 2021, OpenAI introduced Dall-E, a multimodal (we will see what this means) system that could create images from a user's text inputs. Finally, various LLMs were released for the general public, starting with OpenAI's ChatGPT in late 2022, followed by Microsoft Co-pilot and Google Bard (now Gemini).

To conclude this section, we live in the decade that will later be recognized as the era of "Machine Learning," so we must learn all we can to be a part of this great field.

1.3 Where is Machine Learning used in Daily Life?

Have you ever wondered how you use machine learning in your daily lives? You will be surprised to know that almost any technical product you use today uses machine learning in some way or another. Here are a few scenarios where ML plays quite a pivotal role, although unseen in our daily lives.

- **Mobile Phones:** Phones are a daily driver for everyone now. Interestingly, whenever you use your phone, an ML model is running almost every time under the hood. For instance, scrolling through reels on Instagram uses several ML models to understand your preferences on ads and content.

- **Content Recommendation:** Most of you use various audio and video streaming services like Netflix and Spotify. Have you ever wondered how they recommend the shows that always fit your taste? They use machine learning to analyze your watching or listening habits and make recommendations based on this data.

- **Navigation and Travel:** Have you ever been lost in a new city and had to rely on Google Maps to find your destination? Guess what? You used machine learning, which enhances GPS technology to predict traffic conditions, suggest optimal routes, and even estimate travel times. So, next time you use maps, remember that a reasonably complex ML algorithm is running in the background to give you directions and suggestions.

- **Personal Assistants:** "Hey Siri," "OK Google!" and "Alexa" are some trendy phrases nowadays, with voice assistant devices becoming ubiquitous. These devices use a blend of different machine learning models to understand and respond to your commands. Whether setting reminders, controlling smart home devices, or getting answers to questions, these assistants learn from each interaction to improve themselves with time.

- **Email filtering:** I have seen my share of spam emails, and I am annoyed when they clog up my mail thread and all my relevant emails are not visible. Hence, most email providers use machine learning to sort out spam and phishing emails. These systems study email content and how senders behave to identify and block harmful emails, helping you keep your inbox safe and clutter-free.

Now that we've explored how ML is utilized in everyday scenarios, let's see what typically makes up a machine learning system and understand the core components that enable these intelligent applications.

1.4 Overview of a Typical ML System

Until now, I have used a lot of complex terms like an ML algorithm or model, training data, etc., which would have been difficult for you to grasp if you had never explored the ML domain. For that reason, let's look at what components make up a machine learning system using a simple analogy to make things a bit more interesting (refer to Figure 1.7).

Figure 1.7	Components of a typical ML system

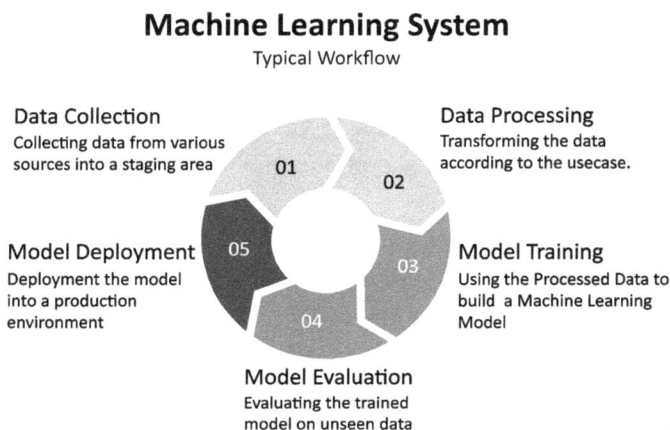

Machine Learning System
Typical Workflow

Data Collection
Collecting data from various
sources into a staging area

Data Processing
Transforming the data
according to the usecase.

Model Deployment
Deployment the model
into a production
environment

Model Training
Using the Processed Data to
build a Machine Learning
Model

01 02 05 03 04

Model Evaluation
Evaluating the trained
model on unseen data

To make things easier, imagine you have just bought a new smartphone and are trying to figure out how it works. Understanding a machine learning system is very similar in many ways. Let's break it down into a few core components.

1. Data Collection

When you initially open your new phone, what is the first thing you do? Personally, I allow the gadget to walk me through how things function, and then I go through the accompanying guide and follow the easy instructions. In ML, data is the material you use to learn new things — the better data you have, the better the learning outcomes will be. This step involves collecting all relevant data that the system will learn from.

2. Data Processing

Once you have all the information from these tutorials, you must create a mind map on how to proceed. You could do the things essential for you first, like setting up the phone's camera if you bought it for its superior cameras. Similarly, in ML, data processing involves cleaning and organizing data. This could be steps like removing errors in data, removing NaN values (a Python® specific term which simply means **not a number**), handling outliers or selecting which parts of the data are most important for learning. We will look at these processing methods in detail in the later chapters.

3. Model Training

Now comes the actual learning part, similar to how you actually start playing with your phone based on the information you have. In ML, this step involves feeding the processed data into an algorithm (a set of rules and calculations), resulting in a "trained model." The model learns from this data by finding patterns and making connections.

4. Model Evaluation

After learning a lot, you should take a test to see how well you know your phone. In ML, the evaluation phase tests how well the resulting model performs. This step checks if the model's predictions and patterns are learned correctly.

5. Deployment

Imagine that the phone you were learning and testing was a prototype, and you work for the company that developed this phone. Once you have figured out everything, you document and upload it on the company's website. This is precisely what deployment is for an ML model. Once you have the evaluated model, you deploy it in the backend for your application to make decisions or predictions in real-world applications, such as recommending what movie you might enjoy or recognizing faces in photos.

Great! You now know about the core components of a machine learning system.

In the next chapter, we will go through the fundamental blocks of machine learning, which include what types of data are used for machine learning models, the basics of Python for ML, some mathematical concepts relevant to ML applications, and much more. Let's take a look at what we learned throughout this chapter.

Chapter Summary

◆ This chapter introduces the term "Machine Learning" by breaking it down into its components—machine and learning—highlighting its basic definition as a machine capable of learning, inspired by Arthur Samuel's checkers-playing program.

◆ An analogy for machine learning is presented as "Data Labeling Machines," emphasizing that these systems compare new data with previous examples to assign labels, making the concept more accessible and less intimidating.

◆ Moreover, the chapter covers the three main learning paradigms in machine learning: supervised learning, where machines learn from input-output pairs; unsupervised learning, which involves pattern identification without explicit labels; and reinforcement learning, akin to training a dog, where desired behaviors are reinforced through rewards.

◆ Additionally, a brief historical overview traces the evolution of machine learning from the early developments in artificial neural networks in 1943 to significant milestones like the creation of Deep Blue and the introduction of major algorithms like Deep Learning and GANs.

◆ The chapter closes by illustrating how machine learning permeates our daily lives, from mobile phones and content recommendations to navigation systems and personal assistants, highlighting the ubiquitous and often invisible role of ML in modern technology. It also describes the core components of a typical ML system.

Glossary

We used numerous terms related to machine learning which you won't know. So, here is a simple glossary of those words for you.

Term	Definition
Algorithm	A set of rules or instructions given to a computer to help it make decisions or solve problems. Used in ML to learn from data.
Artificial intelligence (AI)	The broader concept of machines carrying out tasks in a way that we would consider "smart". ML is a subset of AI.
Data	Information used by ML systems to learn. Can include numbers, words, images, clicks, etc.
Deep Learning	A subset of ML that uses complex neural networks with many layers, good at learning from large amounts of data.
Deployment	The stage in ML where a trained model is made available for practical use, such as in an app or software.
Generative Adversarial Networks (GANs)	A type of AI model used in unsupervised learning where two neural networks compete to generate new data.
Input-output pairs	In supervised learning, the pairing of input data (like images or text) with the correct output (like labels), which the model learns to predict.
Machine learning (ML)	A field of computer science that focuses on building systems that can learn from and make decisions based on data.

Quiz

Let's test how much you know about machine learning after going through this chapter.

1. **What is machine learning primarily about?**
   a. Programming machines to perform high-level computations
   b. Enabling machines to learn from data and make decisions
   c. Designing machines that require human intervention
   d. Creating machines that function exactly like humans

2. **The term "machine learning" was coined by**
   a. Marvin Minsky
   b. Arthur Samuel
   c. John McCarthy
   d. Geoffrey Hinton

3. **What was the first machine that could learn which was also mentioned in the chapter?**
   a. A chess-playing robot
   b. A checkers-playing program
   c. A data-sorting computer
   d. A language processing machine

4. **Which option from the ones given below is not a machine learning paradigm?**
   a. Supervised learning
   b. Unsupervised learning
   c. Reactive learning
   d. Reinforcement learning

5. **Which process do you refer to as "training" in machine learning?**
   a. Collecting data
   b. Programming a machine
   c. The process in which the machine learns from data
   d. The process of testing the machine

6. **Supervised Learning involves:**
   a. Machines creating data
   b. Machines finding patterns without labels
   c. Input-output pairs for machine training
   d. Rewarding machines for correct behavior

7. **Unsupervised learning is used to:**
   a. Identify patterns in data without explicit labels
   b. Label new data based on past examples
   c. Train machines using labeled data
   d. Teach machines to perform specific tasks

8. **What does reinforcement learning involve?**
   a. Machines making decisions based on past mistakes
   b. Machines learning from input-output pairs
   c. Machines learning to maximize performance through rewards
   d. Machines learning to follow explicit instructions

9. **What significant event involving AI occurred in 1997?**
   a. Introduction of the MNIST dataset
   b. IBM's Deep Blue defeated a chess champion
   c. The first use of the term "deep learning"
   d. The invention of GANs

10. The Perceptron, introduced in 1958, is a foundational model for:

a. Supervised learning

b. Unsupervised learning

c. Reinforcement learning

d. Neural networks

Answers	1 – b	2 – b	3 – b	4 – c	5 – c
	6 – c	7 – a	8 – c	9 – b	10 – d

Chapter 2

Mastering the Fundamentals of Machine Learning

KEY LEARNING OBJECTIVES

- Identify the various flavors of data available and how they affect the overall goal of training a machine learning model.
- Have a firm grasp on the key mathematical concepts essential for machine learning.
- Recognize the primary Python packages used in machine learning.
- Apply basic Python programming skills in practical machine learning tasks.

This chapter will take you through the fundamentals that we will be using throughout this book. In the last chapter, we learnt how vital data is for machine learning, so we will first cover the common types and formats of data and discuss various sources for each briefly. It's always said that to master ML, one needs to be proficient with math. Well, not exactly true, but you do need a basic understanding of some key mathematical concepts. So next, we will cover those concepts briefly here and provide some good resources if you haven't covered any of the mentioned topics in additional resources. Once we are clear on the theoretical aspects, we will delve into the practical side! We will talk about the go-to programming language for ML and the one we will use throughout this book: "Python." We will go through the main packages we will use throughout this journey we have embarked on.

That's right! We will train our very first machine learning model in this chapter.

2.1 Types of Data in Machine Learning

In the modern world, data is all around us. Every smart gadget we use produces enormous volumes of data every day. Machine learning is essentially the field which figures out how to use this obtained data to gain some valuable knowledge and insights. Before delving into the different types of data, let's see what data is.

Data is nothing but a grouping of numerical values and facts that can be processed efficiently. A data collection is often referred to as a "dataset."

As we all know, there are various formats of data that we are exposed to everyday. Can you think of some? Well, let's see: images, videos, tables, text and audio are the most common types we encounter on a daily basis.

However, all the real world data is captured in a variety of ways with the primary goal of capturing some information about a real world phenomenon; for instance, a temperature sensor capturing the temperature values to get an idea of how hot or cold the atmosphere is. Considering the absolute basics, data can broadly be categorized into two types: Numerical and Categorical. Don't let the terminology overwhelm you; together, let's go over them and determine what they mean.

Figure 2.1 **Different types of data in machine learning**

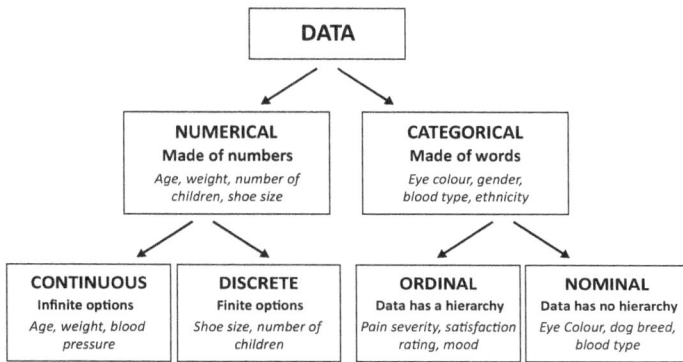

DATA			
NUMERICAL Made of numbers *Age, weight, number of children, shoe size*		**CATEGORICAL** Made of words *Eye colour, gender, blood type, ethnicity*	
CONTINUOUS Infinite options *Age, weight, blood pressure*	**DISCRETE** Finite options *Shoe size, number of children*	**ORDINAL** Data has a hierarchy *Pain severity, satisfaction rating, mood*	**NOMINAL** Data has no hierarchy *Eye Colour, dog breed, blood type*

Numerical Data

As the name implies, numerical data is all about numbers. This includes everything that can be expressed as a number or a sequence of numbers. It can be further classified into two types based on the type of representation.

1. **Continuous data:** Imagine that you are measuring the temperature using a sensor. You get a new reading every second, which can have little to huge variation, depending on the conditions. This value can be anything in a given range, which in our case may be 0 to 50. This is referred to as *continuous data.*

2. **Discrete Data:** Now think about counting the number of books on your shelf. You can have 20 books or 21 books, but not 20.5 books. Discrete data is all about distinct, separate values.

Categorical Data

Categorical data deals with categories or groups. It's not about numbers but rather different labels or names. There are two kinds:

1. **Nominal Data:** This is the simplest form of categorical data. It's just about different names without any specific order. For instance, the types of fruits: bananas, oranges, and

apples. There's no inherent ranking here – one fruit isn't "higher" than the other.

2. **Ordinal Data:** Now, this type does have a specific order. Think about movie ratings: good, better, best. There's a clear ranking or order, even though the differences between them aren't numerically defined.

You now have an understanding of the basic data types that we will come across in the later chapters when talking about data for different use cases. While we are on this topic, do you remember what a dataset is? (If you don't, you will have to read more thoroughly).

Datasets are generally represented or characterized with the following terms (take a look at Figure 2.2):

Figure 2.2   **Dataset characterization**

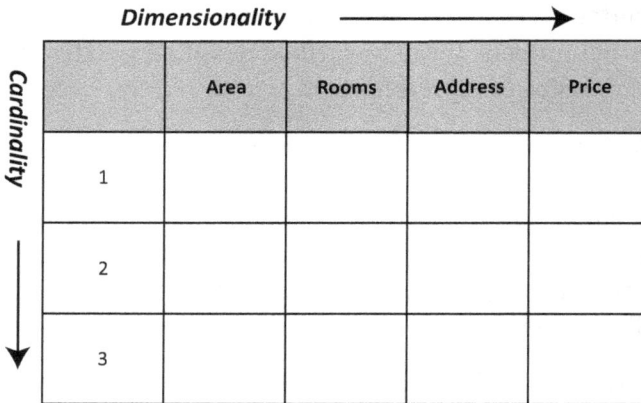

		Area	Rooms	Address	Price
	1				
	2				
	3				

Dimensionality →

Cardinality ↓

- The number of samples in a dataset is termed as the "cardinality" of the dataset.
- The number of characteristics (generally called *features*) is described as the "dimensionality" of that data.

As we approach the conclusion of this section, it is important to address a concept that frequently emerges in the context of real-world machine learning projects: "Big Data." In the simplest words, *an enormous amount of data is referred to as Big Data.*

The primary reason for this characterization is that we need to use some different methods and frameworks to process this amount of data efficiently.

Now that you know about what data is in machine learning, let's explore how this framework actually learns from it. (Hint, it's not rocket science! In fact, you yourself would have used this secret ingredient with several problems.) Well, it's **Math!**

2.2 Math and Machine Learning

Figure 2.3 **How math is used in various stages of ML**

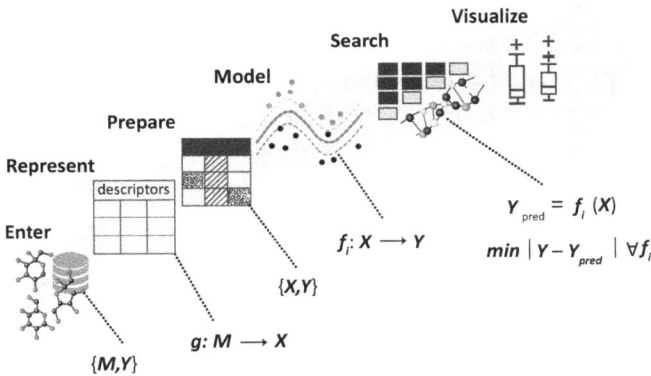

You don't have to be an expert in math to understand machine learning. But, having a firm grasp of a few fundamental ideas will not only make your journey much more pleasurable, but it will also enable you to comprehend how machine learning functions on a technical level. Comparable to owning a map when touring a new place, it enables you to make sense of your location and direction.

So, why is math important in machine learning? Well, at its core, machine learning is all about learning from data, and math is the language we use to describe those patterns. Whatever machine learning related task you are trying to do, math is there to guide you. Now, a question you might have: Math is not a small domain, so what should I focus on, specifically for machine learning? Well, I am your guide as math is for machine learning. So, let me help you with this.

2.2.1 Linear algebra: The foundations

Linear algebra is one of the most important foundational blocks on which machine learning is based. It is the basis for numerous models and applications in ML. In actuality, many of the apps you use today rely on the principles of linear algebra. For example, your phone uses these principles to process photos it receives in order to produce the ideal photograph. Let's examine these principles in more detail.

At the core of linear algebra are vectors and matrices, which is what we use in different types of data in machine learning. Vectors can be thought of as a point with some weight and direction, while matrices are grid-like arrangements of numbers that can represent more complex structures such as images and datasets. For instance, an image can be represented as a matrix where each element corresponds to a pixel value. Each row and column of the matrix represents the spatial dimensions of the image (refer Fig. 2.4).

| Figure 2.4 | **How images are represented as matrices** |

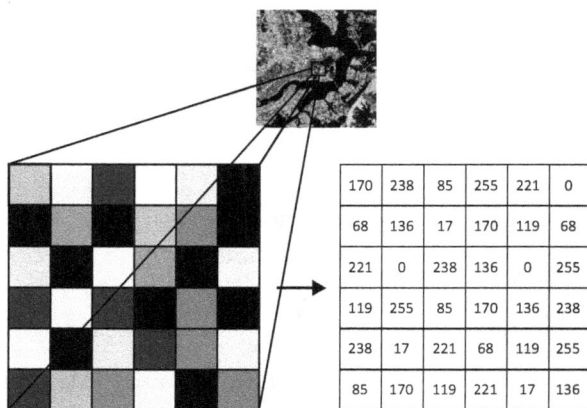

170	238	85	255	221	0
68	136	17	170	119	68
221	0	238	136	0	255
119	255	85	170	136	238
238	17	221	68	119	255
85	170	119	221	17	136

Source: Analysis of Emotions From Body Postures Based on Digital Imaging - Scientific Figure on ResearchGate. Available from: https://www.researchgate.net/figure/Matrix-for-certain-area-of-a-grayscale-image-17_fig3_325569674 [accessed 22 Nov 2024]

Although representing the data using these tools is powerful, what makes this thing magic is the ability to apply various transformations on these vectors and matrices. For instance, matrix multiplication serves as a foundation on which the core concept of neural networks is based upon (don't worry, we will cover them in detail in the later chapters).

Apart from this, some other essential operations in linear algebra are:

1. **Dot Product:** The dot product of vectors is used to measure similarity, which is fundamental in algorithms like k-nearest neighbors and more recently, in using RAG (Retrieval Augmented Generation) for LLM-based applications.

2. **Eigenvalues and Eigenvectors:** This is a very simple yet powerful concept. They are used in PCA (Principal Component Analysis) to find the most important aspects of data (for instance, the difference in the size of handwritten digits to identify them) so that we can focus more on them.

To conclude with this section, I would just like to say this: linear algebra is a language used to describe and solve problems in machine learning. Its concepts are not only theoretical but also highly practical, as they are implemented in various machine learning libraries and frameworks such as NumPy, which we will be covering in our next section. For now, let's move onto the next important mathematical concept: *Calculus.*

2.2.2 Calculus: Way an ML model learns

Before you start biting your nails, we're not talking about solving complex integrals here. In machine learning, calculus helps us understand how a ML model learns and improves. Specifically, concepts like derivatives and gradients are crucial for optimization.

When you're training a model, you're essentially trying to find the best pattern in your data and calculus helps us understand how small changes in the model's parameters affect the outcome, guiding us towards the optimal configuration. So, let's take a look at the fundamental concepts of calculus that are important for machine learning.

1. **Derivatives:** Although the term may seem advanced, it just shows how a function changes over time with respect to something. For example, if the price of a stock sky-rocketed after a news article, we can use this concept to figure out just how much the article changed the price of that stock over a particular time period. In machine learning, derivatives are used to understand how changes in a model impact its performance and in turn, determine the best model.

2. **Gradients:** Let's consider the example above; the price of a stock doesn't depend on just one factor but numerous things. How to consider the impact of all these factors? Well, that is what gradients are. A gradient is a vector that contains the partial derivatives of a function (usually our model's loss function) with respect to all its features. In the context of ML, it is used by the model to figure out the most optimum path to get to the ideal solution.

We now know that calculus helps our model learn from the data. Now, the obvious question you would have is: "How?". Let's answer that now.

Whenever we learn something at school, we have an assignment or tests to assess our knowledge. Similarly, when a model learns something, it has something called a loss function, which helps assess its performance (do note that in case of supervised learning, we already have the answer key, i.e. the labels). So, everytime our model learns something, we use this loss function to assess its performance and then compute the gradient and derivatives based on each feature or column to see how well our model is learning. This gradient information helps us update the parameters of the model in such a way that reduces the loss function.

Overall, calculus is indispensable for understanding and improving machine learning models. It helps you train models that learn from data and make wise judgments by serving as a link between abstract mathematical ideas and real-world applications. Let's now examine probability and statistics, the last item in our mathematics toolkit.

2.2.3 Probability and statistics: Making accurate predictions

Everybody has done an assignment or test where they were unsure of the exact answer and had to "guess" their way through the question. Well, how certain are you that your guess would be correct? This is what probability is all about: dealing with uncertainty and making predictions. Understanding probability is essential for algorithms that rely on data to make judgments. In contrast, statistics facilitates the interpretation of data, the detection of patterns, and the testing of theories. It's similar to using hints to solve a problem as a detective does. Let's examine their foundations in more detail.

Probability

The mathematical instrument used to calculate the likelihood of an event occurring is called "*probability*." Probability in machine learning is all about forecasts and choices based on available data. For example, consider creating a model that can look at a patient's medical records to predict if he has cancer.

There are numerous machine learning models that we will cover in the coming chapters that are actually based on various probabilistic models, which essentially try to solve the problem from a probabilistic point of view. If you ever studied probability, you would know about Bayes Theorem. There is an actual machine learning model that uses this as it's basis called the *Naive Bayes Classifier* (don't worry about it now, just remember the name. We will get into the details later).

Statistics

As discussed before, this is a mathematical tool that can help you quantify things, which essentially means measure things in numbers. There are two widely categorized types of statistics that we will discuss now: Descriptive and Inferential Statistics.

Descriptive Statistics

Descriptive statistics help us understand and describe the features of a dataset. There are various measures that are used in practice. Here are some basic and popular ones:

- **Mean:** The average value of the data.
- **Median:** The middle value for a list of sorted values.
- **Standard Deviation:** It is a metric that is used to measure the amount of variation in your data. In addition to providing you with a brief summary of the features of the data, this can also help you spot some extremely helpful trends and patterns. For example, you can determine whether a given feature has a high number of null values by looking at how that feature's average value is affected.

Inferential Statistics

This category deals with making actual predictions about the data. Its tools include advanced analytical tools like confidence intervals, hypothesis testing, etc. For instance, in hypothesis testing, we use statistical tests to determine whether observed patterns in the data are statistically significant or if they occurred by chance.

In summary, Feature Selection—the process of choosing the best features—and prediction-making using the input data are the main applications of this mathematical tool. You can turn raw data into insightful understandings and create reliable machine learning models that function well in real-world situations by having a solid understanding of probability and statistics.

That was quite an extensive theoretical section. Interestingly, we did not use a single numerical value, aside from the numbering of the figures, throughout the entire chapter! Now that we have covered the theory, it's time to transition into the practical aspect, which many of you have likely been anticipating:

coding. For the entirety of this book, we will focus on Python as the primary programming language.

2.3 Introducing Python and Other Essential Tools

Now that we have a solid understanding of the fundamental aspects of what machine learning is based upon, let's take a drive through the practical tools we will be using throughout this book to perform numerous experiments which will help you become someone who can really say: "I know what machine learning is and how to train ML models!"

As for anything related to computers, to write things that they understand, you need something called a programming language. Now, there are numerous options which are available, some very old and some considerably new, designed for specific applications. However, for machine learning, two languages in particular stand out: Python and R. For this book, we will be sticking with Python as in my opinion, it's just easier to learn and has a very active community of developers (so there is always something new). In this section, we will walk through the steps of setting up a Python environment on your local system and then go through some essential libraries (library is just a collection of code packaged together) that we will be using for machine learning tasks.

Here are some key advantages of Python which gives it the upper edge when compared to other operating systems:

- **Simple to learn:** Python is a great option for novices because of its compact and straightforward syntax (the way to write code). With a short learning curve, even beginners may rapidly pick up the language and begin writing their own code because it's just so simple and can be easily interpreted.

- **Huge corpus of libraries:** Python's large ecosystem of importable libraries and packages makes development much easier. That means that most of the things you think of have already been implemented by someone and can be used just by writing a single line of code.

- **Independent platform:** There are so many operating systems available in the market right now. For instance, what do you use on your personal computer? They all process code differently. However, Python is a flexible and cross-platform language compatible with Windows, macOS, and Linux, among other operating systems. Developers may write code once and have it seamlessly distributed across a range of platforms because of its platform independence.

- **Active developer community:** As previously noted, there is a thriving Python developer community. Because of the vibrant community, Python is kept abreast of industry developments and developers may readily access tools, tutorials, and support as needed.

Now that we know why Python is the right choice for ML, let's start by seeing how to install Python on different operating systems available right now.

2.3.1 Installing Python

Installing Python on your systems is really easy. There are numerous tutorials available on the internet that can take you through the entire process interactively and in an easy-to-understand manner. Hence, instead of going through the entire process, I have compiled a list of some tutorials (both videos and blogs) that can be found in the Online Resources.

You can simply go through these tutorials and complete the installation of Python on your own system.

Note: *The tutorials I share are for a particular version of Python (I have chosen the version which is second to the most recent one keeping in mind the stability aspect). However, the installation process remains the same for different versions with only a few exceptions, which you can easily find about by googling. Also, for Windows users, I would suggest using Anaconda for managing your Python development environment.*

Once you have Python successfully set up on your system, move to the next section where we explore some really popular machine learning related libraries available in Python with instructions on how to install them and some starter code to write our very first program! Please note that I would recommend that you use a code editor like **VS Code or Sublime Text** to write your code and execute them. The overall interface of these applications is really easy to understand and fun to work with.

2.3.2 ML Libraries for Python

As discussed in the last section, one of the major advantages of Python is the vast collection of libraries that it provides for various applications. ML being one of the primary use cases for Python, has numerous libraries. Some are developed for a very specific application like face recognition while others are just the base frameworks that can be used to create numerous applications.

In this section, we will cover the three most important Python libraries that every beginner should absolutely use. Interestingly, each library will be used to fulfill an important theoretical aspect we discussed in the earlier content.

NumPy: coding math!

NumPy (**Numerical Python)** is the package for *performing numerical computations* in Python. It provides us with the various mathematical devices we went through in the last section. It provides support for numerous data types like arrays, matrices, and many mathematical functions as well (logarithmic, exponential, etc).

However, there are other options available for this as well (again, an advantage of having an active community). So, why would one choose NumPy?

1. **Convenience:** First and foremost, NumPy is one of the most comprehensive libraries available for all things math-related in Python. It supports a vast range

of mathematical functions that are easy to implement, making complex calculations and tasks much simpler and more efficient.

2. **Efficiency:** Apart from this, NumPy has computationally efficient implementations of most math functions (mostly state of the art implementations) which makes it possible for us to deal with large amounts of data on our personal machines as well.

To install numpy on your system, you just need to type a very simple command in your terminal window:

```
pip (or pip3) install numpy
```

"pip" in the command is Python's very own package manager which allows you to connect to the website where all the Python packages are stored and download them onto your system. Once you have successfully installed NumPy, you can use the package in your code. Let's write our very first code file!

The first step is to import the numpy library. Python has the *"import"* command for this. Then, let's define an array and print it on the Python console (this is where the things you print in the code appear).

```
# Importing the numpy library
import numpy as np
# Creating a numpy array
arr = np.array([1, 2, 3, 4, 5])
# Printing the array
print("Array:", arr)
# Accessing a particular element of the array
print("Element at index 2:", arr[2])
```

Don't worry about writing this code on your system (although I would recommend that you do that to learn Python) as I will be providing all of this code in this book's GitHub repository. If you have done everything as instructed, you should be able to successfully run this code and see the following output in your terminal window by executing the following command (make sure you are in the same directory as your file):

```
python(3) numpy_introduction.py    # Change the file name
accordingly
```

Writing and executing your first Python code

```
numpy_introduction.py > ...
1  # The Machine Learning Book by Vibrant Publishers
2  # Author: Dhairya Parikh
3  # Date: 4th June 2024
4  # File Description: This file contains the first
     program for the introduction to numpy.
5  # The program demonstrates the creation of a numpy
     array and accessing a particular element of the
     array.
6
7  # Importing the numpy library
8  import numpy as np
9  # Creating a numpy array
10 arr = np.array([1, 2, 3, 4, 5])
11 # Printing the array
12 print("Array:", arr)
13 # Accessing a particular elepent of the array
14 print("Element at index 2:", arr[2])
15
```

The output for the above code snippet would be as follows:

```
v1042-wn-rt-a-55-80:Chapter 2 dhairyaparikh$ python3
numpy_introduction.py
    Array: [1 2 3 4 5]
    Element at index 2: 3

v1042-wn-rt-a-55-80:Chapter 2 dhairyaparikh$
```

Perfect! We now have NumPy all set up on our systems. Let's move to the next library: **Pandas**.

Pandas: The data manipulation framework

Figure 2.5   **Pandas in Python (Tabular Data Manipulation)**

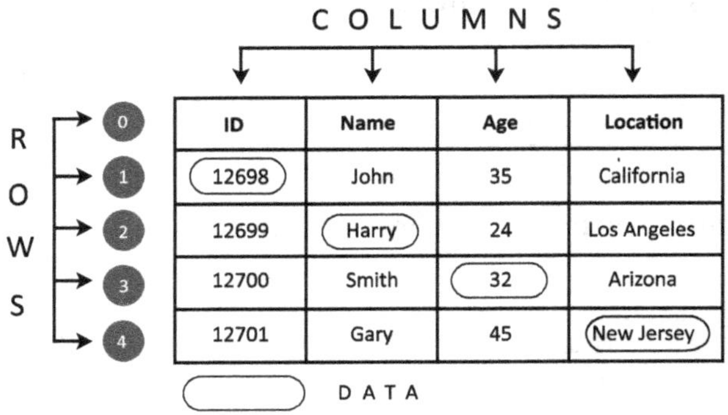

Source: *"What Is Pandas in Python? Pandas Introduction." Board Infinity. Accessed November 21, 2024. https://www.boardinfinity.com/blog/what-is-pandas-in-python-pandas-introduction/.*

As discussed before, we generally work with tabular data when building ML applications. So, you will often need tools that will allow you to manipulate things within this table to create things that are important for building our model. That is exactly what pandas does! Pandas is a really powerful library for data manipulation and analysis, providing data structures like **DataFrames** which are great for handling tabular data.

As before, let's consider the two primary aspects which makes pandas one of the most important ML Python libraries:

1. **Data wrangling (manipulation):** Pandas makes it easy to clean, manipulate, and analyze data. In other words, it's like *"Excel on steroids"* but with the power and flexibility of Python although there are strengths and weaknesses of both the software packages.

2. **Handling various data types:** It can handle various data formats such as CSV, Excel, SQL, Parquet, databases, and more. In short, any structured data format can be easily handled by pandas. Moreover, there are always new improvements and features, thanks to the active developer community.

Installing pandas using the pip package manager is as easy as before. You just need to execute this one command in your terminal:

```
pip install pandas
```

Once you are done with this, we can write our very first code where we use the pandas package to create a very simple DataFrame and show the first row of this data.

```
# Importing the pandas library
import pandas as pd
# Creating a pandas dataframe
df = pd.DataFrame({'A': [1, 2, 3, 4, 5], 'B': [6, 7, 8,
9, 10]})
# Accessing the first few rows of the dataframe
print("First few rows of the dataframe:")
print(df.head(2))
```

The given code snippet simply creates a DataFrame with two columns and five rows. Then, we just print the first two rows of the data (number of rows can be specified by adding a number on the .head() call).

First Python program using pandas

```
pandas_introduction.py > ...
1    # The Machine Learning Book by Vibrant Publishers
2    # Author: Dhairya Parikh
3    # Date: 4th June 2024
4    # File Description: This file contains the first
     program for the introduction to pandas.
5    # The program demonstrates the creation of a pandas
     dataframe and showing the first few rows of the
     dataframe.
6
7    # Importing the pandas library
8    import pandas as pd
9
10   # Creating a pandas dataframe
11   df = pd.DataFrame({'A': [1, 2, 3, 4, 5], 'B': [6, 7,
     8, 9, 10]})
12
13   # Accessing the first few rows of the dataframe
```

```
14   print("First few rows of the dataframe:")
15   print(df.head(2))
```

The output for the above code snippet would be as follows:

```
v1042-wn-rt-a-55-80:Chapter 2 dhairyaparikh$ python3
pandas_introduction.py
First few rows of the dataframe:
   A  B
0  1  6
1  2  7

v1042-wn-rt-a-55-80: Chapter 2 dhairyaparikh$
```

Finally, let's end this section with the last library: matplotlib.

Matplotlib: It's all about visualization!

Figure 2.6   **Visualization Toolkit for Python**

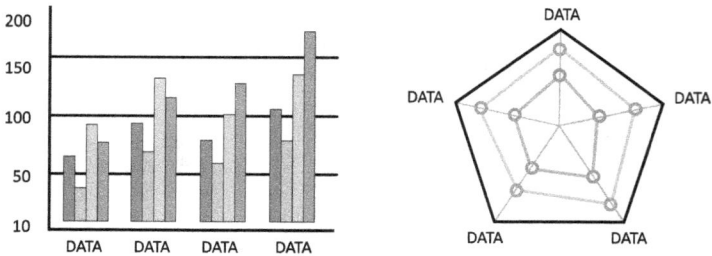

Source: 360DigiTMG. "Matplotlib: A Comprehensive Guide to Data Visualization in Python." 360DigiTMG Blog. Accessed December 12, 2024. https://360digitmg.com/blog/ matplotlib.

Until now, we have printed everything on the Python console as plain text. Although the text provides us with information, oftentimes it is really difficult to discern the meaning of text. We need something like graphs and other forms of visualizations to effectively analyze and present the data. Well, Python has a specific tool for this purpose: **matplotlib**.

Matplotlib is one of the most widely used plotting libraries for Python. It's like having a magic wand that turns your data into beautiful plots and graphs.

So, let's see what exactly Matplotlib does and why should you use it?

Visualization framework: The flexibility of Matplotlib is remarkable. Matplotlib can be used to construct any type of plot including basic line plots, bar charts, scatter plots, histograms, and even intricate 3D displays. It's the go-to resource for turning unprocessed data into visual insights, which makes it simpler to see patterns in the data that aren't immediately apparent.

Extensive customization: One of Matplotlib's greatest features is its capacity to allow you to alter any single element of your plots. You have total control over everything including font sizes, colors, and label designs. This implies that you can produce some incredibly interesting and educational visuals.

Community and integration: There are a ton of tutorials, examples, and support available for Matplotlib due to its big and vibrant community. It also easily interfaces with other libraries, including pandas and NumPy, which are frequently utilized in machine learning processes. Plotting your data directly from these libraries is now simpler as a result.

For example, you can use another Python package called Seaborn, which is actually built on top of Matplotlib, to allow even more modifications and plot styles.

These are just a few reasons why Matplotlib is a favorite among data scientists and ML enthusiasts. As before, to get started with Matplotlib, you need to install it. This can be done easily using Python's package manager, pip.

```
pip install matplotlib
```

Once installed, you can start using Matplotlib in your code. Let's create a simple plot to see Matplotlib in action.

```
# Importing the matplotlib library
import matplotlib.pyplot as plt

# Creating some data
x = [1, 2, 3, 4, 5]
y = [2, 3, 5, 7, 11]

# Creating a simple line plot
plt.plot(x, y)

# Adding a title and labels
plt.title("First Python Plot!")
plt.xlabel("X-axis")
plt.ylabel("Y-axis")

# Displaying the plot
plt.show()
```

When you run this code, a window will pop up displaying a line plot of the data points you provided. It's a simple example, but it demonstrates the basic workflow of creating plots with Matplotlib.

First lot with Python using Matplotlib

```
matplotlib_tutorial.py > ...
6
7  # Importing the matplotlib
library
8  import matplotlib.pyplot as
plt
9
10 # Creating some data
11 x = [1, 2, 3, 4, 5]
12 y = [2, 3, 5, 7, 11]
13
14 # Creating a simple line plot
15 plt.plot(x, y)
16
17 # Adding a title and labels (Customizations)
18 plt.title("First Python Plot!")
19 plt.xlabel("X-axis")
20 plt.ylabel("Y-axis")
21
22 # Displaying the plot
23 plt.show()
24
```

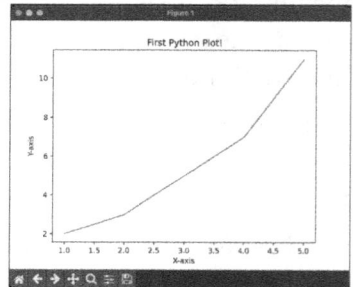

The output for the above code snippet would be as follows:

```
v1042-wn-rt-a-55-80:Chapter 2 dhairyaparikh$ python3
matplotlib_tutorial.py
2024-06-04 17:58:35.330 Python [89569:754143] WARNING:
Secure coding is not enabled for restorable state! Enable
secure coding by implementing NSApplicationDelegate.
applicationSupportsSecureRestorableState: and returning
YES.
```

Pro Tip

Always remember to call plt.show() at the end of your
plotting code to display the plot. If you forget this
step, you won't see your plot!

You ought to have Matplotlib installed and operational on your computer by now. This is the first step in learning Python data visualization. We will delve further into the process of producing more intricate and educational visuals in the next chapters.

This marks the end of this chapter. In the next chapter, we will start exploring the very first machine learning algorithms and write code to create our very first ML model, so get excited!

Chapter Summary

◆ In the beginning, we explored different types of data which are divided as Categorical (Nominal and Ordinal) and Numerical (Continuous and Discrete). You need to be able to understand these differences so that you know which models and machine learning techniques are appropriate.

◆ We reviewed some of the underlying mathematics (calculus, linear algebra, probability and statistics) that machine learning uses as well. We base these ideas to understand how machine learning algorithms operate and how we can optimize them effectively.

◆ Then we delved into the practical side of things. Python was introduced as the primary programming language for this book. We discussed its advantages that make it the ideal choice for machine learning. Following that, we went through the guide on installing Python on different operating systems.

◆ Finally, we introduced three essential Python libraries:

   ■ **Numpy:** an array, matrix, and multiple mathematical function supporter for numerical computing.

   ■ **Pandas:** a tool for data analysis and manipulation that makes working with structured data formats like SQL, Excel, and CSV simple.

   ■ **Matplotlib:** a tool for data visualization that lets us generate a variety of plots and charts.

Glossary

Term	Definition
Python	A programming language widely used in machine learning for its simplicity and extensive libraries.
NumPy	A Python library for numerical computing, supporting arrays, matrices, and various mathematical functions.
Pandas	A Python library for data manipulation and analysis, providing data structures like DataFrames.
Matplotlib	A Python library for creating data visualizations such as plots and charts.
Library	A collection of code packaged together for reuse, providing specific functionality.
Package Manager (pip)	A tool used to install and manage Python libraries and packages.

Quiz

1. **What is the primary purpose of data in machine learning?**
    a. To decorate machine learning models
    b. To provide input for training models
    c. To replace human intelligence
    d. To create random numbers

2. **What are the two main types of numerical data?**
    a. Continuous and discrete
    b. Nominal and ordinal
    c. Positive and negative
    d. Large and small

3. **Which type of data deals with categories that have a specific order?**
    a. Continuous data
    b. Discrete data
    c. Nominal data
    d. Ordinal data

4. **What does the term "dimensionality" refer to in a dataset?**
    a. The number of rows
    b. The number of columns
    c. The number of characteristics or features
    d. The number of categories

5. **What is "big data"?**
   a. Data that is visually large
   b. Data that cannot fit on a single hard drive
   c. An enormous amount of data requiring special processing methods
   d. Data that is stored in big files

6. **Which branch of mathematics is essential for understanding machine learning models and involves vectors and matrices?**
   a. Calculus
   b. Probability
   c. Linear Algebra
   d. Statistics

7. **What is a vector in linear algebra?**
   a. A type of data
   b. A programming language
   c. An entity with magnitude and direction
   d. A statistical measure

8. **How is a matrix used in machine learning?**
   a. To store text data
   b. To create complex algorithms
   c. To represent data structures such as images and datasets
   d. To design neural networks

9. **Which operation measures the similarity between two vectors?**
   a. Matrix multiplication
   b. Dot product
   c. Eigenvalues
   d. Gradient descent

10. What does a gradient represent in machine learning?

 a. A matrix transformation

 b. A vector of partial derivatives

 c. A data collection technique

 d. A programming concept

Answers	1 – b	2 – a	3 – d	4 – c	5 – c
	6 – c	7 – c	8 – c	9 – b	10 – b

Chapter 3

Supervised Learning: Starting with the Basics

KEY LEARNING OBJECTIVES

- Understand and implement linear regression for continuous output prediction problems.
- Apply logistic regression to both binary and multi-class classification tasks.
- Select appropriate evaluation metrics for different supervised learning scenarios.
- Interpret the results of various evaluation metrics to gauge model performance.
- Recognize the strengths and limitations of the algorithms we just learnt and the need for some advanced techniques.

This chapter will introduce you to the foundational concepts of machine learning, starting with Supervised Learning. We will be focusing on two fundamental algorithms and essential evaluation metrics. We will start by exploring **linear regression**, one of the most simplistic learning techniques for machines. You will learn how this simple yet powerful algorithm works, its mathematical underpinnings, and how to implement it in practice. Next, we'll delve into **logistic regression**, extending our understanding beyond continuous value prediction (by entering the realm of classifications). You will discover how this algorithm can be applied to classification problems and gain insights into its inner workings.

Finally, we will cover crucial evaluation metrics for supervised learning. You will learn how to assess the performance of your models accurately and choose the right metrics for different types of problems.

By mastering these basics, you will build a solid foundation for understanding more complex supervised learning algorithms in future chapters. Let's begin our journey into the world of supervised learning by knowing more about a model that anyone who has worked on machine learning would have used at some point: "Linear Regression".

3.1 A Refresher on Supervised Learning

As discussed in the earlier chapters, supervised learning is when we provide both the data and its corresponding label to the algorithm and with numerous such examples, it eventually learns what type of data yields which label. Take a look at this figure we reviewed in the first chapter.

Figure 3.1　Supervised learning - A visual representation

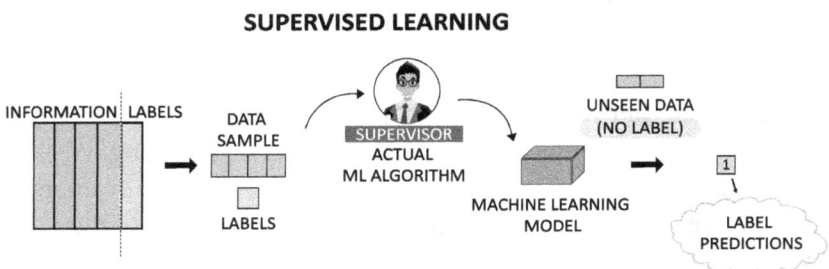

SUPERVISED LEARNING

In this chapter, we will cover some very basic yet important supervised learning algorithms and see how they actually work. Now that you have a better understanding on what this type of learning is, let's start with Linear Regression!

3.2 Linear Regression: The Starting Point

As before, let's break down the name to understand its significance. The name of the algorithm is composed of two words: **"Linear"** and **"Regression"**. Let's understand what these words mean individually:

Linear: This word signifies a straight line relationship in Mathematics.

Regression: A statistical technique used to measure the correlation between two different variables (which will be featured in our case).

Well, this gave us a much better idea on what the algorithm does. Essentially, given some data and its label, it tries to model the label as a linear equation (i.e. equation of a line) in terms of the data. So, the number we predict can be any real number (as the label can be any number). Let's take an example to understand it in a better way. Imagine you're trying to guess how much a house costs based on its size. You might think, *"Well, bigger houses usually cost more."* That's the basic idea behind linear regression - finding a "straight" (Hence, the word linear) line that best fits your data.

| Figure 3.2 | **Linear Regression Intuitively** |

Linear Regression in a Nutshell

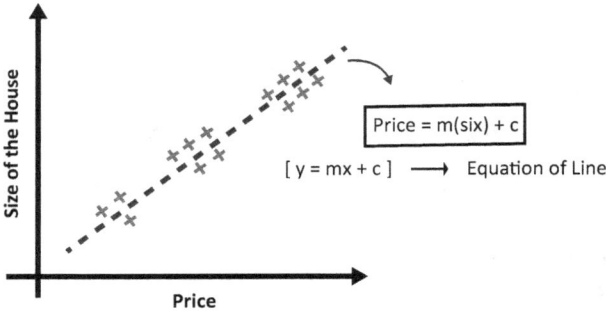

Linear regression is like drawing the best "line of best fit" through a bunch of data points as shown above. It's a way to model the relationship between two things:

1. An input variable/variables (often called x)

2. An output variable (often called y)

The above example is very basic as it just has one input variable (size) that is used to predict the price. In real world applications, we have numerous features that impact the price of a house. For instance, number of bedrooms, type of house (apartment or house), etc are important descriptors (terminology alert: they describe the reasons for the price of the house) variables. So, the actual equation of the line will be something like this:

$$y = w0 + w1 \cdot x1 + w2 \cdot x2 + \ldots\ldots\ldots + wn \cdot xn$$

The w's are called the model parameters and the x's are the different features. Hence, the task of the algorithm is to find the best w values so that the price can be represented in terms of the features (x values). Perfect! Now, you have an intuitive understanding of Linear Regression. Let's see how it actually works under the hood.

3.2.1 How linear regression works?

Now let's examine how Linear Regression functions inside. Before we get started, it's crucial to understand that this model's simplicity depends on its assumption that the feature variables—also known as independent variables—and the label, or dependent variable, have a linear relationship.

Defining the Problem

So, let's learn how linear regression actually works using an example. Consider the above case of housing prices, but let's make things a bit more interesting and choose some additional features. Here is a snapshot of the dataset we will be considering.

No. of Bedrooms	Size (in sq ft)	Price (in thousands of dollars)
4	3500	600
2	1500	380

Now, let's define this as a Supervised Learning problem. Here, our task is to predict the price of a house given its size and the number of bedrooms it has. So, in this case our features will be "No. of Bedrooms" and "Size" while the price will be our label or the target variable. Now, as we saw above, let's define our problem mathematically in terms of a linear equation:

X: Feature Variables (x1 - No. of Bedrooms, x2 - Size)

Y: Target Variable (y - price)

Linear Equation:

$$h(X, w) = w0 + w1x1 + w2x2$$

Perfect, we can mathematically represent the data as an equation of a line (or a plane in 2D). Here, the function h is defined as the **hypotheses** function. We can even plot these points in 3D to analyze the data and draw the line as we did in the last section. However, what if we have more than 10 feature variables (or 1000's?)? It is not a feasible technique and it would be a challenging task for the computer to teach this. So, the question is how do we make the computer learn?

Well, taking a look at the equation we defined above, the only things that we can control or set ourselves are the w's (also called the parameters of the model). We have to somehow teach the computer how to learn the linear pattern of the data and set the w's such that we can just put in the new values of x1 and x2 and get a prediction of the price. Note that this prediction will be based on the data we used to find these ideal parameter values. There are several ways to learn these but we will take a look at the most standard way used in Linear Regression: "Least Squares".

Linear Regression Math

This section will walk you through the mathematical aspects of this model, whose primary goal is to learn the best parameters given some data and the "target" (Supervised Learning, remember?). One reasonable method would be to make h(x) close to y, at least for the training samples. To define this mathematically, for each value of the w's, how close the h(x) is to the corresponding y. We define this function as J(w), which is the **Least Squares Function** for Linear Regression:

$$J(w) = \frac{1}{2} \sum_{i=1}^{m} \left(h_w \left(x^{(i)} \right) - y^{(i)} \right)^2$$

If you think of it, it is kind of a *cost* function, which penalizes the values more which are not close to each other, thereby learning the parameter values which favor them being close to each other. Now, let's see how the model actually learns these w values. For that, we will take out an important tool from our mathematical toolbox: "**Gradients**".

Mathematically speaking, our goal is simple: **"We want to choose w so as to minimize J(w)"**. To solve this, we can use the concepts of optimization and gradients (don't worry about the words, the actual working is simple). We first start with some randomly chosen w values and then go through the data we have and gradually change the w values to make the J(w) value smaller and smaller *based on our training data*. To select by how much we should change the w values, we use the Gradient Descent algorithm. Here is how we change the value of w:

Gradient Descent Algorithm

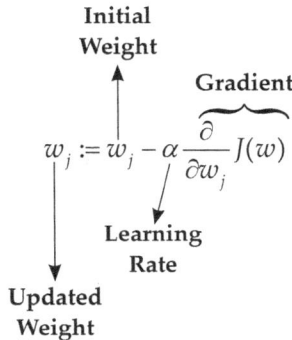

$$w_j := w_j - \alpha \frac{\partial}{\partial w_j} J(w)$$

Initial
Weight

Gradient

Learning
Rate

Updated
Weight

Let's break down this equation to understand it's working. As you know, there is a weight parameter for every feature so the above mentioned equation actually runs for each of these parameters. At every update step, the partial derivative (refer to the basics of Differentiation) of the cost function is computed with respect to a particular parameter wj and then it a product of it and the **learning rate** (defines by how much do you want to reduce the value) is subtracted from the initial parameter/weight value at the start of the update step. This is a natural algorithm that takes steps in the direction of steepest decrease of J, which is our ultimate goal.

We know our cost function, so we can easily compute the partial derivative using a bit of mathematics as shown below.

$$\frac{\partial}{\partial w_j} J(w) = \frac{\partial}{\partial w_j} \frac{1}{2} \left(h_w(x) - y \right)^2$$

$$= 2 \cdot \frac{1}{2} \left(h_w(x) - y \right) \cdot \frac{\partial}{\partial w_j} \left(h_w(x) - y \right) \cdot$$

$$= \left(h_w(x) - y \right) \cdot \frac{\partial}{\partial w_j} \left(\sum_{i=0}^{n} w_i x_i - y \right)$$

$$= \left(h_w(x) - y \right) x_j$$

As you can see, differentiating the cost function is actually very simple using the chain rule (that is differentiating the whole term [(h - y)^2] first followed by differentiation of the inner term [h(x)]). Now, we can simply substitute this value into our Gradient Descent update rule to get our final equation.

$$w_j := w_j - \alpha \left(h_w(x) - y \right) x_j$$

The above rule allows the model to learn the parameters of the model. In simple terms, **we adjust our model more when it makes big mistakes and adjust it less when it makes small mistakes.** This helps the model learn efficiently and improve over time (yes, we run it several times to make it better). Great! We finally have our algorithm which we can use to learn things about our data and predict something.

Now, let's implement whatever we have learnt here and code our very first machine learning model.

3.2.2 Coding linear regression from scratch

The time you all were waiting for is finally here! We will be writing code to implement and train our very first machine learning model: Linear Regression. For this section, we will use a very popular dataset: **"Boston House Pricing Dataset"** (link provided in the Online Resources) It is an open source and simple dataset which has a bunch of descriptors about houses along with its price. We will train a model on this dataset and see how it actually performs.

So, let's get started. Just remember that we are doing everything from scratch so we will only be using the Matplotlib, Numpy and Pandas packages for this exercise. Also, we will be using Jupyter Notebook for this exercise (My personal preference is using Google Collaboratory for this).

Importing the Libraries and Loading the Dataset

Let's import the libraries we need first and then load the dataset.

Importing the required libraries

```
import numpy as np
import pandas as pd
import matplotlib.pyplot as plt
```

Loading the Dataset

```
# Load the dataset
url
"https://archive.ics.uci.edu/ml/machine-learning-
databases/housing/housing.data"
column_names = [
    'CRIM', 'ZN', 'INDUS', 'CHAS', 'NOX', 'RM', 'AGE',
'DIS', 'RAD', 'TAX', 'PTRATIO', 'B', 'LSTAT', 'MEDV'
]
data = pd.read_csv(url, delim_whitespace=True,
names=column_names)

# Display the first few rows
data.head()
```

This will load the dataset we want into a pandas Dataframe and print out the first 5 records.

	CRIM	ZN	INDUS	CHAS	NOX	RM	AGE	DIS	RAD	TAX	PTRATIO	B	LSTAT	MEDV
0	0.00632	18.0	2.31	0	0.538	6.575	65.2	4.0900	1	296.0	15.3	396.90	4.98	24.0
1	0.02731	0.0	7.07	0	0.469	6.421	78.9	4.9671	2	242.0	17.8	396.90	9.14	21.6
2	0.02729	0.0	7.07	0	0.469	7.185	61.1	4.9671	2	242.0	17.8	392.83	4.03	34.7
3	0.03237	0.0	2.18	0	0.458	6.998	45.8	6.0622	3	222.0	18.7	394.63	2.94	33.4
4	0.06905	0.0	2.18	0	0.458	7.147	54.2	6.0622	3	222.0	18.7	396.90	5.33	36.2

Here are some more details about the dataset columns:

Variables

There are **14** attributes in each case of the dataset. They are:

1. **CRIM** - per capita crime rate by town
2. **ZN** - proportion of residential land zoned for lots over 25,000 sq.ft.
3. **INDUS** - proportion of non-retail business acres per town.
4. **CHAS** - Charles River dummy variable (1 if tract bounds river; 0 otherwise)
5. **NOX** - nitric oxides concentration (parts per 10 million)
6. **RM** - average number of rooms per dwelling
7. **AGE** - proportion of owner-occupied units built prior to 1940
8. **DIS** - weighted distances to five Boston employment centres
9. **RAD** - index of accessibility to radial highways
10. **TAX** - full-value property-tax rate per $10,000
11. **PTRATIO** - pupil-teacher ratio by town

12. **B** - 1OOO(Bk - 0 .63)^2 where Bk is the proportion of blacks by town

13. **LSTAT** - % lower status of the population

14. **MEDV** - Median value of owner-occupied homes in $1000's

So, the **MEDV** column is our target column while the rest are features which will help us. Hence, we will have 14 parameters in our model in total (13 features + one intercept w0). However, before we start anything, let's code our model.

Implementing the Linear Regression Model

Step 1: Initialize Parameters

As discussed in the theory above, we need to initialize the weights and set certain things like the **learning rate** and **number of iterations** (i.e. number of times you want to run the Update rule). For that, we will need to split our dataset into features and labels (X and Y notations).

```
# Separate features and labels
X = data.drop('MEDV', axis=1)
y = data['MEDV']
# Add a bias term (column of ones) to the features
X = np.c_[np.ones(X.shape[0]), X]
# Initialize weights
w = np.zeros(X.shape[1])
# configure Learning Rate and Iterations
learning_rate = 0.01
iterations = 1000
```

Step 2: Define the Hypothesis Function

Next, let's define the h(x) function we defined above (which represents our target variable as a linear equation of the features). It is simply the dot product between our weight parameters and the features.

```
# Defining the Hypothesis Function
def hypothesis(X, w):
    return np.dot(X, w)
```

Great, now we will define the **least squares cost function** for Linear Regression.

Step 3: The Cost Function

We will now implement the cost function J(w) we defined in the previous section. Note that this function will actually use our Hypothesis function.

```
def cost_function(X, y, w):
    m = len(y)
    return (1 / (2 * m)) * np.sum((hypothesis(X, w) - y) ** 2)
```

Step 4: The Gradient Descent Algorithm

Finally, the most important part based on which our model will learn: Gradient Descent. We will now implement it with Python so that we can update our weights based on our derived update rule.

```
def gradient_descent(X, y, w, learning_rate, iterations):
    m = len(y)
    cost_history = np.zeros(iterations)

    for i in range(iterations):
        w = w - (learning_rate / m) * np.dot(X.T,
(hypothesis(X, w) - y))
        cost_history[i] = cost_function(X, y, w)

    return w, cost_history
```

Great, we have successfully coded our Linear Regression model. Next, let's train our model on the dataset we loaded in the last step. But before we do that, we will need to pre-process the data.

Data Preprocessing and Model Training

Step 1: Data Preprocessing

As discussed before, preprocessing the data is a very crucial step in machine learning. It results in better performance and generalization of our model. For this exercise, we will normalize the features for better performance. Apart from this, if you have created a custom dataset, you might have to take care of NaN values and perform some essential data cleaning steps which remove outliers that could hurt the overall model predictions.

```
# Add a bias term (column of ones) to the features
X = np.c_[np.ones(X.shape[0]), X]

# Convert to numpy arrays
X = X.values
y = y.values
```

Step 2: Model Training

We are finally here! We will now train our first ML model. That is just executing the gradient_descent function but still, it is a major milestone. You can finally say that you have trained your very own machine learning model.

```
w, cost_history = gradient_descent(X, y, w, learning_
rate, iterations)

print("Weights after training:", w)
print("Final value of the Cost Function:",
cost_history[-1])
```

This will print out the values of your model weights and the final value of the cost function J as shown below.

```
Weights after training: [14.28507047 -0.59488568
0.45444082 -0.56208316 0.78614539 -0.4367987 0.661591
-2.27392334]
Final value of the cost Function: 47.49792532562944
```

These values are well and good but how will we know that our model actually learnt something? Well, let's see how our cost function value changes with the number of iterations to get a better idea of this learning process (remember, our ultimate goal was to minimize the cost function).

Step 3: Visualizing the Learning Process

For this, we will use the matplotlib library and plot a scatter plot between the cost function and the number of iterations. The code for the same is given below.

```
plt.plot(range(iterations), cost_history, 'b.')
plt.xlabel('Iterations')
plt.ylabel('Cost')
plt.title('Cost Function J(w)')
plt.show()
```

Cost Function J(w)

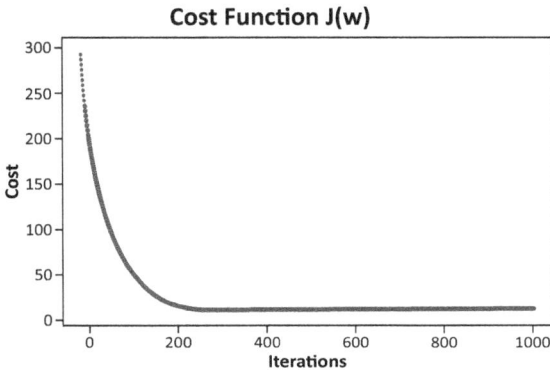

As you can see in the graph on the right, the value of the cost function is gradually decreasing, meaning our model is learning from the training data!

Now, let's test our model by choosing some records from our dataset, predicting their price values and comparing them to the original values.

Step 4: Making Predictions with our model

We will use the parameters obtained from the model training process (which is essentially our model) to make predictions on the first 5 records of our dataset and compare them to the original ground truths (another name for the target variable value).

```
def predict(X, w):
    return hypothesis(X, w)

predictions = predict(X, w)
print("Predictions:", predictions[:5])
print("Actual values:", y[:5])
```

Output

```
Predictions: [30.596 24.96 30.741 28.979 28.359]
Actual values: [24. 21.6 34.7 33.4 36.2]
```

Although the model doesn't perform as well as expected, it's a great starting point. However, how do we quantify this performance? The answer to this is **Evaluation metrics,** which we will be covering later in this chapter.

The predictions we got on this simple dataset suggest that this model is fairly simple and may not be enough in real word applications. On the flip side, it is really fast, which may be a critical requirement for certain applications. So, I would just like to conclude with the statement: *"Even though you may never use Linear Regression in a real ML problem, it is essential to know about it as it forms the foundations for more complex models"*. That was all for Linear Regression. Next, we will take a look at our first classification algorithm: "**Logistic Regression**".

3.3 Logistic Regression: The Fundamental Classifier

Similar to how we broke down the term "Linear Regression" for its relevance, let's analyze the word Logistic regression. This name consists of two words: "Logistic" and "Regression". Let's understand what these terms mean individually:

Logistic: Refers to the logistic function, also known as the **sigmoid function** (See figure 3.3). This function outputs a value between 0 and 1, making it ideal for binary classification tasks where we want to predict probabilities as a probability measure falls in the same range.

Figure 3.3   **Visualizing the Sigmoid Function**

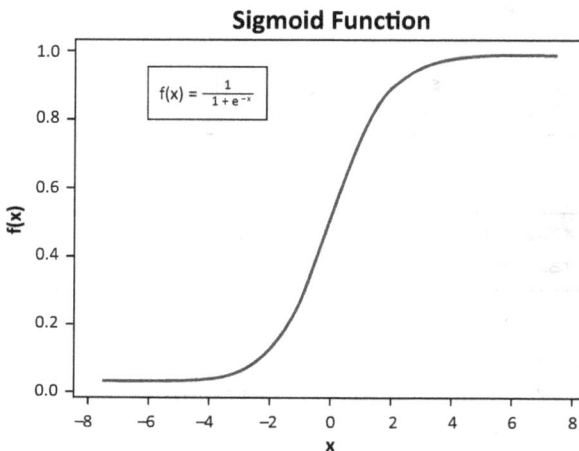

Sigmoid Function

$$f(x) = \frac{1}{1+e^{-x}}$$

Regression: It may sound like a relationship akin to linear regression, but with logistic-regression it actually refers to the process of estimating parameters for the logistic function.

Simply from the name, we can deduce that logistic regression assumes a logistic function to solve problems of classification through regressive analysis. Essentially, given some data and its label, logistic regression models the probability that a given input point belongs to a particular class. It is the same as drawing the line but instead of fitting the data, we find the line which separates the labels.

Figure 3.4	Logistic Regression Interpretation

Logistic Regression

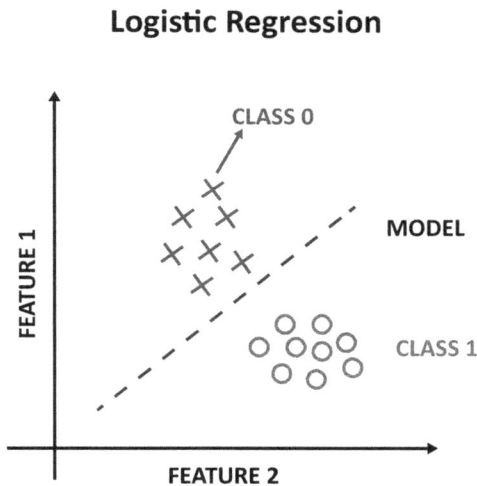

Now, let's understand this with a very basic example. Consider a case where you're trying to predict whether an email is spam or not spam (Spam mails are annoying, right?). Each email has specific identifiers, such as the presence of particular keywords, the length of the email, and the sender's address (this is an important one). Logistic regression helps you find a boundary that separates the spam emails from the non-spam ones (like the line shown in the image above). *The logistic functi*on converts the input data to a probability value between 0 and 1, indicating how likely it is that an email is spam.

So, logistic regression is all about finding the decision boundary between classes. As before, this is a way to model the relationship between:

- Input variables (often called features or predictors)
- Output variable (often called a response or target, which is binary)

Let's consider a simple example with one input variable (x). The logistic regression model can be represented as:

$$P(y = 1 \mid x) = \sigma(x) = \frac{1}{1 + e^{-(w_0 + w_1 x)}}$$

Here, $P(y=1 \mid x)$ is the probability that the output y is 1 (e.g., spam) given the input x. The w's are the model parameters that logistic regression aims to learn as was the case with Linear Regression. So, the only difference between Linear and Logistic Regression will be the cost function used. Let's dive deeper by understanding the algorithm mathematically.

3.3.1 How does Logistic Regression work?

Now that we have an intuitive understanding, let's see how logistic regression actually works.

Defining the Problem

Consider the task of predicting whether a student passes or fails based on their study hours and attendance. Here's a snapshot of the dataset:

Study Hours	Attendance (%)	Pass (1) / Fail (0)
10	90	1
5	70	0

In this problem, the features we will be considering are "Study Hours" and "Attendance," while the outcome we want to predict is "Pass/Fail". Mathematically, the logistic regression model can be defined as:

- X: Feature Variables (x1 - Study Hours, x2 - Attendance)
- Y: Target Variable (y - Pass/Fail, you can consider it 0/1 as shown)

The logistic function, or the sigmoid function, can convert any real-valued number into a number in the range [0, 1]. It's like probability, right? That's exactly the idea! The equation of the logistic function as shown above is:

$$\sigma(z) = \frac{1}{1 + e^{-z}}$$

In the context of logistic regression, the equation of "z" is defined as follows:

$$z = w_0 + w_1 x_1 + w_2 x_2$$

Thus, the model can be written as:

$$P(y = 1 \mid X) = \sigma\left(w_0 + w_1 x_1 + w_2 x_2\right)$$

Our task is to learn the **parameters w** that maximize the likelihood of our observations (how often does the desired observation occur). This process is called **maximum likelihood estimation**.

Logistic Regression Math

Logistic regression aims to find the best-fitting model to describe the relationship between the binary (or as we will later see, categorical) dependent variable and one or more independent variables (i.e. the features). To achieve this, we define a cost (or loss) function, often called the log-loss or binary cross-entropy loss, which is used to measure the performance of our model.

The log-loss (log as in *logarithm*) function for logistic regression is defined as:

$$J(w) = -\frac{1}{m} \sum_{i=1}^{m} \left[y^{(i)} \log\left(\hat{y}^{(i)}\right) + \left(1 - y^{(i)}\right) \log\left(1 - \hat{y}^{(i)}\right) \right]$$

Here, *m is the number of training examples*, y(i) is the actual label, and y_hat(i) is the predicted probability that y=1.

Our objective here is to minimize this cost function, which will help us find the optimal parameter values. Similar to linear regression, we use the Gradient Descent algorithm to minimize the cost function:

$$w_j := w_j - \alpha \frac{\partial}{\partial w_j} J(w)$$

Where α is the learning rate, and the partial derivative of the cost function with respect to wj can be derived as:

$$\frac{\partial}{\partial w_j} J(w) = \frac{1}{m} \sum_{i=1}^{m} \left(\hat{y}^{(i)} - y^{(i)} \right) x_j^{(i)}$$

By iteratively updating the weights using the above rule, the algorithm converges to the optimal weights that minimize the cost function.

The logistic cost function is given by:

$$J(w) = -\frac{1}{m} \sum_{i=1}^{m} \left[y^{(i)} \log\left(\hat{y}^{(i)}\right) + \left(1 - y^{(i)}\right) \log\left(1 - \hat{y}^{(i)}\right) \right]$$

The predicted probability is:

$$\hat{y}^{(i)} = \sigma\left(z^{(i)}\right) = \frac{1}{1 + e^{-w^T x^{(i)}}}$$

To find the gradient, we compute the partial derivative of J(w) with respect to wj:

$$\frac{\partial J(w)}{\partial w_j} = \frac{\partial}{\partial w_j} \left(-\frac{1}{m} \sum_{i=1}^{m} \left[y^{(i)} \log\left(\hat{y}^{(i)}\right) + \left(1 - y^{(i)}\right) \log\left(1 - \hat{y}^{(i)}\right) \right] \right)$$

$$= -\frac{1}{m} \sum_{i=1}^{m} \left[\frac{\partial}{\partial w_j} \left(y^{(i)} \log\left(\hat{y}^{(i)}\right) + \left(1 - y^{(i)}\right) \log\left(1 - \hat{y}^{(i)}\right) \right) \right]$$

$$= -\frac{1}{m} \sum_{i=1}^{m} \left[y^{(i)} \left(\frac{1}{\hat{y}^{(i)}} \frac{\partial \hat{y}^{(i)}}{\partial w_j} \right) + \left(1 - y^{(i)}\right) \left(\frac{1}{1 - \hat{y}^{(i)}} \frac{\partial \left(1 - \hat{y}^{(i)}\right)}{\partial w_j} \right) \right] .$$

$$= -\frac{1}{m} \sum_{i=1}^{m} \left[y^{(i)} \left(\frac{1}{\hat{y}^{(i)}} \hat{y}^{(i)} \left(1 - \hat{y}^{(i)}\right) x_j^{(i)} \right) + \left(1 - y^{(i)}\right) \left(\frac{1}{1 - \hat{y}^{(i)}} \left(-\hat{y}^{(i)}\right) \left(1 - \hat{y}^{(i)}\right) x_j^{(i)} \right) \right]$$

$$= -\frac{1}{m} \sum_{i=1}^{m} \left[y^{(i)} \left(\left(1 - \hat{y}^{(i)}\right) x_j^{(i)} \right) - \left(1 - y^{(i)}\right) \left(\hat{y}^{(i)} x_j^{(i)} \right) \right]$$

$$= \frac{1}{m} \sum_{i=1}^{m} \left(\hat{y}^{(i)} - y^{(i)} \right) x_j^{(i)}$$

Therefore, the partial derivative of the logistic cost function with respect to wj is:

$$\frac{\partial J(w)}{\partial w_j} = \frac{1}{m} \sum_{i=1}^{m} \left(\hat{y}^{(i)} - y^{(i)} \right) x_j^{(i)}$$

So, the Gradient Descent Algorithm for Logistic Regression will be as follows:

$$w_j := w_j - \alpha \frac{1}{m} \sum_{i=1}^{m} \left(\sigma \left(w^T x^{(i)} \right) - y^{(i)} \right) x_j^{(i)}$$

By iteratively updating the weights using the above rule, the algorithm converges to the optimal weights that minimize the cost function. That was Logistic Regression Math for you. You now have a solid understanding of how the algorithm actually works.

Now comes the fun part. Let's code Logistic Regression from scratch!

3.3.2 Coding logistic regression from scratch

Let's implement logistic regression using Python. For this section, we'll use a simple custom dataset based on the example we discussed above and follow the steps of defining the model, initializing parameters, and using gradient descent for optimization as we did in Linear Regression.

Importing the Libraries and Loading the Dataset

First, let's import the necessary libraries as before. We will only use the fundamental ML libraries in Python throughout this Chapter.

```
import numpy as np
import pandas as pd
import matplotlib.pyplot as plt
```

Next, we will create a simple dataset based on our example above:

```
# Creating a simple dataset
data = {
    'Study Hours': [10, 5, 8, 12, 3],
    'Attendance': [90, 70, 80, 95, 60],
    'Pass': [1, 0, 1, 1, 0]
}
df = pd.DataFrame(data)
X = df[['Study Hours', 'Attendance']].values
y = df['Pass'].values
```

Implementing the Logistic Regression Model

Step 1: Initialize Parameters

As before, we need to initialize the weights and set certain parameters like the learning rate and the number of iterations for our model.

```
# Add a bias term (column of ones) to the features
X = np.c_[np.ones(X.shape[0]), X]

# Initialize weights
w = np.zeros(X.shape[1])

# Configure Learning Rate and Iterations
learning_rate = 0.01
iterations = 1000
```

Next, let's define our actual model.

Step 2: Define the Sigmoid Function

First, we need to define the primary function on which the model is based, i.e. **sigmoid function**:

```
def sigmoid(z):
    return 1 / (1 + np.exp(-z))
```

Step 3: The Cost Function

Next, let's implement the cost function for logistic regression:

```
def cost_function(X, y, w):
    m = len(y)
    h = sigmoid(np.dot(X, w))
    return -1/m * np.sum(y * np.log(h) + (1 - y) *
np.log(1 - h))
```

Step 4: The Gradient Descent Algorithm

Now, we need to define how our model learns, i.e. *the Gradient Descent Algorithm*.

```
def gradient_descent(X, y, w, learning_rate, iterations):
    m = len(y)
    cost_history = np.zeros(iterations)

    for i in range(iterations):
        w = w - learning_rate/m * np.dot(X.T,
    (sigmoid(np.dot(X, w)) - y))
        cost_history[i] = cost_function(X, y, w)

    return w, cost_history
```

Great, we have successfully coded our Logistic Regression model. Next, let's train our model on the dataset we created:

Model Training and Evaluation

Now, let's train our first classification model using the functions we defined above.

```
w, cost_history = gradient_descent(X, y, w,
learning_rate, iterations)
print("Weights after training:", w)
print("Final value of the Cost Function:",
cost_history[-1])
```

Making Predictions with Our Model

Finally, we use the trained model to make predictions on our training dataset itself and see how it performs.

```
def predict(X, w):
    return sigmoid(np.dot(X, w)) >= 0.5

predictions = predict(X, w)
print("Predictions:", [1 if pred == True else 0 for pred
in predictions])
print("Actual values:", y)
```

The output shows that our model really performs well:

Figure 3.5 **Model Predictions Output and Comparison with actual labels**

```
def predict(X, w):
    return sigmoid(np.dot(X, w)) >= 0.5

predictions = predict(X, w)
print("Predictions:", [1 if pred == True else 0 for pred in predictions])
print("Actual values:", y)

Predictions: [1, 0, 1, 1, 0]
Actual values: [1 0 1 1 0]
```

This shows that our model performs perfectly for the training data. However, this doesn't actually mean that the model is actually good as the model has actually learnt the training data and we are predicting on the same dataset. It is like giving you the question paper for a test before you actually attempt it.

So, the obvious next question you should have is, "how do I assess the performance of my model?". Well, that is what we will see in the next section: some mathematical metrics that will have you quantify your model's performance.

3.4 Evaluation Metrics in Supervised Learning

Exams are really important to test your learning on anything. In the same way, it is crucial to test the performance of machine learning models to have an idea of their effectiveness in the real world. Now the question is, how? An important thing to note is that we need some data which the model hasn't actually seen to truly measure its performance, the same way we have questions not directly related to the text we used to prepare for it. Another thing to note is the type of metric we use will depend upon the problem we are trying to solve as well (for instance, regression and classification problem will have different metrics)

As we just discussed Logistic Regression, let's start with some basic but powerful evaluation metrics.

3.4.1 Evaluating Classification Algorithms

Here is a refresher on what the goal of a classification problem is: *"Given some data, the algorithm predicts if the data falls under a certain group for a defined group of target values (also called labels)"*. For instance, in the implementation of Logistic Regression, we took an example where we trained the model to predict if a student will pass the course given some data about him.

Before we start discussing the metrics, I want you to take a few minutes and think logically on what some useful measure can be for this. Did you get a chance to do this? Reading the problem, the most obvious measure that comes in my mind is to check if what the model predicted is the same as the actual label value. If that is the case, our model is good, otherwise it needs improvement. Well, that is exactly what the first evaluation metric does.

Accuracy (The Fundamental Performance Metric)

Most of you would have heard about this already. It is a fairly fundamental but effective metric where we want to measure the quality of our predictions. The formula for this is as follows:

$$\text{Accuracy} = \frac{\text{Number of Correct Predictions}}{\text{Total Number of Predictions}}$$

Although this metric is quite useful in normal scenarios, its simplicity can be costly in cases where our training dataset has values of a particular class dominating the data. **Can you think of such a case?** Well, if you create a dataset for people who have defrauded the bank, there will be very less people with a label of "yes" and a majority of the data will be about people who haven't committed fraud. *In such cases, accuracy can be misleading as if 90% of the data has label 0 values, an algorithm predicting 0 no matter the data will have a 90% accuracy score!.*

Hence, we will need some better evaluation metrics to capture useful information for models trained on these types of datasets. For more fine grained and detailed evaluation, we consider the 4 possible cases given the predicted and actual labels and develop some really interesting metrics from those values.

Precision (Positives - Right or Wrong)

Precision is another important metric for evaluating the **accuracy of the positive predictions** made by the model. It is defined as the ratio of actual truly positive predictions to the total number of positive predictions (both true positives and false positives). The formula for precision is:

$$Precision = \frac{True\ Positives}{True\ Positives + False\ Positives}$$

Precision is critical in situations when the number of false positives is significant, such as spam detection or medical diagnostics. Precision score assures that when the model predicts a favorable outcome, it is more probable that the model is correct.

Recall (Sensitivity of the Model)

Recall, sometimes called sensitivity or true positive rate, assesses the model's ability to properly detect all relevant events. It is determined as the ratio of genuine positive predictions to total positives (true positives and false negatives combined). Recall can be calculated with this formula:

$$Recall = \frac{True\ Positives}{True\ Positives + False\ Negatives}$$

Recall is crucial in situations where missing a positive instance has critical consequences like in healthcare or fraud detection. High recall ensures that the model captures most of the actual positive cases, *reducing the likelihood of overlooking important instances.*

F1-Score (Weighing both Precision and Recall)

We discussed scenarios where precision and recall could be important metrics for evaluation. However, what about cases where we need both? The F1 Score is a single metric that balances both aspects of the model's performance. It is particularly useful when dealing with imbalanced datasets, where precision and recall might provide opposite insights. The F1 Score is nothing but the harmonic mean of precision and recall. The formula for this metric is as follows:

$$\text{F1 Score} = 2 \times \frac{\text{Precision} \times \text{Recall}}{\text{Precision} + \text{Recall}}$$

Hence, F1 Score provides a more nuanced assessment of a model's performance by combining precision and recall, guaranteeing that equal weight is given to both the accuracy of positive predictions and the capacity to recognize all positive cases.

Confusion Matrix (Visualizing Model Performance)

We previously talked a lot about the different prediction categories but the question is how to actually get them for analysis?. An extensive tool that offers thorough insight into a classification model's performance is the Confusion Matrix. It is, essentially, a table that shows how well the model's predictions match the actual outcomes. The table is set up as follows:

	Predicted Positive	**Predicted Negative**
Actual Positive	*True Positive (TP)*	*False Negative (FN)*
Actual Negative	*False Positive (FP)*	*True Negative (TN)*

Predicted Positive and **Predicted Negative** are the model's predictions. **Actual Positive** and **Actual Negative** are the true labels.

The cells in the table represent:

- **True Positive (TP):** Correctly predicted positives.
- **False Negative (FN):** Actual positives incorrectly predicted as negatives.
- **False Positive (FP):** Actual negatives incorrectly predicted as positives.
- **True Negative (TN):** Correctly predicted negatives.

This is used to compute different kinds of performance metrics like Accuracy, Precision, recall and F1-Score With a confusion matrix, you can identify where your model is going wrong. This in turn allows you to make useful tweaks and modifications on your model such that it achieves better results.

That was all for this section. Note that these are just a few performance metrics that can be practically used. In practice, there are numerous metrics like AUC (**A**rea **U**nder the **C**urve) which can be really useful. Next, let's take a look at some metrics that would be useful for regression problems.

3.4.2 Regression Evaluation Metrics

Imagine you're an engineer at a large company, and your job is to predict how much your product will sell based on how much you spend on advertising. Every dollar spent on advertising could mean a new customer coming through your door, so it's important that your predictions are as accurate as possible.

To tackle this, you've built a regression model to make these predictions. But now comes the crucial part—how do you know if your model is actually working well? To figure that out, let's dive into some key metrics that will give you a clear picture of how effective your model really is:

Mean Absolute Error (MAE)

MAE represents the average difference between your predicted sales and the actual sales. It's like checking how far off each prediction is, without worrying if you're over or under (because we compute the absolute value). For instance, If your predictions are off by $200 over the original value on average, your MAE would be 200.

The formula for MAE is as follows:

$$MAE = \frac{1}{n}\sum_{i=1}^{n}\left|y_i - \hat{y}_i\right|$$

From the formula, you can see that it sums the absolute value of difference between each true output and the predicted value and then averages that value (hence the word mean).

Mean Squared Error (MSE)

MSE is quite similar to MAE with one key difference; it gives more weight to larger errors. By squaring the differences before averaging them, it emphasizes big mistakes. So, it essentially means that bigger mistakes would be given much more importance. So, if your prediction errors are sometimes way off, MSE might show a higher value, emphasizing the impact of those outliers.

The formula for MSE is given as follows:

$$MSE = \frac{1}{n}\sum_{i=1}^{n}\left(y_i - \hat{y}_i\right)^2$$

Here, y is the actual label while y_hat is the predicted values. The formula shows how to calculate this error over n records.

Root Mean Squared Error (RMSE)

RMSE, as the name suggests, is the square root of the Mean Squared Error value, , bringing the error back to the same units as your actual data, making it easier to interpret this error value. For instance, if your RMSE value comes out to be 225, it means your predictions are $225 off from actual sales on average.

The formula for RMSE is just the square root of the MSE, as shown below:

$$RMSE = \sqrt{\frac{1}{n}\sum_{i=1}^{n}\left(y_i - \hat{y}_i\right)^2}$$

The notations are the same as they are for MSE.

R-squared (Coefficient of Determination)

R-squared score shows how much of the variation in the predictions our model can explain. An R-squared of 1 means perfect predictions, while 0 means no predictive power. So, the range of this value is between 0 and 1. For instance, an

R-squared of 0.85 suggests that 85% of the variability in sales can be explained by your model's input. The formula for this is as follows:

$$R^2 = 1 - \frac{\sum_{i=1}^{n}\left(y_i - \hat{y}_i\right)^2}{\sum_{i=1}^{n}\left(y_i - \overline{y}\right)^2}$$

The value y_bar is the mean value for the true label values, y and y_hat are the true and predicted labels.

3.4.3 Choosing the Right Metric

So, let's summarize what we learnt from this section on evaluation metrics. The most important thing is that the choice of evaluation metric depends on the specific requirements of your problem:

- For **regression-related** problems, measures such as MAE, MSE, RMSE, and R-squared provide information on the model's prediction accuracy and size of error.

- For **classification** tasks, accuracy measures overall performance, whereas precision, recall, and F1-Score provide a more thorough picture of the model's handling of positive and negative classifications. The confusion matrix provides a comprehensive perspective, whereas ROC-AUC assesses the model's performance at all classification levels.

Hence, by understanding the problem and appropriately applying the chosen evaluation metrics, you can accurately assess the performance of your supervised learning models and make informed decisions on how to improve them. Taking a look at the basic algorithms, you should know by now that the data we have in the real world is very different from the datasets we used in this chapter. So, we will need much more complex models with advanced mathematical foundations to solve more complex problems.

Regardless, this foundational knowledge will be crucial as we explore more advanced algorithms and techniques in future chapters.

Chapter Summary

This chapter introduced you to your very first machine learning models: **Linear and Logistic Regression.** Here is a comprehensive summary of everything you learnt:

◆ We looked at the basic ideas behind supervised learning and emphasized its importance in machine learning. This part laid the foundation for more complex subjects by clearly explaining how models learn from labeled input.

◆ Next, We delved into the topic of linear regression and went over its mathematical foundations and principles. We illustrated the simplicity and efficiency of this method by showing how it can anticipate continuous outcomes using real-world instances. Finally, we implemented our very first model in Python on a fairly simple yet interesting dataset about property prices.

◆ The chapter went on to discuss logistic regression and provided examples of how to use it for classification tasks. We talked about the differences between this technique and linear regression as well as its applicability to different classification settings. We implemented this classification algorithm in Python as well, that too from scratch!

◆ Finally, we discussed key evaluation metrics for supervised learning and explained their significance in assessing model performance. This knowledge is critical for determining the appropriate metric for various types of problems and ensuring accurate model evaluation.

Glossary

Term	Definition
Supervised Learning	A type of machine learning where models learn from labeled input-output pairs.
Linear Regression	An algorithm used to predict continuous outcomes based on the linear relationship between variables.
Logistic Regression	A classification algorithm used to predict categorical outcomes, particularly in binary tasks.
Evaluation Metrics	Measures such as accuracy, precision, and recall used to evaluate model performance.
Gradient Descent	An optimization algorithm that minimizes the cost function by iteratively adjusting parameters.
Cost Function	A function that quantifies the error between predicted and actual values in a model.
Parameters	Coefficients in a model that are adjusted during training to minimize the cost function.

Quiz

1. What is Supervised Learning?
   a. Learning without labels
   b. Learning from labeled data
   c. Learning from data clusters
   d. Learning from anomalies

2. Which algorithm is used for continuous value prediction?
   a. Logistic Regression
   b. Decision Tree
   c. Linear Regression
   d. Random Forest

3. What does the term "regression" in linear regression refer to?
   a. Classification tasks
   b. Correlation between variables
   c. Clustering data points
   d. Dimensionality reduction

4. In logistic regression, what type of outcomes are predicted?
   a. Continuous
   b. Discrete
   c. Ordinal
   d. Categorical

5. **Which metric is NOT used for model evaluation in supervised learning?**

    a. Accuracy

    b. Precision

    c. Recall

    d. Entropy

6. **What is the main purpose of the cost function in linear regression?**

    a. To maximize accuracy

    b. To minimize errors

    c. To classify data

    d. To cluster data

7. **What does the gradient descent algorithm optimize?**

    a. Loss function

    b. Number of features

    c. Learning rate

    d. Number of iterations

8. **What is the role of features in a model?**

    a. Predict the target variable

    b. Act as labels

    c. Serve as weights

    d. Optimize the cost function

9. **What is the primary goal of logistic regression?**

    a. Predict continuous values

    b. Predict categorical outcomes

    c. Minimize errors

    d. Maximize clusters

10. **Which algorithm assumes a linear relationship between variables?**

    a. Logistic Regression

    b. K-Nearest Neighbors

    c. Linear Regression

    d. Naive Bayes

Answers	1 – b	2 – c	3 – b	4 – d	5 – d
	6 – b	7 – a	8 – a	9 – b	10 – c

This page is intentionally left blank

Chapter **4**

Going Beyond the Basics: Exploring Non-Linear Models

> ## KEY LEARNING OBJECTIVES
>
> - Grasp the core principles behind Decision Trees, K-Nearest Neighbors, and Support Vector Machines.
> - Implement these models in Python and use them to solve real-world problems.
> - Assess how well these models perform and understand their advantages and limitations.
> - Choose the right model for different types of machine learning tasks.

This chapter will dive into some of the most fundamental models of machine learning as we move towards more advanced concepts, introducing the concept of **non-linearity**. We are going to kick things off with Decision

Trees—a fascinating tree-based method for tackling supervised learning problems. Essentially, it's like asking a series of if-else questions to split data into smaller, more manageable chunks until we reach a conclusion. We'll break down how Decision Trees operate, explore their key components, weigh their pros and cons, and even roll up our sleeves to implement them in Python.

Next up, we'll dive into K-Nearest Neighbors (KNN), an intriguing model that skips the training phase entirely and instead makes predictions based on how close data points are to each other. We'll walk through how KNN works, discuss its strengths and weaknesses, and, of course, get hands-on with some coding examples.

Finally, we'll explore Support Vector Machines (SVM), a powerful tool known for creating optimal decision boundaries using something called kernel functions. We'll unpack the theory behind SVMs, why they matter, and show you how to implement them in Python with practical examples.

With these concepts under your belt, you'll be ready to tackle more complex machine learning challenges in the chapters ahead. So, let's get started with our first model: Decision Trees.

4.1 Decision Trees: Unraveling the Tree Structure

In this section, we will learn about **Decision Trees**. The first question you would have is, what is with the name? Well, let's break it down! *"Decision"* is the word used when you have to make a choice and the word "tree" refers to creating a tree based structure which is dependent on your choices. Below is a very simple example which solves a very very important question: "What should I eat today?".

Figure 4.1 **Tree of questions**

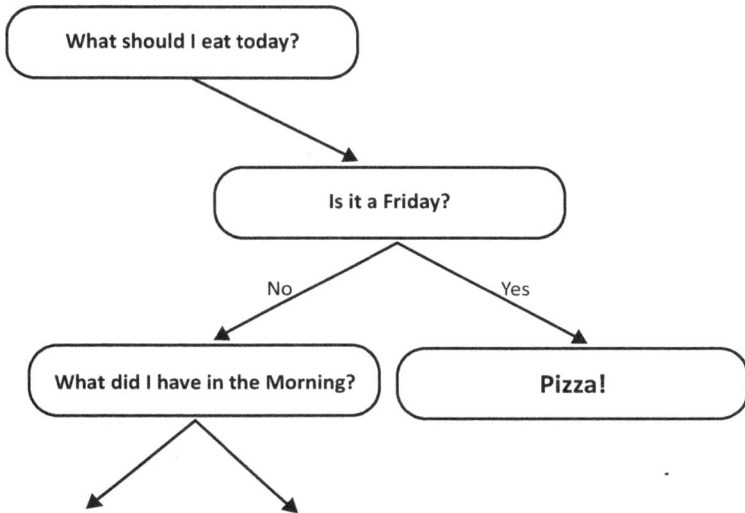

Well, as always, the question remains open ended and we will probably end up thinking about it for hours and then end up with Pizza anyways (at least for me). But, the point I wanted to make was that Decision trees can be interpreted simply as "Asking a bunch of questions to the data and based on the answers, making a decision". Well, the next question you might have is this is some simple so why do so much research and work to understand it? Well, although the concept is very intuitive, the challenging thing about this algorithm is "What questions to ask the data?". So, with this intuitive understanding, let's dive into some of the more complex concepts about this algorithm.

4.1.1 How Decision Trees Work?

Everything discussed above is well and good but how can we use these trees for machine learning? Well, let's see that now. Decision Trees actually work on the input data by dividing them into parts based on the some input data values. This process is repeated again and again and different questions are asked to finally create a tree-like structure. Each node in the tree represents a feature (input value), each branch represents a decision rule (i.e. the question), and each leaf node represents an outcome (onto the next question!). Seeing that I have used a lot of new terms in the above explanation, I feel I should also cover what these components are so that you won't be confused when you see them in the later parts of this section:

1. **Target Variable and Initial Distribution:** Suppose our goal is to check whether or not a customer will purchase a product. So, the outcome for this case would be the decision to "buy" or "not buy". The product's initial sales provide us with the information about the number of buyers and non-buyers.

2. **Root Node:** Root Node is the first node in the tree based structure, i.e. where the decision making starts. It selects the most effective way to divide the data, such as giving a pitch of the most appealing features of the product we want to sell.

3. **Decision Nodes:** Following the root node, these are the locations where the data is further divided by asking what you might think of as follow up questions. To more precisely sort the data, each decision node poses a different question. Remember, the end goal is to perfectly divide the different classes. That is where the concept of purity comes in.

4. **Purity of Nodes:** Nodes may be pure or impure. For A mix of classes (such as buyers and non-buyers) characterize an impure node. There is only one class (all buyers or all non-buyers) in a pure node. Nodes should be as pure as feasible for Decision trees to be good.

5. **Leaf Nodes (Terminal Nodes):** The ends of the tree are called leaf nodes. Based on the path the data took through the tree, these pure nodes are utilized to produce the final prediction, such as if a customer will purchase the product.

| Figure 4.2 | Breaking down a decision tree |

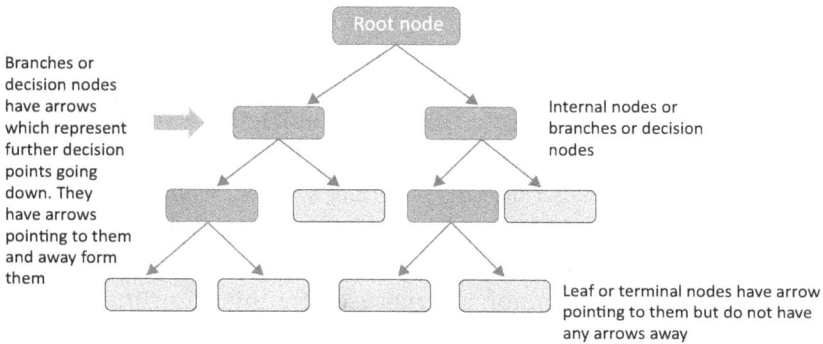

Source: *Shailey Dash, Decision Trees Explained — Entropy, Information Gain, Gini Index, CCP Pruning,* Towards Data Science. *Accessed December 12, 2024. https://towardsdatascience.com/decision-trees-explained-entropy-information-gain-gini-index-ccp-pruning-4d78070db36c.*

Let's understand this better with a very basic example. Consider that we have a dataset of people who are either 'fit' or 'not fit', and we have some personal data about them like age, diet, and exercise frequency. A Decision Tree can be built to check if a person is fit by asking specific questions about them like:

- Is the person under 30 years old?
- Do they exercise more than 3 times a week?
- Do they follow a healthy diet?

Based on the answers to these questions, which by the way are asked in a *particular order* (remember, order is important here as we go from top to bottom), we can say if people are **'fit' or 'not fit'**. The tree construction starts from the root node (the first question) and moves downwards, asking questions at each stage and splitting the dataset until it reaches a conclusion at the leaf nodes.

Great job! We now have an idea of how things work from a machine learning perspective, let's understand how the algorithm works under the hood? By that, I mean how things work from a mathematical standpoint (great, Math again!). Don't worry, I will make things as simple as possible while not missing anything important.

4.1.2 Decision Trees: A Mathematical Perspective

Fundamentally speaking, creating an efficient decision tree is all about choosing the right questions (or splitting conditions) for your data. This means that *each branch of the tree ideally contains data points that are as similar to each other as possible.* To achieve this, Decision Trees use various metrics to decide the best way to split the data. The most common metrics used for this algorithm are **Gini Impurity, Information Gain, and Entropy**. Let's cover each of them to understand their significance.

Gini Impurity

When creating Decision Trees, the Gini Impurity measurement is used to calculate how a dataset's features should split nodes to form the tree. More specifically, a dataset's Gini Impurity is a number between 0 and 0.5 that represents the probability that newly collected, random data would be incorrectly classified if its class label were chosen at random based on the dataset's class distribution. I know it sounds complicated but the only thing you need to know is that lower the impurity value, the more pure the node would be (node as in a particular stage in the tree and pure means all the datasets will be of the same class, which is our goal).

The formula for Gini Impurity is:

$$Gini(D) = 1 - \sum_{i=1}^{C} p_i^2$$

where:

- D is our data (i.e. the whole dataset).
- C is the number of classes for our classification problem.
- p_i is the probability of an element being classified as a particular class i.

Let's understand this equation with an example. Consider a case where we have a dataset with two classes, say "Pass" and "Fail", and the probabilities of an element being classified as

"Pass" and "Fail" are 0.6 and 0.4 respectively. To calculate the Gini Impurity value for this case, we will use the formula given above:

$$Gini(D) = 1 - (0.6^2 + 0.4^2) = 1 - (0.36 + 0.16) = 0.48$$

This is considered a very high value of impurity and the probabilities for both classes are quite close to 0.5 (which is a pure random guess, you can't do worse than this). So, the extreme cases for this value can be obtained as follows:

$Gini(D) = 0 \rightarrow$ When records for only one class are present (probability for that class is 1 and 0 for the other classes)

$Gini(D) = 0.5 \rightarrow$ When the classes are equiprobable (all the probabilities are 0.5)

Having said that, let's see how the value looks visually. We already know that as the probability values for a particular class are between 0 and 1, the overall Gini Impurity value is between 0 and 0.5. Let's use Python to draw the graph so we can practice coding while we learn!

```
import numpy as np
import matplotlib.pyplot as plt

# Define the probability range
p = np.linspace(0, 1, 100)

# Calculate Gini Impurity
gini_impurity = 1 - (p ** 2 + (1 - p) ** 2)

# Plot the Gini Impurity curve
plt.figure(figsize=(8, 6))
plt.plot(p, gini_impurity, label='Gini Impurity',
color='blue')
plt.xlabel('Probability of Class 1')
plt.ylabel('Gini Impurity')
plt.title('Gini Impurity Curve')
plt.legend()
plt.grid(True)
plt.show()
```

Running this code will plot the Gini Impurity values for 100 probability values (which are generated using the numpy's linspace function). The plot looks something like this:

Figure 4.3   **Visualizing Gini Impurity**

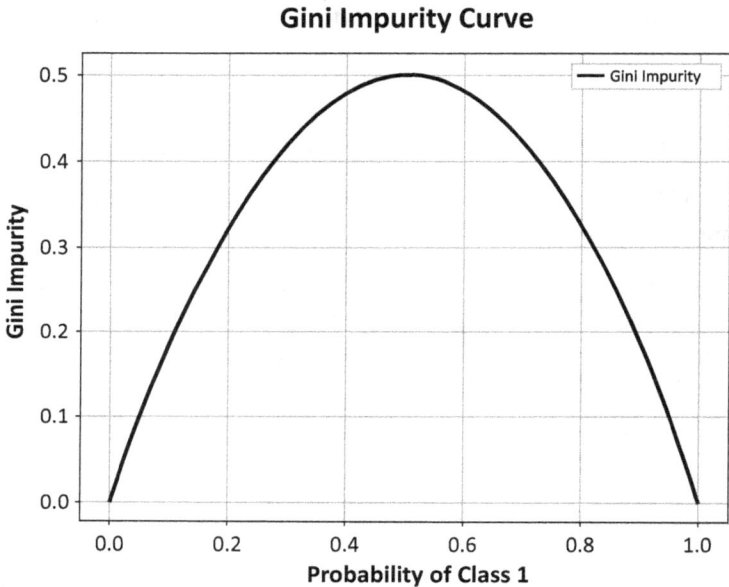

Gini Impurity Curve

The figure confirms our observations about the minimum and maximum gini values. Next, let's cover some basic concepts of Entropy and Information Gain.

Entropy - Physics in machine learning

Entropy comes from physics and means a measure of randomness in a system. Let's see its official definition that we can find with a simple google search:

*"Entropy is a scientific concept that is most commonly associated with a state of disorder, randomness, or uncertainty. The term and the concept are used in diverse fields, from classical thermodynamics, where it was first recognized, to the microscopic description of nature in statistical physics, and to the principles of **information theory.**"*

The term information theory is something we are interested in! From a Decision tree standpoint, entropy is used to measure the impurity of a certain node (more diverse the set of classes of a node, larger the entropy value). It can be considered as an alternative to Gini Impurity as the purpose of both these terms is the same: finding out the potential best split for the data.

Here is the mathematical formulation of entropy:

$$Entropy(D) = -\sum_{i=1}^{C} p_i \log_2(p_i)$$

where:

- D is our data (i.e. the whole dataset).
- C is the number of classes for our classification problem.
- p_i is the probability of an element being classified as a particular class i.

Let's take the same example we did for Gini Impurity and calculate the Entropy:

$$Entropy(D) = -\left(0.6\log_2 0.6 + 0.4\log_2 0.4\right)$$
$$0.6\log_2 0.6 \approx 0.6\times(-0.737) = -0.442$$
$$0.4\log_2 0.4 \approx 0.4\times(-1.322) = -0.529$$
$$Entropy(D) = -(-0.442 - 0.529) = 0.971$$

Great! This also gives us an idea about the range of possible values for Entropy: 0 to 1 (because *log 0.5 = -1 and log 1 = 0*). Hence, same as for Gini index (another name alert!) the maximum value occurs when there are an equal number of class instances after a decision (probability of 0.5) and a pure node results in zero entropy (intuitively speaking, there is no uncertainty in this case, hence the zero entropy).

Having explained the concept of Entropy, let's see how the values look visually.. Let's use Python to draw the graph as we did in the last section!

```
import numpy as np
import matplotlib.pyplot as plt

# Define the probability range
p = np.linspace(0, 1, 100)

# Calculate Entropy
entropy = - (p * np.log2(p + np.finfo(float).eps) + (1 -
p) * np.log2(1 - p + np.finfo(float).eps))

# Plot the Entropy curve
plt.figure(figsize=(8, 6))
plt.plot(p, entropy, label='Entropy', color='green')
plt.xlabel('Probability of Class 1')
plt.ylabel('Entropy')
plt.title('Entropy Curve')
plt.legend()
plt.grid(True)
plt.show()
```

Running this code will plot the Entropy values for 100 probability values (which are generated using the **numpy.linspace** function). The plot will look something like this:

Figure 4.4   **Visualizing Entropy**

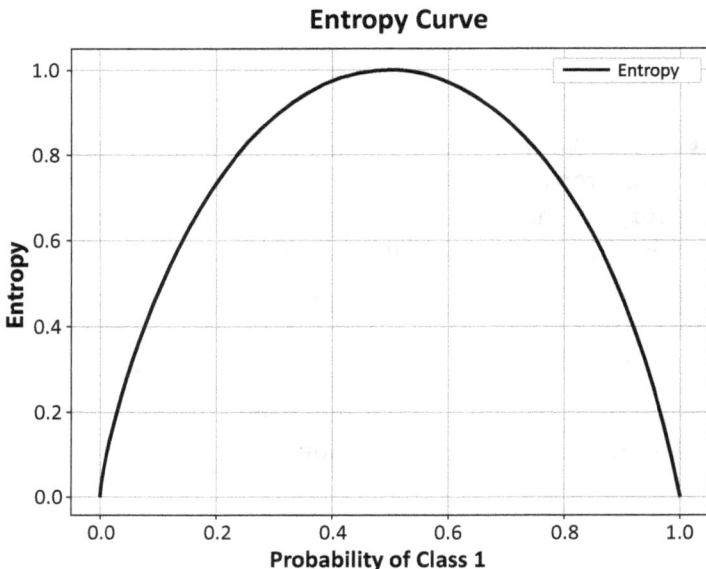

Entropy Curve

This visual representation helps us understand how Entropy behaves as the probability of a class changes. At extreme probabilities (close to 0 or 1), the Entropy is low, indicating a more certain prediction. When the probabilities are equal (0.5), the Entropy is at its maximum, indicating maximum uncertainty, as we discussed in the last paragraph.

Now, you know about two of the most widely used metrics in Decision Trees. But these just help you measure the uncertainty at a given node. The question is, why do we use this information to decide what is the best way to split the given dataset. That is where Information gain comes in.

Information Gain

As the name suggests, this is a concept of information theory which is used to quantify or measure the gain of information. In the context of machine learning and Decision Trees, we use this to measure the change in entropy or gini index to ascertain how important a given feature split is.

Figure 4.5 **How information gain is calculated**

Information Gain

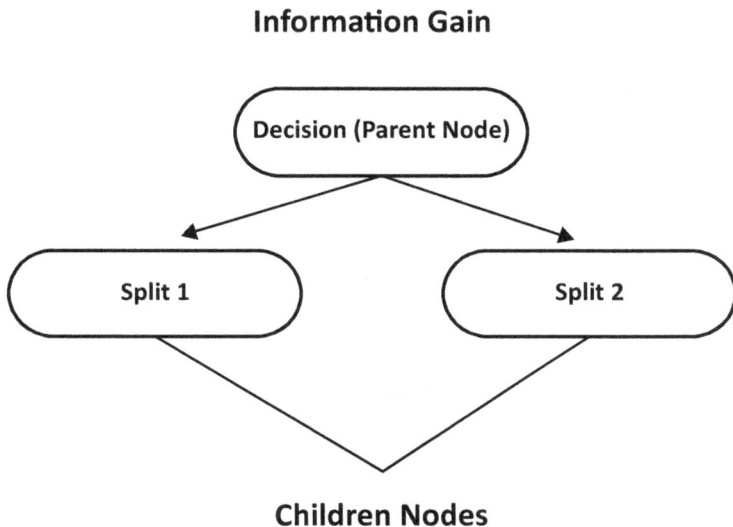

```
Decision (Parent Node)
         │
    ┌────┴────┐
    ▼         ▼
 Split 1   Split 2
```

Children Nodes

Based on the above image, we can see that the nodes resulting from a decision split are called children nodes. Hence, the way we compute Information gain is:

$$\text{Information Gain}(D, A) = \text{Entropy}(D) - \sum_{v \in Values(A)} \frac{|D_v|}{|D|} \cdot Entropy\left(D_v\right)$$

In this formula:

- D represents the dataset. D represents the dataset.
- A is the attribute for which information gain is being calculated.
- *Entropy*(D) denotes the entropy of the dataset D.
- *Values*(A) represent the possible values of attribute A.
- D_v represents the subset of the dataset D where attribute A has value v.

So, what essentially happens at each step of the Decision tree is that the algorithm chooses the feature which gives the maximum information gain until we get to all pure leaf nodes (perfect separation). Now, after the math, let's get to the fun part. We will take an example problem and solve it together both using mathematics and concurrently code it. Note that for this tutorial, I will introduce you to a very interesting and useful package which you must know as a machine learning enthusiast: **"scikit-learn"**. Let's start!

4.1.3 Decision Trees in Practice!

Defining the Problem

Let's predict whether it will rain today based on two weather attributes: "Outlook" and "Humidity". Outlook is the weather forecast for the day and Humidity is a categorical measure of the humidity for the day. Our goal is to build a Decision Tree that can perfectly classify whether it will rain or not using these two features. Note that to keep things simple, both the features we are using are categorical features.

Here is the dataset we will be using for this example:

Outlook	Humidity	Rain Today
Sunny	High	No
Sunny	High	No
Overcast	High	Yes
Rainy	High	Yes
Rainy	Normal	Yes
Rainy	Normal	No
Overcast	Normal	Yes
Sunny	High	No
Sunny	Normal	Yes

Now, let's create the same dataset in Python using the pandas library.

```
import pandas as pd

# Creating a simplified weather dataset
data = {
    'Outlook': ['Sunny', 'Sunny', 'Overcast', 'Rainy',
'Rainy', 'Rainy', 'Overcast', 'Sunny', 'Sunny'],
    'Humidity': ['High', 'High', 'High', 'High',
'Normal', 'Normal', 'Normal', 'High', 'Normal'],
    'Rain Today': ['No', 'No', 'Yes', 'Yes', 'Yes', 'No',
'Yes', 'No', 'Yes']
}

df = pd.DataFrame(data)
df.head(10)
```

The output for this code (I would always suggest you to use **Jupyter Notebook**) will be your dataset as a table:

	Outlook	Humidity	Rain Today
0	Sunny	High	No
1	Sunny	High	No
2	Overcast	High	Yes
3	Rainy	High	Yes
4	Rainy	Normal	Yes
5	Rainy	Normal	No
6	Overcast	Normal	Yes
7	Sunny	High	No
8	Sunny	Normal	Yes

Now, before you build a Decision Tree classifier in Python, let's do some math and solve this problem with our minds. Just to let you know, I would be using Gini Index for all the calculations but you can take it as an exercise to do the same with Entropy (Exercise 4.1).

Decision Tree By Hand

To build our Decision tree, we'll compute the Gini Index for each possible split and choose the ones that result in pure nodes (i.e. Gini Index of 0). Just for you, here is the formula for Gini Index:

$$Gini(D) = 1 - \sum_{i=1}^{C} p_i^2$$

Let's start by computing the Gini Index for the entire dataset for our target variable: "Rain Today".

- Number of instances where "Rain Today = Yes": 5

- Number of instances where "Rain Today = No": 4

Hence, the total size of our dataset is 9 records (D = 9). Let's compute the Gini Index now:

$$Gini(D) = 1 - \left(\left(\frac{5}{9} \right)^2 + \left(\frac{4}{9} \right)^2 \right)$$

$$Gini(D) = 1 - \left(\frac{25}{81} + \frac{16}{81} \right)$$

$$Gini(D) = 1 - \frac{41}{81} = \frac{40}{81} = 0.4938$$

Let's select the condition for the next split. First, we will choose the Outlook feature and compute the Gini Index for different categories that it has: Sunny, Overcast and Rainy.

Split by Outlook

Let's compute the Gini Index values for each category to select which would be the best fit. First, let's start with Sunny.

Sunny:

- Number of instances where "Outlook = Sunny": 4
- Number of instances where "Rain Today = Yes": 2
- Number of instances where "Rain Today = No": 2

The Gini Index would be as follows:

$$\text{Gini}\left(D_{\text{Sunny}}\right) = 1 - \left(\left(\frac{2}{4}\right)^2 + \left(\frac{2}{4}\right)^2\right)$$

$$\text{Gini}\left(D_{\text{Sunny}}\right) = 1 - (0.25 + 0.25)$$

$$\text{Gini}\left(D_{\text{Sunny}}\right) = 1 - 0.5 = 0.5$$

Overcast:

- Number of instances where "Outlook = Overcast": 2
- Number of instances where "Rain Today = Yes": 2
- Number of instances where "Rain Today = No": 0

The Gini Index would be as follows:

$$\text{Gini}\left(D_{\text{Overcast}}\right) = 1 - \left(\left(\frac{2}{2}\right)^2 + \left(\frac{0}{2}\right)^2\right)$$

$$\text{Gini}\left(D_{\text{Overcast}}\right) = 1 - (1 + 0)$$

$$\text{Gini}\left(D_{\text{Overcast}}\right) = 0$$

Rainy:

- Number of instances where "Outlook = Rainy": 3
- Number of instances where "Rain Today = Yes": 1
- Number of instances where "Rain Today = No": 2

The Gini Index would be as follows:

$$\text{Gini}\left(D_{\text{Rainy}}\right) = 1 - \left(\left(\frac{1}{3}\right)^2 + \left(\frac{2}{3}\right)^2\right)$$

$$\text{Gini}\left(D_{\text{Rainy}}\right) = 1 - \left(\frac{1}{9} + \frac{4}{9}\right)$$

$$\text{Gini}\left(D_{\text{Rainy}}\right) = 1 - \frac{5}{9} = \frac{4}{9} \approx 0.4444$$

Based on all the obtained values, we can clearly see that we will get the maximum information gain if we choose the condition "Outlook = Overcast" as it will result in an information gain of 0.5.

$$\text{Information Gain} = \text{Gini}_{\text{parent}} - \text{Gini}_{\text{children}} = 0.5 - 0 = 0.5$$

Perfect, now let's choose the condition for our next split. Let's explore the Humidity feature now.

Split of Humidity

Note that we will perform this split only on the records where the Outlook is not Overcast as we already have a pure node for that condition. So, the remaining records we have will have an Outlook of either Sunny or Rainy. Let's choose the Rainy condition given our objective to find if it's going to Rain today and solve this problem further:

Humidity = High:

- Number of instances where "Humidity = High": 2
- Number of instances where "Rain Today = Yes": 1
- Number of instances where "Rain Today = No": 1

The Gini Index in this case will be as follows:

$$\text{Gini}\left(D_{\text{Rainy, High}}\right) = 1 - \left(\left(\frac{1}{2}\right)^2 + \left(\frac{1}{2}\right)^2\right)$$

$$\text{Gini}\left(D_{\text{Rainy, High}}\right) = 1 - (0.25 + 0.25)$$

$$\text{Gini}\left(D_{\text{Rainy, High}}\right) = 1 - 0.5 = 0.5$$

Humidity = Normal

- Number of instances where "Humidity = Normal": 1
- Number of instances where "Rain Today = Yes": 0
- Number of instances where "Rain Today = No": 1

The Gini Index in this case will be as follows:

$$\text{Gini}\left(D_{\text{Rainy, Normal}}\right) = 1 - \left(\left(\frac{0}{1}\right)^2 + \left(\frac{1}{1}\right)^2\right)$$

$$\text{Gini}\left(D_{\text{Rainy, Normal}}\right) = 1 - (0 + 1)$$

$$\text{Gini}\left(D_{\text{Rainy, Normal}}\right) = 0$$

Perfect, we now have one more perfect split for the condition where Humidity = Normal and Outlook = Rainy. This solves our overall Decision tree! Now, for the fun part, let's try to solve the same problem but with code by training a Decision Tree Classifier on this dataset using scikit-learn. As a bonus, we will also look at how it solves the problem and what our final decision tree looks like.

Coding a Decision Tree Classifier

We are finally at the point everyone of you was waiting for (trust me, I also hate the math part most times but it is really important to understand what goes on internally). Let's train a Decision Tree Classifier in Python.

As mentioned before, we will use the Scikit Learn library for this task instead of doing everything from scratch as I want to make things easier for you. Let's start by importing the required libraries and defining our dataset.

```
# Import the required libraries
from sklearn.tree import DecisionTreeClassifier
from sklearn.tree import plot_tree
import matplotlib.pyplot as plt

# Define features and target variable
X = df[['Outlook', 'Humidity']]
y = df['Rain Today']
```

Note that we already created our dataset and stored it as a Dataframe called **"df"**. Now we know that all our variables are categorical so we can convert them from string to numbers using this very simple "get_dummies" function for pandas. All it does is convert your features into categorical variables. Under the hood, it does something called one hot encoding. Let's understand this with an example; consider a column that stores the color and has three possible values: Red, Green and Blue. Now, **one hot encoding** this column will result in the following:

Color		Color_Red	Color_Green	Color_Blue
Red		1	0	0
Green	→	0	1	0
Blue		0	0	1

Apart from this, there is also an alternate method to use categorical variables in ML known as **label encoding**, which assigns a unique label to each possible value. So, let's convert the categorical variables in this example using one hot encoding using the "get_dummies" function.

```
# Convert categorical variables to numerical
X = pd.get_dummies(X)
```

Now, let's define a new Decision Tree Classifier (as this problem is for classifying, there is a Regressor as well for Regression problems) for our data and let's keep the maximum depth (how deep the tree can go) as 3 and set a random state of 42 so that if you run the same code on your end with the same number, you will get the same results as me.

```
# Initialize Decision Tree classifier. Random state for
reproducibility
clf = DecisionTreeClassifier(max_depth=3,random_state=42)
```

We will now train this classifier on our input data using the fit() command. (Trust me, the library is so simple. You can train a machine learning model in less than 5 lines of code!).

```
# Fit the classifier
clf.fit(X, y)
```

We have successfully built our Decision Tree. Let's first see how the tree looks using the plot_tree function that scikit-learn provides.

```
# Plot the Decision Tree
plt.figure(figsize=(10, 6))
plot_tree(clf, feature_names=X.columns, class_names=clf.
classes_, filled=True)
plt.title("Decision Tree Classifier for Rain Prediction")
plt.show()
```

The tree will look something very similar to what we computed when we solved the same question mathematically in the last section, which shows that you now understand completely how a Decision tree is trained!

Figure 4.6   **Decision tree for our dummy dataset**

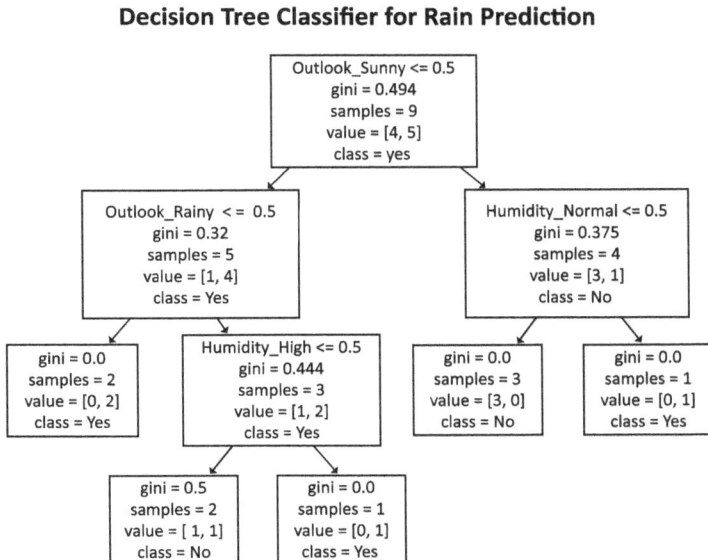

Decision Tree Classifier for Rain Prediction

This concludes this section of implementing the Decision Tree algorithm both by hand and in Python. Let's discuss some important things about this algorithm based on what we have learnt before we start the next one.

4.1.4 Some Important Things about Decision Trees

As you saw in the previous sections, this is a very intuitive yet effective machine learning algorithm which is seemingly simple but is quite complex under the hood. It essentially maps your entire training data with the goal of perfectly separating it. However, this poses a very interesting challenge which we have discussed in the earlier chapters: **Overfitting.** Yes, as it essentially maps your *Training Data* in a tree based structure to perfectly separate only that data, it is very much prone to overfitting on that data. (not generalization)

So, if you encounter any combination of features that was not part of your train set, the classifier fails to correctly predict an outcome. Can you think of some ways to avoid this problem? Well, one way I can think of is not separating the data perfectly so we can get a somewhat generalized solution. Well, that is what the depth parameter does. We can control how deep a tree we would like to build. But, the downside of a shallow tree is that it may perform badly if there are a lot of features and it doesn't even have decent separation between classes. To solve this, there is a concept called **Pruning.** Ideally, it involves training the tree completely and then removing the lower most splits which result in the least gain or any other condition (there are numerous ways to do this).

Figure 4.7   What is Pruning?

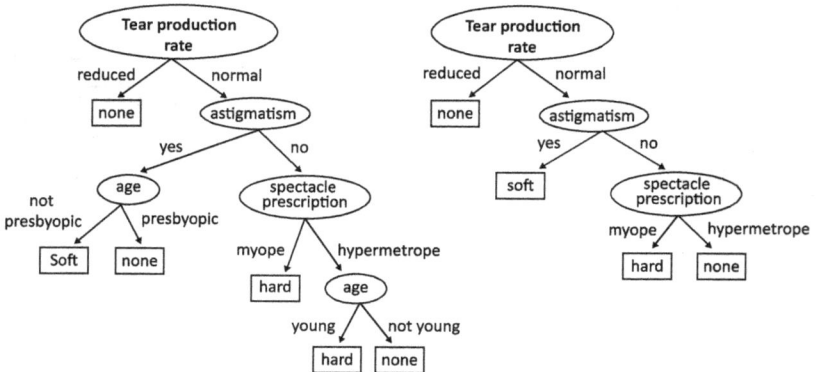

Source: Decision Trees, Carnegie Mellon University, Accessed 12th December, 2024.
https://www.cs.cmu.edu/~bhiksha/courses/10-601/decisiontrees/

Having said these things, let's review the advantages and disadvantages on this algorithm:

Advantages:

- Decision Trees are very easy to interpret, making them ideal for decision-making processes where you need an explanation for your choice.

- One key advantage of these models is that they can model non-linear relationships unlike the traditional linear models, which many real-world problems exhibit.

- Decision Trees can effectively handle missing values and are quite robust to outliers.

Disadvantages/Limitations:

- **Overfitting:** Decision Trees can easily overfit the training data, especially when the tree is very deep as discussed.

- **Bias:** They can be biased if the majority values are from a single class. Techniques like pruning and ensemble methods (This is what the next chapter is about!) can help mitigate these issues.

To conclude, in this section, we delved deep into Decision Trees, understanding their structure, the mathematics behind them, and how to implement them in Python. We explored how they split data based on attributes to make decisions, the metrics used to evaluate splits, and the practical steps to build and evaluate a Decision Tree model. Decision Trees are powerful and intuitive models, making them a great choice for many machine learning tasks despite their limitations.

In the next section, we will explore K-Nearest Neighbors, another fundamental model with its unique approach to solving classification problems. Let's continue our exploration!

4.2 K-Nearest Neighbors: Finding Friends in Data

"Imagine you just moved to a new city and are looking for a good restaurant to try. You ask a few of your new neighbors for recommendations. You notice that a particular restaurant is mentioned most frequently by your neighbors, so you decide to go there for dinner." This simple process of making a decision is how the Nearest Neighbors algorithm works.

Figure 4.8	How nearest neighbours algorithm works?

NEAREST NEIGHBOURS ALGORITHM

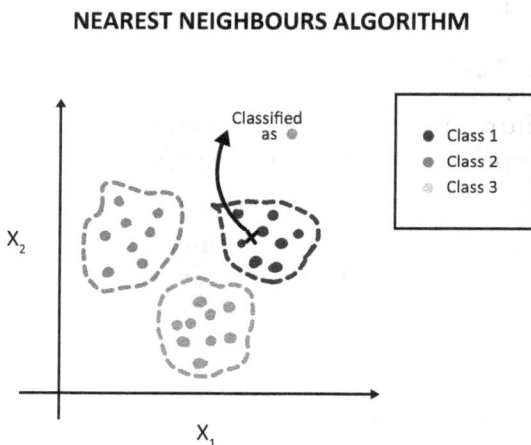

K-Nearest Neighbors (KNN) is a basic and intuitive machine learning algorithm that is used for classification as well as regression tasks. Its simplicity and efficacy have made it popular among newbies and experienced data scientists alike. At its core, KNN is built on the premise of similar things being close to each other. In other words, similar data points (as in data points with the same target outcome for a classification problem) are near each other when plotted.

One of the most unique aspects of K-nearest neighbors is that it belongs to an instance-based learning type, where the model does not explicitly learn a mathematical model from the training data. Rather, it memorizes the training dataset and makes predictions based on how similar new data points are to stored ones. Sometimes this approach is called "**lazy learning**" because until there's a need for it to make predictions, there isn't much work done by the algorithm.

We will now delve deeper into understanding how this works.

4.2.1 How K-Nearest Neighbors Works?

The core idea of KNN is straightforward. KNN uses the 'k' nearest data points in the training set to predict a new data point by finding out which of these neighbors has the most common target/ label. Have a look at this step-by-step explanation of how it is done:

Figure 4.9   **How the KNN Algorithm works?**

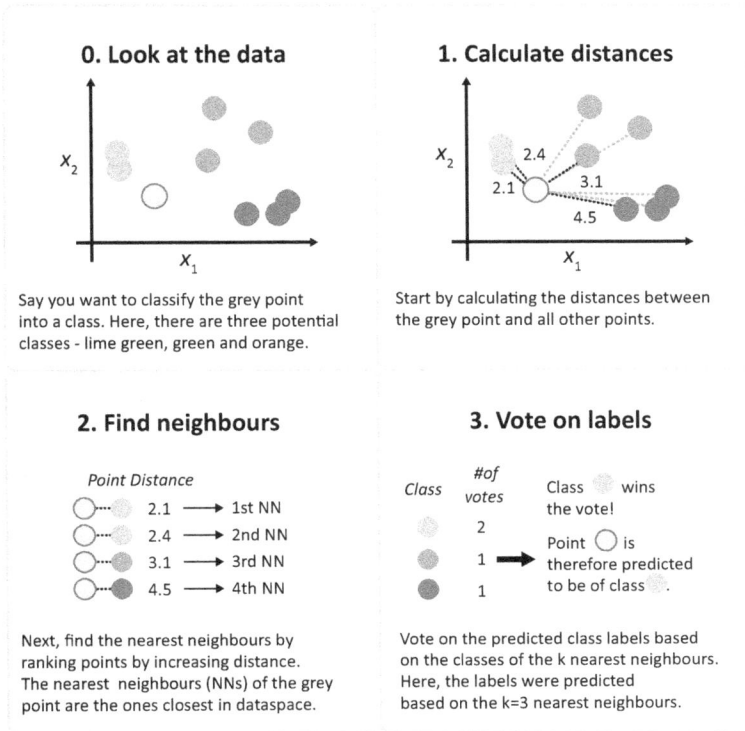

0. Look at the data

Say you want to classify the grey point into a class. Here, there are three potential classes - lime green, green and orange.

1. Calculate distances

Start by calculating the distances between the grey point and all other points.

2. Find neighbours

Point Distance		
	2.1 →	1st NN
	2.4 →	2nd NN
	3.1 →	3rd NN
	4.5 →	4th NN

Next, find the nearest neighbours by ranking points by increasing distance. The nearest neighbours (NNs) of the grey point are the ones closest in dataspace.

3. Vote on labels

Class	#of votes
	2
	1
	1

Class ○ wins the vote!

Point ○ is therefore predicted to be of class ○.

Vote on the predicted class labels based on the classes of the k nearest neighbours. Here, the labels were predicted based on the k=3 nearest neighbours.

Source: Antony Christopher, K-Nearest Neighbor, Towards Data Science, Accessed 12th December, 2024. https://medium.com/swlh/k-nearest-neighbor-ca2593d7a3c4

1. **Choose the number of neighbors (k):** This is an important step since the value of 'k' can have a big effect on how well the algorithm performs. A low k might create a model that is very sensitive to noise in the data (overfitting) while a high k may make the model overly simple (underfitting).

2. **Calculate distance:** Calculate distances between the new data point and all points in the training set. Common methods for finding distances are Euclidean, Manhattan, and Minkowski.

3. **Find out k-nearest neighbors:** Identify 'k' points from the training set which are closest to this new data point. It is these neighbors who will be used to predict.

4. **Make a prediction:** For classification, the prediction is the class that is most common among the 'k' neighbors. For regression, the prediction is the average of the values of the 'k' neighbors.

Let's use another example to better understand this: Suppose you have a dataset of house pricing characterized by features like size, number of bedrooms, and distance to the city center, and you want to predict the price of a new house not in the dataset. Using KNN, you find the 'k' houses in the dataset that are most similar to the new house based on these features and the predicted price of the new house would be the average price of these 'k' similar houses.

Next, let's cover some basic mathematical concepts about distances that will help us understand the overall algorithm better.

4.2.2 Distances Explained: Mathematically

While KNN is simple, it's important to understand the core mathematical concepts that it works on, especially the distance metrics used to determine the similarity between data points.

Euclidean Distance: The most commonly used distance metric (you must have learnt and used it at some time during your school tenure for sure). It's the straight-line distance between two points in Euclidean space. It is the square root of the sum of squared point-to-point difference for each dimension.

$$d(x,y) = \sqrt{\sum_{i=1}^{n}(x_i - y_i)^2}$$

Manhattan Distance: Also known as L1 distance, it's the sum of the absolute differences between the points. This is a different take on the concept of distances and it is particularly useful in certain situations (as always, it depends on the dataset you are using).

$$d(x,y) = \sum_{i=1}^{n}|x_i - y_i|$$

Do you see some relation between the two formulae? Yes, the core values are the same, just the power on those values is different. So, let's generalize this and write what you get.

Minkowski Distance: This is a generalization of various distance metrics. It can be represented using the following formula:

$$d(x,y) = \left(\sum_{i=1}^{n}|x_i - y_i|^p\right)^{1/p}$$

Where p determines the type of distance:

- When $p = 1$, it's the formula for Manhattan distance.

- When $p = 2$, it's the formula for Euclidean distance.

Now, let's implement KNN in Python using the scikit-learn library's pre-defined functions.

4.2.3 Practical Implementation of K-Nearest Neighbors

In this section, we will complete a practical implementation of the K-Nearest Neighbors (KNN) algorithm using Python together. For this, we'll use the Iris dataset for this tutorial and visualize how the KNN classifier makes predictions, including showing the decision boundaries.

Import Necessary Libraries

First, we need to import the necessary libraries for our implementation. These include NumPy for numerical operations, Matplotlib and Seaborn for plotting, and Scikit-learn for the KNN classifier, the dataset and to compute the accuracy score for analyzing our model performance.

```
import numpy as np
import matplotlib.pyplot as plt
import seaborn as sns
from matplotlib.colors import ListedColormap
from sklearn import neighbors, datasets
from sklearn.metrics import accuracy_score
```

Configure Plot Settings and ColorMaps

We'll set up some matplotlib configurations for our plots to ensure they are displayed properly. We'll also define color maps for plotting the decision boundaries and the scatter plot.

```
plt.rcParams["figure.figsize"] = [7.00, 3.50]
plt.rcParams["figure.autolayout"] = True
cmap_light = ListedColormap(['orange', 'cyan',
'cornflowerblue'])
cmap_bold = ['darkorange', 'c', 'darkblue']
```

Load the Dataset

Now, we will load the Iris dataset, which is included in Scikit-learn's datasets module (so it's really easy to load it). We'll use only the first two features (sepal length and sepal width) to make the visualization simpler and more intuitive. For the number of neighbors for this algorithm, we will choose 10 so that we don't under fit or overfit on the data (more about this in the next section).

```
n_neighbors = 10
iris = datasets.load_iris()
X = iris.data[:, :2]
y = iris.target
```

Visualize the Dataset

Before training the classifier, let's create a scatter plot of the dataset to see how the data points are distributed. Each point is colored according to its class for better interpretation of the differences in the values based on the class.

```
plt.figure()
sns.scatterplot(x=X[:, 0], y=X[:, 1], hue=iris.
target_names[y], palette=cmap_bold, alpha=1.0,
edgecolor="black")
```

The plot will be as follows, showing a somewhat visible distinction between the three classes.

Figure 4.10 Iris Dataset Scatter Plot (First 2 features)

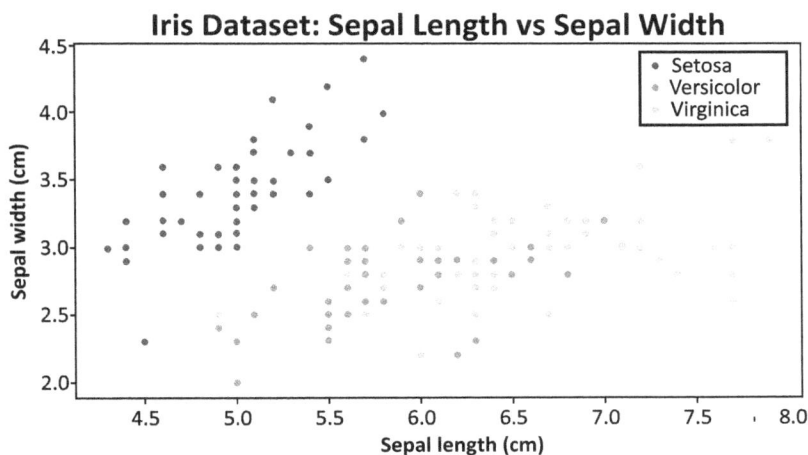
Iris Dataset: Sepal Length vs Sepal Width

Train the KNN Classifier

Now let's train our Machine Learning model using the scikit-learn library. We will create an instance of the KNeighborsClassifier with **n_neighbors** set to 10 (defined above) and fit it to our dataset.

```
clf = neighbors.KNeighborsClassifier(n_neighbors,
weights='uniform')
clf.fit(X, y)
```

Great, we now have our trained classifier. Let's see how it performs by computing the accuracy score on our training dataset.

```
# Make predictions
y_pred = clf.predict(X)

# Evaluate the model
accuracy = accuracy_score(y, y_pred)
print(f'Accuracy: {accuracy * 100:.2f}%')
```

This model will give you an accuracy score of 84.67%, which is fairly good for such a simplistic model. Now, let's see how it actually does by seeing how the classes are actually separated (i.e. the decision boundary).

Plot the Decision Boundaries

First, using our trained classifier, we predict the class for each point in the dataset and create a grid of these points. Then, we'll plot the decision boundaries using **contourf** to show which regions of the plot belong to which class.

```
Z = clf.predict(np.c_[xx.ravel(), yy.ravel()])
Z = Z.reshape(xx.shape)
plt.figure()
plt.contourf(xx, yy, Z, cmap=cmap_light)

sns.scatterplot(x=X[:, 0], y=X[:, 1], hue=iris.target_
names[y],
                palette=cmap_bold, alpha=1.0,
edgecolor="black")

plt.xlim(xx.min(), xx.max())
plt.ylim(yy.min(), yy.max())

plt.title("3-Class classification (k = %i, 'uniform' = '%s')"
          % (n_neighbors, 'uniform'))

plt.xlabel(iris.feature_names[0])
plt.ylabel(iris.feature_names[1])

plt.show()
```

This will give you a very informative plot which will show you what will be the predicted class for each possible datapoint on the grid (seperated with different colors).

Figure 4.11 KNN Classifier Decision Boundary Plot

3 - Class classification (k = 10, 'uniform' = 'uniform')

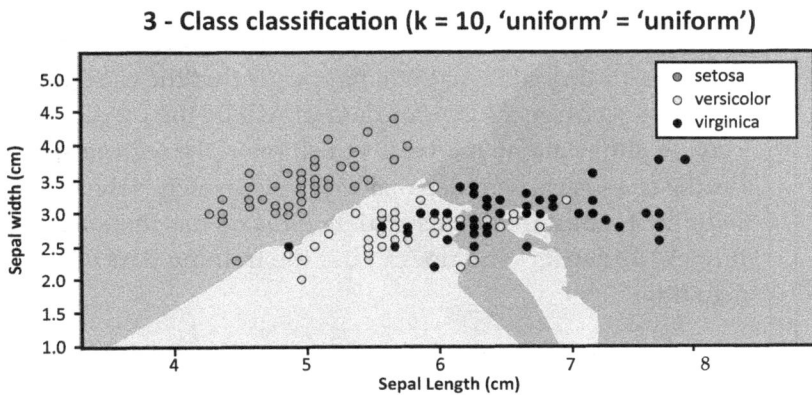

Great, now you know how to build your own KNN classifier as well. You have 4 different models in your ML toolkit now, each with a unique working strategy of its own. Before we move on to the last classifier of this chapter, let's summarize a few important points about the KNN classifier as we did for Decision trees.

4.2.4 About the KNN Classifier

In the last few sections, we learnt how this classifier works, the mathematics that forms the basis of this algorithm and how to create our very own model in Python. Based on what we learnt, what observations can we make about this algorithm as a whole. Well, here is an important observation about this algorithm which will allow you to see it in a whole new way.

Importance of the value of k: The only parameters that we can control in this algorithm are the values of k and the type of distance that we use (there are other things you can control, but let's keep things simple). Particularly, the value of "k" is very important as it is what governs your overall model. Intuitively speaking, let's consider two edge cases:

1. **If k is small:** If it is a small value (less than 3) then what will happen is the class of the point in the training set closest to

the datapoint will be assigned, always. That means that the data will try to "**overfit**" the training set.

2. **If k is large:** If the k value is large, say in the order of the size of your dataset, what will happen is that the class with the most occurrences in your dataset will be the predicted class of your data no matter it's position in the feature space (as the class is chosen by a majority vote, which is the class with the highest mode). Essentially, this means that our model "**underfits**" and doesn't use the training data at all in actuality.

Having said that, let's summarize this algorithm by stating its main advantages and disadvantages.

Advantages

- **Simplicity:** KNN is easy to understand and implement. There's no complex mathematical model to learn.

- **No Training Period:** KNN is a lazy learner, meaning it doesn't have a training phase, which can save time for some applications.

- **Versatility:** KNN can be used for both classification and regression tasks.

Disadvantages

- **It is Computationally Expensive:** As the dataset grows, the algorithm becomes slower and more memory-intensive because it stores all the training data. Calculating the distance between the new data point and all existing points is time-consuming as well.

- **It is Sensitive to Irrelevant Features:** KNN can be affected by irrelevant or redundant features since it relies on distance calculations and these features will contribute to that to some degree at least. Feature selection and normalization are essential to improve its performance.

- **Choice of 'k':** As discussed above, the performance of KNN is highly dependent on the choice of 'k'. A poor choice can lead to inaccurate predictions. Cross-validation is often used to select the optimal value of 'k'. (Terminology alert: Cross-validation is a technique used to evaluate how well a machine learning model generalizes to unseen data. It works by splitting the dataset into multiple parts (called "folds"), training the model on some of them, and testing it on the remaining part. This process is repeated several times, and the results are averaged to get a more reliable estimate of model performance.)

- **Curse of Dimensionality:** Despite the complex term, all it means is that as the number of dimensions in the data increases, the concept of distances changes greatly and hence, the core concept of the algorithm (that points close together are similar) no longer holds. *(Head over to our Online Resource page to read more about it.)*

To summarize, K-Nearest Neighbors is a fairly powerful and straightforward algorithm that can be effectively used for both classification and regression tasks. Its simplicity and intuitiveness makes it a great choice for people who are just starting machine learning. However, as will all the algorithms, it's important to be aware of its limitations and consider these when choosing it for your application. Next, let's start with another interesting algorithm: **SVM.**

4.3 Support Vector Machines: The Magic of Margins

Remember what we did in Logistic Regression? We drew a line to separate the data points of two or more different classes. However, one thing to note is that for a given dataset, there may be several lines which perfectly separate it. However, there will be one solution which best separates this dataset. The question is, how to find this best line? In other words, that is exactly what SVMs do: **they try to find the best line or surface that divides two classes.**

Today, Support Vector Machines are probably the most well-known and the most commonly used robust supervised learning models for classification and regression. Moreover, skeptics simultaneously believe that SVM is a "black box", due to its apparent mysteriousness and its gripping and non-obvious mathematical background. SVMs are known for their ability to find the optimal separating hyperplane (also known as maximum-margin hyperplane) and work immensely well and are formidable at classification and regression in high-dimensional domains, where almost all ML models are useless. Hence in this chapter we shall take a look at SVMs from a conceptual and philosophical perspective, derive the underlying mathematics of SVMs, and finally create an SVM Classifier from scratch in Python.

And so, let me start with outlining what this algorithm is all about.

4.3.1 How SVM Works?

At the heart of SVMs lies the concept of finding the optimal separating line that separates the classes. Let's break down some key terms and concepts that are crucial to understanding the fundamentals of this algorithm:

- **Hyperplane:** It is a generalized plane that can be represented in higher dimensions. For instance, in 2 dimensions, this hyperplane will simply be a line.. The final goal of SVMs is to find the hyperplane that best separates the classes.

- **Margin:** The margin is the distance between the hyperplane and the nearest data points from each class. SVM aims to maximize this margin, ensuring that the boundary is as far away from the nearest points as possible, thereby finding the best hyperplane.

- **Support Vectors:** The data points that are closest to the hyperplane and influence its position with respect to the other points are called support vectors. These points are critical as they define the margin.

Figure 4.12	Idea behind SVMs

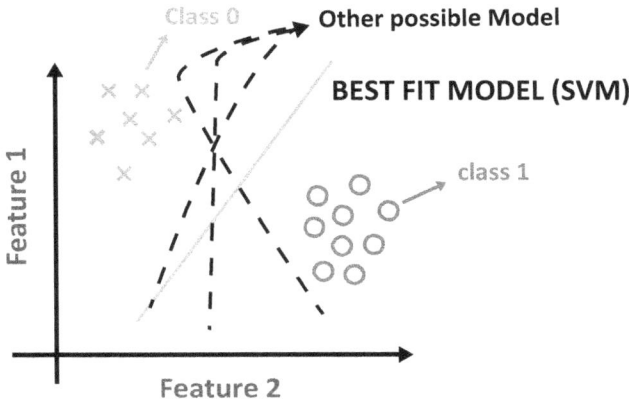

There's a 2D representation (as shown above): let's have two classes of training examples, each class in red or blue dots. We need to draw a line to separate the dots. A good line is one that separates the classes but, even better, it should separate the classes with a big margin (as much as possible). Because we try to do that, the separation will be as robust as possible, which is what any SVM does. Let's consider a very simple example Instead, let's have a dataset where we want to separate cats from dogs: we have an image of each class, and each image is a list of features (e.g., each image is a 2D list of items such as weight, height and ear length, etc). In a 2D feature space, each image is a point. The SVM will find the optimal line (or hyperplane) that separates the cats from the dogs with the maximum margin, ensuring accurate and robust classification as shown in the above image by the green line.

Now, let's understand the mathematics that allows us to apply these concepts in practice on real world datasets.

4.3.2 Mathematics behind SVMs

The true power of SVMs lies in their mathematical foundation, which ensures that the model finds the optimal hyperplane between different classes with maximum margin. So, let's dive into the math that makes this possible. Don't worry, I will try to keep things as simple as possible for you. The first step to solving anything is formulating and understanding the problem, so let's do that.

Given a training dataset with n samples $(x_1, y_1), (x_2, y_2), , (x_n, y_n)$, where x_i are the features and y_i is the class label, the goal is to find a hyperplane defined by $wx + b = 0$ that best separates the classes.

Now, let's start by defining the margin for the given dataset.

Margin: The margin is the distance between the hyperplane and the nearest data points from each class. This distance from a point x_i to the hyperplane is given by:

$$\text{Margin} = \frac{|w \cdot x_i + b|}{\|w\|}$$

SVM aims to maximize this distance. For the points on the margin, the distance is 1, so:

$$y_i\left(w \cdot x_i + b\right) \geq 1$$

Now, based on the above points, let's define the optimization problem that will allow us to solve this problem defined for the SVM algorithm. Intuitively speaking, to maximize the margin, we need to minimize $\|w\|$ subject to the following constraint of $y_i\left(w \cdot x_i + b\right) \geq 1$. This can be formulated as a convex optimization problem:

$$\min_{w,b} \frac{1}{2}\|w\|^2 \text{ subject to } y_i\left(w \cdot x_i + b\right) \geq 1$$

Now that we have the problem, let's see how we can actually solve it. For this, we will use the concept of **Lagrange Multipliers**, which convert a constrained optimization problem (the conditions in the above equation are called constraints) to an unconstrained problem. Hence, Introducing Lagrange multipliers $\alpha i \geq 0$ for each constraint, we get the Lagrangian:

$$L(w, b, \alpha) = \frac{1}{2}\|w\|^2 - \sum_{i=1}^{n} \alpha_i\left[y_i\left(w \cdot x_i + b\right) - 1\right]$$

Now, to keep things simple, I will skip a few steps to avoid any confusion. By taking derivatives of the Lagrangian with respect to w and b, and setting them to zero, we derive the dual form for SVM, which can be written as follows:

$$\max_{\alpha} \sum_{i=1}^{n} \alpha_i - \frac{1}{2}\sum_{i=1}^{n}\sum_{j=1}^{n}\alpha_i\alpha_j y_i y_j \left(x_i \cdot x_j\right) \text{ subject to } \sum_{i=1}^{n}\alpha_i y_i = 0 \text{ and } \alpha_i \geq 0$$

The solution to this dual problem gives us the optimal Lagrange multipliers, which in turn provide the weights w and the bias b of the hyperplane. The interesting thing about this form of the solution is that the Lagrange Multiplier values αi will be non-zero only for the support vectors, which is fairly intuitive if you think about it; they are the points based on which our margin is actually defined. Now, a question you would have is, isn't this still a Linear classifier if we use the $wx + b = 0$ to define our solution? Yes, this is indeed the case and hence, this formulation is called "Hard Margin SVM". But with some very small yet powerful changes, we can make this problem capable of forming non-linear solutions as well. The way we do this intuitively is allowing our classifier to make some mistakes and penalizing these mistakes in some way. That is the basic idea behind "Soft Margin SVMs".

Another very powerful trick that makes this one of the more successful algorithms is the "**Kernel Trick**". In most practical use cases, the data is not linearly separable. SVMs handle this using the kernel trick, which maps the data into a higher-dimensional space where it becomes linearly separable. This allows us to solve a variety of non-linear and complex problems. Some of the most common kernels are:

- **Linear Kernel:** $K\left(x_i, x_j\right) = x_i \cdot x_j$
- **Polynomial Kernel:** $K\left(x_i, x_j\right) = \left(x_i \cdot x_j + c\right)^d$
- **Gaussian (RBF) Kernel:** $K\left(x_i, x_j\right) = \exp\left(-\gamma \| x_i - x_j \|^2\right)$

That was all the math I could cover without confusing you guys. I know it's a lot but trust me, understanding this is very crucial to understand the SVM algorithm as a whole. Now, for the fun part, let's implement the SVM algorithm in Python and run it on the same dataset we used in the last section: Iris dataset.

4.3.3 Implementing SVM in Python

Let's implement an SVM classifier using Python and the scikit-learn library. We will use the Iris dataset to demonstrate the workings of the algorithm. As always, let's start by importing all the required libraries for this tutorial.

As always, we will use numpy for numerical operations, matplotlib for creating visualizations and scikit-learn for the SVM algorithm and model evaluation.

```
import numpy as np
import matplotlib.pyplot as plt
from sklearn import datasets
from sklearn.model_selection import train_test_split
from sklearn.svm import SVC
from sklearn.metrics import accuracy_score
```

Next, let's load the dataset. For this section, we will select only 2 of the three classes to make it a binary classification problem (for better visualization) and finally divide the dataset into training and testing sets (testing set is the data on which the model is not trained but is tested) so that we can assess our model's performance effectively after training.

```
# Load the dataset
iris = datasets.load_iris()
X = iris.data[:, :2]  # We will use only the first two
features
y = iris.target

# For simplicity, we will only classify two classes
X = X[y != 2]
y = y[y != 2]

# Split the data into training and testing sets
X_train, X_test, y_train, y_test = train_test_split(X, y,
test_size=0.3, random_state=42)
```

Next, let's train a Hard margin or Linear SVM Classifier on the training set. We can do this with two very simple commands. Once the training is complete, let's make predictions on the test set.

```
# Train the SVM model with a linear kernel
model = SVC(kernel='linear')
model.fit(X_train, y_train)

# Predict the labels of the test set
y_pred = model.predict(X_test)
```

Great! We now have our very first SVM model. Let's test to see how it performs on the test set. Let's compute the accuracy score using sklearn's accuracy_score function.

```
# Evaluate the model
accuracy = accuracy_score(y_test, y_pred)
print(f'Accuracy: {accuracy * 100:.2f}%')
```

Surprisingly, you should get a 100% test accuracy, which is very impressive considering that we solved the problem with only 2 features. So, let's dive a bit deeper and see what the decision boundary for this case looks like by plotting it.

```
# Function to plot the decision boundary along with the
margin boundaries
def plot_decision_boundary_with_margins(X, y, model):
    x_min, x_max = X[:, 0].min() - 1, X[:, 0].max() + 1
    y_min, y_max = X[:, 1].min() - 1, X[:, 1].max() + 1
    xx, yy = np.meshgrid(np.arange(x_min, x_max, 0.01),
                         np.arange(y_min, y_max, 0.01))
    Z = model.predict(np.c_[xx.ravel(), yy.ravel()])
    Z = Z.reshape(xx.shape)

    plt.contourf(xx, yy, Z, alpha=0.8)
    plt.scatter(X[:, 0], X[:, 1], c=y, edgecolors='k',
marker='o')
    plt.scatter(model.support_vectors_[:, 0], model.
support_vectors_[:, 1],
                s=100, facecolors='none', edgecolors='r')

    # Plot the decision boundary
    ax = plt.gca()
    xlim = ax.get_xlim()
    ylim = ax.get_ylim()
```

```
# Create grid to evaluate model
xx = np.linspace(xlim[0], xlim[1], 30)
yy = np.linspace(ylim[0], ylim[1], 30)
YY, XX = np.meshgrid(yy, xx)
xy = np.vstack([XX.ravel(), YY.ravel()]).T
Z = model.decision_function(xy).reshape(XX.shape)

# Plot decision boundary and margins
ax.contour(XX, YY, Z, colors='k', levels=[-1, 0, 1],
alpha=0.5,
            linestyles=['--', '-', '--'])

    plt.title('SVM Decision Boundary with Support Vectors
and Margins')
    plt.xlabel('Feature 1')
    plt.ylabel('Feature 2')
    plt.show()

# Plot the decision boundary with margins
plot_decision_boundary_with_margins(X_train, y_train,
model)
```

This code snippet will plot the training dataset's points along with the decision boundary created with the help of the support vectors in the training dataset. The support vectors will be marked as well. The plot will look something like this:

Figure 4.13 **SVM Classifier Decision Boundary WRT the Training Data**

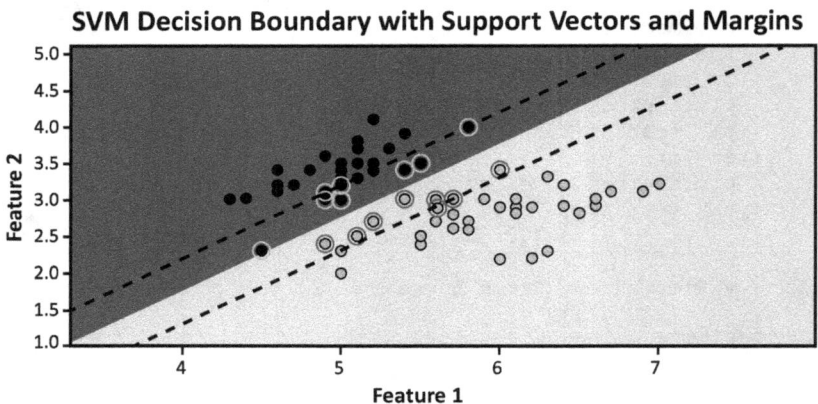

The points circled red are the support vectors and the dotted lines are the derived left and right margins. Great! We have successfully implemented the SVM classifier. Now, let's take a look at some of the most important observations about the Support Vector Machines (SVM) algorithm based on what we covered above and discuss its various advantages and disadvantages.

4.3.4 SVMs - Observations, Advantages and Disadvantages

Observations

- **Support Vectors:** The points highlighted as support vectors are critical in defining the decision boundary. Only these points influence the position of the hyperplane.

- **Decision Boundary:** The decision boundary is linear in the case of a linear kernel, but choosing different kernels (like the RBF (Radial Basis Function) kernel) can help you get non-linear boundaries, giving you the ability to solve more complex problems.

- **Margin:** The margin is maximized, ensuring robust separation between classes.

Advantages of SVM

- **Effective in High-Dimensional Spaces:** SVMs are particularly effective in higher dimensions where algorithms like KNN and Decision trees struggle to perform well.

- **Robustness:** They are effective in cases where the classes are well-separated and even where they aren't, they are robust enough to be able to handle this (check out what Soft SVMs are on the internet as an exercise.)

- **Flexibility with Kernels:** The kernel trick allows SVMs to handle nonlinear classification problems effectively.

Disadvantages of SVM

- **Computational Complexity:** Training an SVM model is computationally very expensive because of its complex loss function, especially with large datasets.

- **Dependency on Choice of Kernel:** The performance of an SVM depends greatly on the choice of the kernel and its parameters. Finding the optimal kernel and parameters can be challenging as you might need to experiment with different setups, which takes a lot of time and resources.

- **Not Suitable for Large Datasets:** Based on what we discussed above, this algorithm might struggle a bit with larger datasets, both in terms of computation time and memory usage. However, if you have no resource constraints, this is the ideal choice.

Support Vector Machines were a game changing tool in the machine learning toolkit when they were first introduced in the 1990's, especially for tasks involving classification. They offered and still offer robust performance and flexibility, which makes them suitable for a wide range of applications.

Chapter Summary

We've reached the end of this chapter, where we've dived deep into three fascinating machine learning algorithms: Decision Trees, K-Nearest Neighbors, and Support Vector Machines. Let's take a moment to recap everything we've covered:

◆ We explored three essential non-linear models— Decision Trees, K-Nearest Neighbors (KNN), and Support Vector Machines (SVM)—and broke down how each one works.

◆ We looked at the details, discussing the core principles, key components, and the pros and cons of each model.

◆ We rolled up our sleeves with hands-on coding examples, showing you how to bring these models to life in Python.

◆ We discussed practical applications, demonstrating how these models can be used to solve real-world problems.

◆ Finally, we covered techniques to evaluate how well these models perform, giving you the tools to know when and how to use each one effectively.

Glossary

Term	Definition
Decision Trees	A tree-based approach to supervised learning, splitting data into subsets based on certain conditions.
K-Nearest Neighbors (KNN)	A model that makes predictions based on the proximity of data points to one another.
Support Vector Machines (SVM)	A powerful model known for creating optimal decision boundaries using kernel functions.
Root Node	The first node in a decision tree, where the decision-making process starts.
Decision Nodes	Nodes in a decision tree where the data is further divided based on specific conditions.

Quiz

1. **What is a Decision Tree?**
   a. A linear regression model
   b. A tree-based approach to supervised learning
   c. A clustering algorithm
   d. A neural network

2. **What does the root node represent in a Decision Tree?**
   a. The end of the decision-making process
   b. The first node where decision-making starts
   c. The node with the highest entropy
   d. A node without any children

3. **What is the main advantage of K-Nearest Neighbors (KNN)?**
   a. It has a high training time
   b. It is a model-free algorithm
   c. It creates complex decision boundaries
   d. It is suitable for large datasets

4. **Which metric is used to measure the purity of a node in Decision Trees?**
   a. Mean Squared Error
   b. Accuracy
   c. Gini Impurity
   d. Log Loss

5. **What is entropy in the context of Decision Trees?**

   a. A measure of purity

   b. A measure of impurity or randomness

   c. A measure of distance

   d. A measure of similarity

6. **How does Information Gain help in building a Decision Tree?**

   a. It measures the accuracy of the model

   b. It reduces overfitting

   c. It helps in deciding the best split by reducing entropy

   d. It measures the distance between data points

7. **What is a Support Vector Machine (SVM) primarily used for?**

   a. Clustering

   b. Classification and regression

   c. Dimensionality reduction

   d. Data preprocessing

8. **What are kernel functions in SVM used for?**

   a. To standardize data

   b. To create non-linear decision boundaries

   c. To normalize data

   d. To reduce data dimensions

9. **What is the key disadvantage of K-Nearest Neighbors (KNN)?**

   a. It is computationally expensive at prediction time

   b. It requires a lot of training data

   c. It is prone to overfitting

   d. It is difficult to interpret

10. Which method can be used to prevent overfitting in Decision Trees?

a. Increasing the depth of the tree

b. Reducing the number of features

c. Pruning

d. Using more data

Answers	1 – b	2 – b	3 – b	4 – c	5 – b
	6 – c	7 – b	8 – b	9 – a	10 – c

This page is intentionally left blank

Chapter **5**

Ensemble Techniques: Improving Prediction Power

KEY LEARNING OBJECTIVES

- Master the fundamental concepts of **Bagging** and **Boosting**.
- Implement these techniques in Python.
- Recognize the strengths and weaknesses of different ensemble methods.
- Apply advanced ensemble models like Random Forests and LightGBM to real-world problems.
- Evaluate and compare the performance of ensemble models.

This chapter will explore various ensemble techniques, which are a set of methods designed to improve the accuracy and robustness of your machine learning models by combining them together in a number of innovative ways. We will begin with *Bagging (Bootstrap Aggregating)*, which is a method that enhances the model's performance by training multiple models on different subsets of the data and combining their predictions in some way based on the problem. You will learn the key principles behind Bagging, its advantages, and see practical implementations in Python.

Next, we will cover Boosting, an ensemble method where models are trained iteratively in a sequential manner, with each new model focusing on the errors made by previous ones. We'll see how Boosting actually works, then go through the various boosting algorithms like AdaBoost and Gradient Boosting, and their practical applications. Finally, we will explore advanced ensemble models which are built using the fundamentals we learnt, including Random Forests and LightGBM. Random Forests combine the simplicity of decision trees with the power of ensemble learning with a few very useful tweaks, while LightGBM is a highly efficient gradient boosting method. We will discuss how these models work, their benefits, and see how to implement them using Python.

By mastering these ensemble techniques, you will significantly enhance your ability to create more robust and accurate machine learning models. Let's begin with our first technique: **Bagging**.

5.1 Bagging: Harnessing the Power of Multiple Models

Welcome to the world of ensemble learning and congratulations on making it here! In this section, we'll dive into one of the most fundamental ensemble techniques: **Bagging, which is short for Bootstrap Aggregating**. Ensemble methods are like a super team in machine learning. Just like how a team of superheroes can tackle a problem better than any single hero, ensemble methods combine multiple models to improve prediction accuracy. The primary objective of this kind of learning is to reduce variability in model predictions and help improve its overall stability. Now, let's take a look at how the algorithm works from a conceptual standpoint.

5.1.1 How does it work?

Let's first examine the real functions of the algorithm before delving into its inner workings. In the simplest of words, creating numerous versions of a model and utilizing them to combine the model results in some way (we will talk about it later) is known as **bagging**. Consider yourself attempting to estimate how many candies are in a jar. The average of several guesses made by different people is probably going to be more accurate than any one prediction if you ask them to estimate the quantity (a very classic yet fascinating example). This is essentially what Bagging does.

Figure 5.1 How does Bagging work?

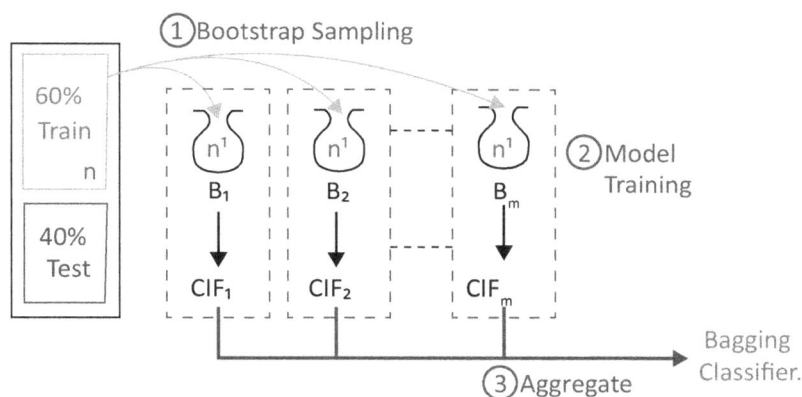

Let's understand the algorithm now. There are three main steps involved:

1. **Bootstrap Sampling:** Generate multiple datasets by randomly sampling from the original dataset with replacement. This means some data points may appear multiple times in a bootstrap sample, while others may not appear at all.

2. **Training:** Train a model on each of these bootstrap samples.

3. **Aggregation:** Combine the predictions of these models. For regression tasks, it will be the average of the predictions, and for classification tasks, it's the majority vote (which is the class that appears the most times).

Now, let's take a very simple example : Your task is to predict house prices based on certain characteristics such as the number of bedrooms, size of the house, location, etc. You have a dataset with this information about 1000 houses. Here's how you can use **Bagging** to create an Ensemble machine learning model:

1. **Bootstrap Sampling:** Create 10 different datasets by randomly sampling from the original 1000 houses. Each bootstrap sample will also have 1000 houses, **but with some duplicates** (i.e. sampling with replacement).

2. **Training:** Train 10 different decision trees (or any other model as the algorithm itself is not dependent on any model) on these 10 datasets.

3. **Aggregation:** For a new house, get the price prediction from each of the 10 models and then take the average (for regression) or majority vote (for classification [just the choice of class which occurs the most]) of these predictions.

This is all well and good but the question you might have is, why do we need this? One reason is that it reduces the variance of our predictions. Each decision tree might be a bit different because they're trained on slightly different data, but when we average their predictions, we get a more robust and accurate result. Next, let's discuss why this algorithm helps in achieving this goal of reducing the variance.

Let's think about the concept of variance. Variance is the amount by which our model's predictions would change if we used a different training dataset. High variability means our model is likely to overfit the training data. Bagging helps reduce this overfitting by training multiple models on different subsets of the data and averaging their predictions. Imagine you're predicting whether it will rain tomorrow. You have a dataset of past weather observations. A single decision tree might get overly attached to specific patterns in your training data, leading to overfitting. By creating multiple decision trees on different subsets of your data (through Bagging), each tree captures different aspects of the data. When you aggregate their predictions, you get a more generalized model that performs better on unseen data.

Perfect, now you are very much aware of how things work from a conceptual standpoint. As always, let's get into the mathematical foundations of this algorithm (which are essentially related to variance reduction).

5.1.2 Theoretical Insights into Bagging

To gain a deeper understanding of Bagging, let's delve into the theoretical aspects. Bagging primarily aims to reduce the variance of the model. By training multiple models on different subsets of the data, we average out the errors of individual models, resulting in a more robust overall model.

Variance Reduction

In statistics, variance measures how much the predictions of a model vary with different training data. High variance models are sensitive to the specific data they are trained on, often leading to overfitting. So, if the model is fed data which is not part of the training set, it will perform poorly on that. Bagging aims to reduce this variance by averaging out the predictions of multiple models.

Consider the formula for the variance of an average:

$$\mathrm{Var}(\overline{X}) = \frac{\sigma^2}{n}$$

where σ^2 is the variance of individual models, and n is the number of models. As n increases, the variance of the average decreases, leading to more stable predictions. We have arrived at a very crucial and important topic in machine learning, which we will be covering now: **Bias-Variance Tradeoff.**

Bias-Variance Tradeoff

This is a very important topic in ML which shows that there is a fundamental tradeoff between **bias (a term for accuracy)** and **variance (another term for generalization).** Bias is the error introduced by approximating a real-world problem (which is essentially what any machine learning problem does). Variance refers to the error introduced by the model's sensitivity to small fluctuations in the training set.

Bagging primarily reduces variance without significantly affecting bias. This is why it works well with high variance models like decision trees, which can overfit to training data. Here is a depiction of what the Bias Variance tradeoff actually looks like:

Figure 5.2   Bias Variance Tradeoff Visualized

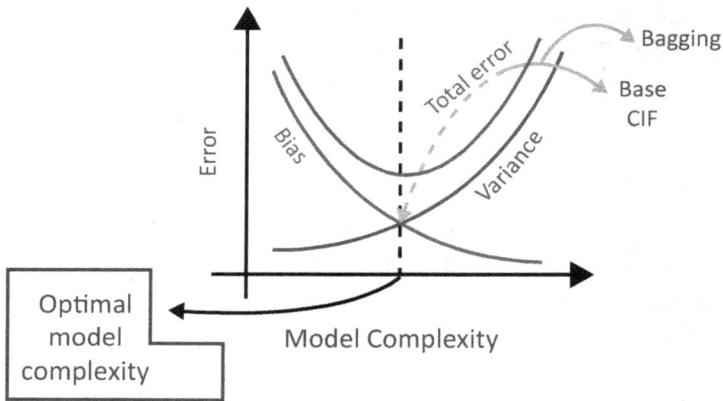

What Bagging helps us achieve is get a balance between the bias and variance by reducing the overall variance of the model. So, it is always preferred to use high variance or overfitted models as the base models as the primary use case of Bootstrap sampling is reducing the variance.

That is all about variance and how Bagging helps with the overall goal of reducing it. Now, before we move on to the practical implementation of the algorithm, let's take a look at how we define this algorithm mathematically.

Bagging Algorithm: Mathematically

For this section, we will consider a very simple example. Let's start with a dataset.

- **Dataset:** Suppose we have a dataset D with 5 samples:

$$D = \{(x_1, y_1), (x_2, y_2), (x_3, y_3), (x_4, y_4), (x_5, y_5)\}$$

- **Bootstrap Sampling:** As the first step for this algorithm, we will sample two different datasets from the original set using the concept of *sampling with replacement*.

$$D_1 = \{(x_1, y_1), (x_3, y_3), (x_5, y_5), (x_2, y_2), (x_3, y_3)\}$$
$$D_2 = \{(x_4, y_4), (x_1, y_1), (x_5, y_5), (x_2, y_2), (x_5, y_5)\}$$

- **Training Phase:** Once we have our datasets ready, we will train multiple models using these different datasets. Hence, at the end of this phase, we will have the following outputs:

$$f_1 = A(D_1)$$
$$f_2 = A(D_2)$$

- **Aggregating Results:** Once we have these models, we can now predict the results for any new data point *x*. There are different ways to do this as discussed above based on the problem we are trying to solve:

Classification Problems: $\hat{y} = \dfrac{1}{B} \sum\limits_{b=1}^{B} f_b(x)$

Regression Problems: $\hat{y} = \text{mode}\{f_1(x), f_2(x), \ldots, f_B(x)\}$

Now you have a clear understanding about the theory behind Bagging too. Let's move on to the fun part: *implementing Bagging in Python!*

5.1.3 Let's Get Practical: Implementing Bagging

Let's see a practical implementation of bagging using two different base models: Decision Tree and K Nearest Neighbours. We'll also compare their performance with the base models and visualize the results. To make things even more interesting, we will also learn how to create a synthetic classification dataset with scikit-learn instead of just using readily available datasets. So, let's start!

Generate a Complex Classification Dataset

We'll create a synthetic dataset with more features and informative patterns to challenge our classifiers. That way, we will get the most out of our machine learning model and at the same time see how they perform.

```python
# Import necessary libraries
from sklearn.datasets import make_classification
import matplotlib.pyplot as plt
import seaborn as sns
import pandas as pd
from sklearn.ensemble import BaggingClassifier
from sklearn.tree import DecisionTreeClassifier
from sklearn.linear_model import LogisticRegression
from sklearn.model_selection import train_test_split
from sklearn.metrics import accuracy_score

# Generate a synthetic dataset
X, y = make_classification(n_samples=2000, n_features=30,
n_informative=20, n_redundant=5, random_state=42)

# Visualize the distribution of the first two features
plt.figure(figsize=(10, 6))
plt.scatter(X[:, 0], X[:, 1], c=y, cmap='viridis', s=10)
plt.title('Scatter plot of the first two features')
plt.xlabel('Feature 1')
plt.ylabel('Feature 2')
plt.show()
```

The make_classification function from sklearn helps with the dataset creation part. We have various options like selecting the total number of features, selecting how many of these features should be important and how many aren't or are just duplicates, etc. Just visit the references section to get a link for this function's documentation or just do a simple google search!

After that, we create a simple scatter plot to visualize the first two features of our dataset. The graph you will generate will be the same as one shown below (any idea how? Hint, we have already discussed this in the earlier section).

| Figure 5.3 | How will your synthetic dataset features look in 2D? |

Scatter plot of the first two features

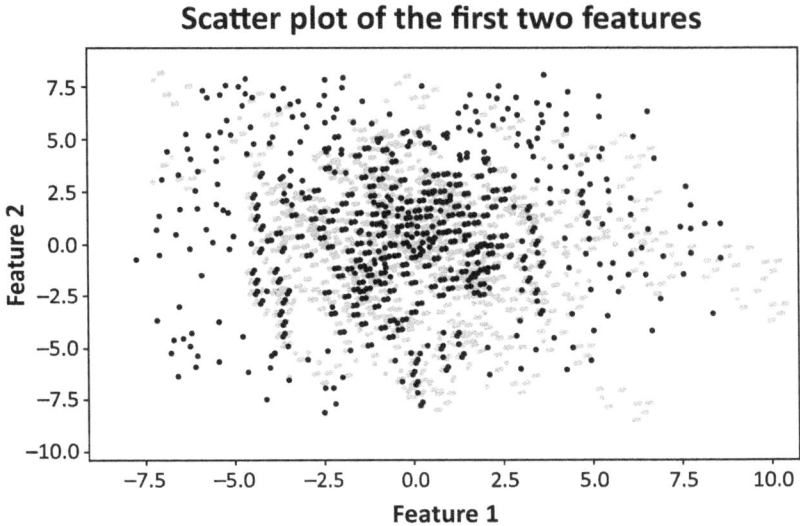

Feature 1

Training Bagging Classifiers with Different Base Models

Next, we will train all the models for this exercise. I am using 2 different base models to show you that the Bagging classifier is indeed model independent and also how it impacts the performance of high variance models. Any ideas on what base models we can use? Well, we already learnt about two models which are either likely to overfit or can be set to overfit: Decision Trees and K Nearest Neighbours (we can tweak the k value).

So, let's do the following:

- Define the Base Models
- Define the Bagging classifier for each of these base models.
- Train different classifiers on our generated dataset after splitting it into train and test sets.

So, let's implement everything stated above.

```
# Split the dataset into training and testing sets
X_train, X_test, y_train, y_test = train_test_split(X, y,
test_size=0.3, random_state=42)

# Create base models
dt_model = DecisionTreeClassifier(random_state=42)
knn_model = KNeighborsClassifier(n_neighbors=3)  # Low
k-value for high variance

# Create bagging classifiers
bagging_dt = BaggingClassifier(base_estimator=dt_model,
n_estimators=50, random_state=42)
bagging_knn = BaggingClassifier(base_estimator=knn_model,
n_estimators=50, random_state=42)

# Train the models
dt_model.fit(X_train, y_train)
knn_model.fit(X_train, y_train)
bagging_dt.fit(X_train, y_train)
bagging_knn.fit(X_train, y_train)
```

Perfect, we now have 4 trained classifiers with different settings. Note that we set the k value for the KNN Classifier to a very small value of 3 to intentionally force it to overfit on our dataset. This way, we will be able to see how Bagging impacts the performance of that model. Let's analyze the performance next by making predictions on the test set and printing out the accuracy scores (also creating a visually appealing bar plot for better analysis):

```
# Make predictions
# Training set predictions
y_pred_dt_train = dt_model.predict(X_train)
y_pred_knn_train = knn_model.predict(X_train)
y_pred_bagging_dt_train = bagging_dt.predict(X_train)
y_pred_bagging_knn_train = bagging_knn.predict(X_train)

# Test set predictions
y_pred_dt = dt_model.predict(X_test)
y_pred_knn = knn_model.predict(X_test)
y_pred_bagging_dt = bagging_dt.predict(X_test)
y_pred_bagging_knn = bagging_knn.predict(X_test)
```

```
# Training set accuracy
accuracy_dt_train = accuracy_score(y_train, y_pred_dt_
train)
accuracy_knn_train = accuracy_score(y_train, y_pred_knn_
train)
accuracy_bagging_dt_train = accuracy_score(y_train, y_
pred_bagging_dt_train)
accuracy_bagging_knn_train = accuracy_score(y_train, y_
pred_bagging_knn_train)

# Test set accuracy
accuracy_dt_test = accuracy_score(y_test, y_pred_dt)
accuracy_knn_test = accuracy_score(y_test, y_pred_knn)
accuracy_bagging_dt_test = accuracy_score(y_test, y_pred_
bagging_dt)
accuracy_bagging_knn_test = accuracy_score(y_test, y_
pred_bagging_knn)

print(f"Decision Tree Accuracy: {accuracy_dt_test:.3f}")
print(f"KNN Accuracy: {accuracy_knn_test:.3f}")
print(f"Bagging Decision Tree Accuracy: {accuracy_
bagging_dt_test:.3f}")
print(f"Bagging KNN Accuracy: {accuracy_bagging_knn_
test:.3f}")

# Visualize the performance of the models
model_names = ['Decision Tree', 'KNN', 'Bagging Decision
Tree', 'Bagging KNN']
train_accuracies = [accuracy_dt_train, accuracy_knn_
train, accuracy_bagging_dt_train, accuracy_bagging_knn_
train]
test_accuracies = [accuracy_dt_test, accuracy_knn_test,
accuracy_bagging_dt_test, accuracy_bagging_knn_test]

x = range(len(model_names))
width = 0.35

plt.figure(figsize=(10, 6))
plt.bar(x, train_accuracies, width, color='blue',
alpha=0.7, label='Train')
plt.bar([i + width for i in x], test_accuracies, width,
color='red', alpha=0.7, label='Test')

plt.title('Training and Testing Accuracies of the
Models')
plt.ylabel('Accuracy')
plt.xlabel('Model')
plt.xticks([i + width/2 for i in x], model_names)
plt.legend()
plt.show()
```

Here is the result after running the above code snippet:

```
Decision Tree Accuracy: 0.753
KNN Accuracy: 0.902
Bagging Decision Tree Accuracy: 0.893
Bagging KNN Accuracy: 0.912
```

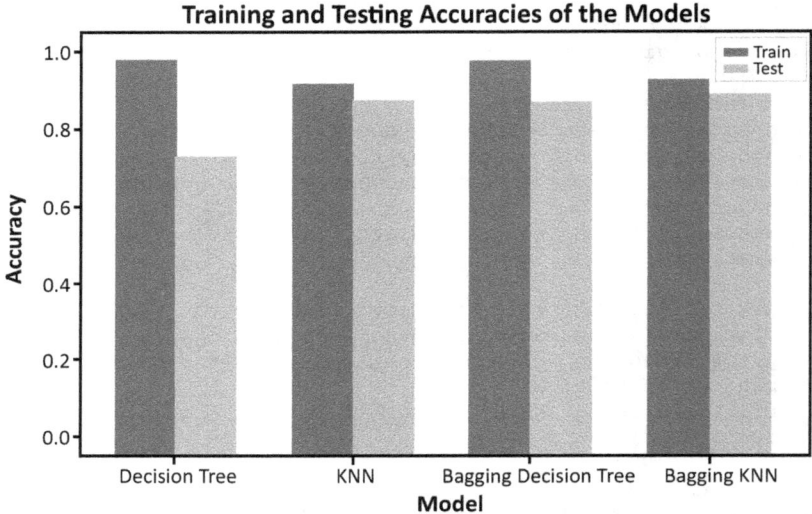

Training and Testing Accuracies of the Models

As you can see, the impact of Bagging can be seen in both the cases, more dominantly in the Decision trees with an accuracy improvement of almost 15% over the base case. There is also an improvement of 1% in the case of KNN Classifier. Moreover, check out the training accuracy values in the plot. The Bagging Classifier helps in that case as well.

Finally, let's store all these results as a table displaying our results for better visibility and easier analysis.

```
# Create a performance table
performance_data = {
    'Model': model_names,
    'Train Accuracy': train_accuracies,
    'Test Accuracy': test_accuracies
}

performance_df = pd.DataFrame(performance_data)
performance_df.head(10)
```

This will create a Pandas Dataframe and store each model's training and testing accuracy. Let's take a look at the actual table.

	Model	Train Accuracy	Test Accuracy
0	Decision Tree	1.000000	0.753333
1	KNN	0.942143	0.901667
2	Bagging Decision Tree	1.000000	0.893333
3	Bagging KNN	0.953571	0.911667

Great, you have successfully implemented Bagging as well. Let's take a step back now and take a look at the bigger picture. Let's focus on some key aspects of this algorithm in the next section.

5.1.4 Bagging Algorithm: Some Key Observations

This section is sort of a conclusion on the Bagging Algorithm we just covered. It will cover some important things about the algorithm like its limitations and how it is different from other ensemble approaches that we will cover in this chapter. So, let's start with the limitations.

Limitations of Bagging

While Bagging (Bootstrap Aggregating) is a powerful tool in our machine learning toolkit, it's important to recognize that it's not without its limitations:

1. **Computational Complexity:** Training multiple models on different bootstrap samples can be quite demanding on your computer's resources, provided it can be done on your personal system. For larger datasets and complex models (i.e. individual models are quite complex), the time and power required becomes pretty significant.

2. **Model Interpretability:** One significant trade-off with Bagging is that while it boosts the overall performance, it

does so at the expense of interpretability. The ensemble models are much more challenging to interpret compared to, say a single, straightforward decision tree.

3. **Bias Variance Trade-off:** Bagging excels at reducing the overall variance of the resulting model. However, it doesn't inherently reduce the bias. If your base model is too simple and under fits the data, Bagging might not provide the performance improvement expected.

4. **Memory Usage:** Because Bagging involves storing multiple models, it can consume a significant amount of memory. This can be a concern if you're working in an environment where memory is limited.

Practical Considerations

When you're using Bagging, it's essential to choose your base model wisely. Look for models that might have high variance but low bias, such as decision trees or KNN with a low k-value, to benefit the most from Bagging. The number of base models, or estimators, you use in your Bagging ensemble can significantly impact performance. Generally, more estimators will improve performance, but also increase computational costs.

Using libraries like scikit-learn can make implementing Bagging much easier and more efficient. Remember to tune the hyperparameters of both your base model and the Bagging algorithm to find the optimal setup for your specific dataset.

Evaluating the performance of your Bagging ensemble with appropriate metrics is crucial. Accuracy is a good starting point, but depending on your problem, precision, recall, and F1-score might provide more insight into how well your model is performing.

Hence, Bagging is a powerful ensemble technique that can significantly enhance the performance of high variance models.

While it has its limitations, understanding when and how to apply Bagging will help you leverage the most out of it. Next, **we'll dive into Boosting**, another ensemble method that offers a different approach to improving prediction power.

5.2 Boosting: Learning from Mistakes

Let's dive into another game-changing technique in our machine learning toolbox: **Boosting**. Like its cousin Bagging, Boosting is an ensemble method that brings together multiple models to amp up prediction accuracy. But here's where it gets interesting - while Bagging is all about reducing variance, Boosting takes on both bias and variance. It's like having a Swiss Army knife for machine learning tasks!

5.2.1 How Does Boosting Work?

So, how does Boosting work its magic? Imagine you're binge-watching your favorite TV series. Each episode builds on the last, filling in gaps and answering questions you didn't even know you had. That's Boosting in a nutshell!

Unlike Bagging, where models are like solo artists doing their own thing, Boosting models are more like a well-coordinated team. They train in sequence, with each model learning from the mistakes of its predecessors. It's like having a relay team where each runner picks up exactly where the last one left off, making the whole team stronger. This is essentially how Boosting works. Let's see what are the steps involved in this algorithm.

The Boosting Algorithm

To understand the Boosting algorithm, let's break it down into three main steps: Initialization, Iterative Training, and Final Prediction.

Figure 5.4   How does Boosting work?

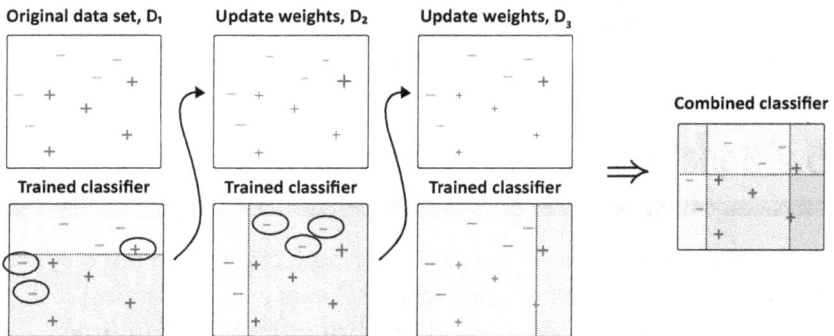

1. **Initialization:** As the primary focus of the Boosting algorithm is reducing the bias, we start with a weak learner, which is typically a simple model that performs slightly better than random guessing (Example can be a Decision tree with a depth of one (essentially asking just 1 question to the data!). Then, we assign equal weights to all training instances.

2. **Training Again and Again:** Next, we train the weak learner on the weighted data. Evaluate its performance and adjust the weights of the training instances based on the errors. Increase the weights of misclassified data points so that the next learner focuses more on them. We repeat this process for a specified number of iterations or until a desired performance is achieved (we can set these things when we define the algorithm).

3. **Final Prediction:** Combine the predictions of all the learners using a weighted majority vote (for classification) or a weighted sum (for regression). The weights are usually based on the accuracy of each learner.

Let's consider a simple example to illustrate Boosting. Suppose we want to classify whether an email is spam or not based on certain features. We start with a weak learner, such as a **decision stump** (terminology alert: it is a decision tree with only one split), which will mostly perform poorly by itself. In the next iteration, we focus on the misclassified emails by the first learner and train another decision stump. This process continues, with each subsequent learner focusing more on the difficult cases. Finally, we combine the predictions of all the learners to get a robust classifier (check the Fig. 5.4 to get a better idea on this).

Now that we have a better understanding of the algorithm in general, let's explore some approaches developed by researchers to improve the overall performance of this algorithm.

Different Takes on Boosting Algorithms

Figure 5.5 Types of Boosting Algorithms

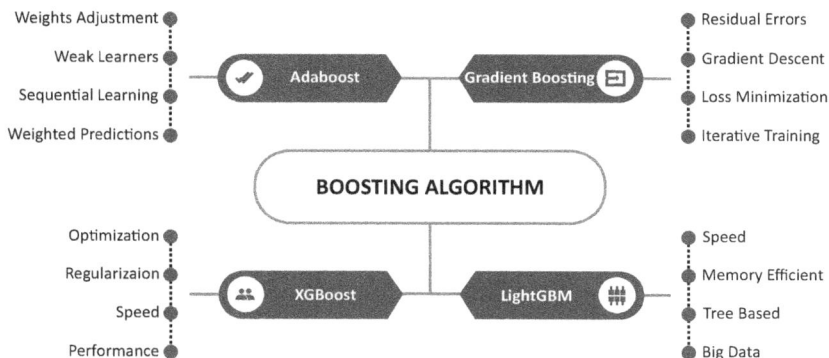

There are several popular Boosting algorithms, each with its unique approach to sequentially training models. Let's cover some of the most popular ones out there.

AdaBoost: The OG of Boosting. It's like a teacher who gives extra attention to struggling students. AdaBoost focuses on misclassified instances, adjusting their importance and combining weak learners' predictions. It's the pioneer of sequential learning.

Gradient Boosting: Think of this as the problem-solving whiz kid. It builds models one after another, each trying to fix the previous one's mistakes. Using gradient descent, it's like a guided missile zeroing in on the best solution for both regression and classification.

XGBoost: The speed demon of the Boosting world. It's Gradient Boosting on steroids, optimized for lightning-fast performance. XGBoost also comes with built-in safeguards against overfitting, making it a reliable workhorse for large datasets.

LightGBM: The efficient multitasker. This algorithm is like a master juggler, handling large-scale and high-dimensional data with ease. It's the go-to choice when you need speed and memory efficiency without sacrificing performance.

5.2.2 Theoretical Insights into Boosting

To gain a deeper understanding of Boosting, let's explore the theoretical aspects that make it so powerful. Boosting primarily aims to reduce both bias and variance, leading to highly accurate models.

Bias and Variance Reduction

Again this! Well, as I said earlier, it is a very important concept in ML so let's take a refresher on what bias and variance are. In the context of machine learning, **bias refers to the error introduced by approximating a real-world problem with a simplified model** (model not capable of approximating such a complex dataset). **Variance, on the other hand, refers to the error introduced by the model's sensitivity to small fluctuations in the training set**. Boosting reduces both bias and variance by combining weak learners in a way that corrects their individual weaknesses (in actuality, the primary focus of the algorithm is reducing the Bias but the final outcome shows a variance reduction as well).

| Figure 5.6 | Bias Variance Tradeoff for Bagging and Boosting |

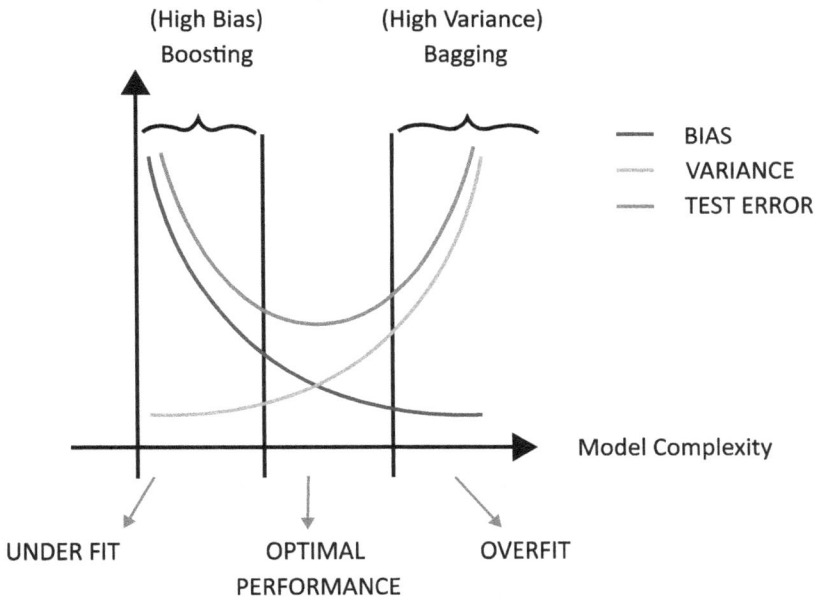

Consider the formula for the weighted sum of predictions in Boosting:

$$\hat{y} = \sum_{m=1}^{M} \alpha_m h_m(x)$$

where α_m is the weight assigned to the m-th learner, $h_m(x)$ and M is the total number of learners. The weights α_m are typically based on the accuracy of each learner. By assigning higher weights to more accurate learners, Boosting effectively reduces the overall bias. Additionally, by focusing on the mistakes of previous learners, Boosting reduces variance, leading to more stable and accurate predictions.

Now that we know how boosting works conceptually, let's define it mathematically (don't worry, I will be brief as I was in the previous section).

Boosting Algorithm: Mathematically

Let's consider a dataset $\{(x_i, y_i)\}_{i=1}^{n}$, where x_i are the features and y_i are the labels. The Boosting algorithm can be summarized in the following steps:

1. Initialize the weights for all training instances $w_i = \dfrac{1}{n}$.

2. For each iteration m from 1 to M:

   - Train a weak learner $h_m(x)$ on the weighted data.
   - Calculate the weighted error rate

   $$\varepsilon_m = \frac{\sum_{i=1}^{n} w_i I\left(y_i \neq h_m(x_i)\right)}{\sum_{i=1}^{n} w_i}$$

   - Compute the weight for the learner. $\alpha_m = \dfrac{1}{2}\ln\left(\dfrac{1-\varepsilon_m}{\varepsilon_m}\right)$
   - Update the weights of the training instances:
   $$w_i \leftarrow w_i \exp\left(-\alpha_m y_i h_m(x_i)\right)$$
   - Normalize the weights.

3. The final model is as follows.

$$H(x) = \text{sign}\left(\sum_{m=1}^{M} \alpha_m h_m(x)\right)$$

This process of training sequentially ensures that each weak learner focuses more on the difficult instances, improving the overall performance of the model (which in turn means reducing the bias and variance of the resultant model.

Great, now you can tell people that you know the math behind boosting too! Let's implement the Boosting algorithm in Python. I will explore multiple boosting models in the next section to show you a comparative study between them.

5.2.3 Implementing Boosting in Python

Let's move on to a practical implementation of Boosting using two popular algorithms: AdaBoost and Gradient Boosting. We'll also compare their performance with a simple decision tree classifier, which will also be our base model. As before, we will generate a simple dataset specific to this problem using scikit-learn's **make_classification** function. So, let's start!

Generating a Synthetic Dataset

We'll start by creating a synthetic dataset to challenge our classifiers. To make things even more interesting, we will use the same dataset we did in the last section to compare the Bagging and Boosting approaches as well.

```python
from sklearn.datasets import make_classification
import matplotlib.pyplot as plt
import seaborn as sns
import pandas as pd
from sklearn.ensemble import AdaBoostClassifier,
GradientBoostingClassifier
from sklearn.tree import DecisionTreeClassifier
from sklearn.model_selection import train_test_split
from sklearn.metrics import accuracy_score

# Generate a synthetic dataset
X, y = make_classification(n_samples=2000, n_features=30,
n_informative=20, n_redundant=5, random_state=42)
```

Training Different Boosting Classifiers

Next, we will train three classifiers: a simple **Decision Tree** model, **AdaBoost** classifier, and **Gradient Boosting** classifier.

```python
# Split the dataset into training and testing sets
X_train, X_test, y_train, y_test = train_test_split(X, y,
test_size=0.3, random_state=42)

# Create base models
dt_model = DecisionTreeClassifier(max_depth=1, random_
state=42)
ada_model = AdaBoostClassifier(base_
estimator=DecisionTreeClassifier(max_depth=1), n_
estimators=50, random_state=42)
gb_model = GradientBoostingClassifier(n_estimators=50,
random_state=42)

# Train the models
dt_model.fit(X_train, y_train)
ada_model.fit(X_train, y_train)
gb_model.fit(X_train, y_train)
```

For this, we first split the dataset into training and testing sets. We then create the three classifiers. The AdaBoost classifier uses decision stumps (decision trees with max_depth=1) as the base learners and both the Boosting classifiers run for 50 iterations. Then, we fit and train a model for each of them.

Evaluating Performance

Now, we will evaluate the performance of the classifiers by making predictions on the test set and calculating the accuracy.

```
# Make predictions on the test set
y_pred_dt = dt_model.predict(X_test)
y_pred_ada = ada_model.predict(X_test)
y_pred_gb = gb_model.predict(X_test)

# Calculate accuracy
accuracy_dt = accuracy_score(y_test, y_pred_dt)
accuracy_ada = accuracy_score(y_test, y_pred_ada)
accuracy_gb = accuracy_score(y_test, y_pred_gb)

print(f"Decision Tree Accuracy: {accuracy_dt:.3f}")
print(f"AdaBoost Accuracy: {accuracy_ada:.3f}")
print(f"Gradient Boosting Accuracy: {accuracy_gb:.3f}")
```

The results for this code will be as follows:

```
Decision Tree Accuracy: 0.645
AdaBoost Accuracy: 0.827
Gradient Boosting Accuracy: 0.872
```

Woah! That is some serious improvement over the base model (15+%). This shows just how powerful Boosting is. Although this performance is really impressive, it's important to note that they don't beat the Bagging Classifier. One of the primary reasons is that we use a very basic high bias model (decision stump) while the base model for Bagging is much more complex where it was allowed to grow fully. Here is a table with accuracy results for all the models we trained in this chapter so that you can compare them better.

Table 5.1	Summarizing Model Performance Results	
Ensemble Technique	**Model**	**Accuracy**
Boosting	Decision Tree (Stump)	64.50%
	AdaBoost	82.70%
	Gradient Boosting	87.20%
Bagging	Decision Tree	75.30%
	KNN	90.20%
	Bagging Decision Tree	89.30%
	Bagging KNN	91.20%

Great, this successfully completes our implementation section for Boosting. Let's cover the essential observations about the boosting algorithm now.

5.2.4 Boosting Essentials

This section will cover the critical observations we made while learning about Boosting in this chapter. Let's start with a simple comparison of the two ensemble methods we have learnt till now.

Bagging vs. Boosting

By comparing these two methods, we will be able to infer that Bagging is great for stabilizing high variance models, making them more reliable. Boosting, on the other hand, is excellent for improving both bias and variance but often requires more time and computational power.

Before we start with the actual comparison, let's take a look at a really great visualization which explains the concepts of these ensemble methodologies using a very simple image.

| Figure 5.7 | Bagging vs Boosting |

Bagging

Boosting

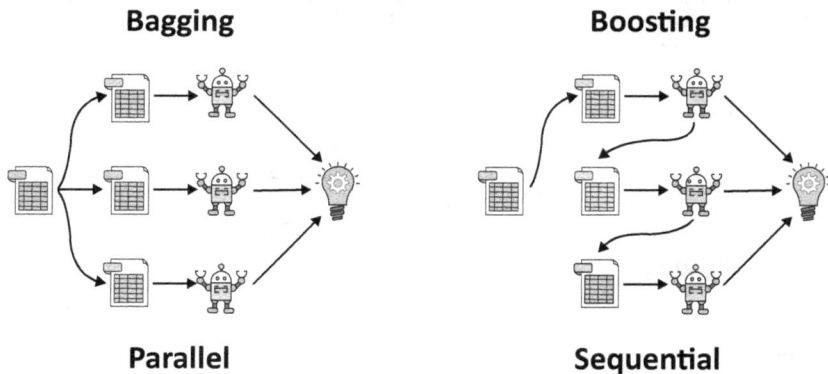

Parallel

Sequential

Source: Dey, Roshmita. "Bagging vs Boosting." Medium, October 17, 2019.
https://medium.com/@roshmitadey/bagging-v-s-boosting-be765c970fd1.

- **Bagging:** In Bagging, we train multiple models independently on different random subsets of our data, and then combine their predictions. This approach helps to reduce variance and make our model more robust. Each model gets the same weight when we combine their predictions.

- **Boosting:** Boosting takes a different approach. Instead of training models independently, Boosting trains them sequentially. Each new model focuses on correcting the errors made by the previous ones. This way, Boosting aims to reduce both bias and variance, often resulting in highly accurate models. However, this sequential training means Boosting can be more computationally intensive and slower than Bagging.

Hence, we saw that the approach of ensembling changes greatly with the application we use it for. Next, let's take a look at the flip side of the coin, which are the limitations of Boosting.

Limitations of Boosting

- **Sensitive to Noisy Data:** Boosting algorithms have a high tendency to overfit on noisy datasets because they place more emphasis on correcting errors from previous iterations. This means that even small amounts of noise can lead to a model that performs well on training data but poorly on unseen data (as there won't be noise in the testing set).

- **It can be a bit of a resource hog:** Boosting models can take a while to train, especially with big datasets. Because each model builds on the last, we can't speed things up by running them all at once like we can with Bagging. This means longer wait times before your model is ready to go.

- **Getting the settings right can be tricky:** Boosting algorithms have quite a few knobs to turn - things like how fast the model learns and how many models to use. Finding the right settings can take a lot of trial and error. It's a bit like tuning a guitar - it takes practice and patience to get it just right.

- **Sometimes it tries too hard:** Boosting focus on fixing mistakes can sometimes backfire. If we're not careful, the model might start memorizing the training data instead of learning general patterns. This is called overfitting, and it's like a student who memorizes test answers but doesn't understand the subject. The model might ace the training data but struggle with new information.

Perfect end to this section! You are now an expert (beginner) at Boosting and Bagging. You understand what ensembling is and how it actually works. Now, let's see some specific algorithms which are based on these ensemble techniques and understand how they further improve on these base algorithms. More specifically, we will focus on two algorithms: **"Random Forests" and "LightGBM"**.

5.3 Advanced Ensemble Models: Introduction to Random Forests and LightGBM

Welcome back, ML Enthusiasts! Now that we've journeyed through the concepts of Bagging and Boosting, it's time to dive into two advanced ensemble models that have revolutionized machine learning: **Random Forests** and **LightGBM**. These models build upon the concepts of Bagging and Boosting, respectively, adding their own unique twists to enhance performance and usability. Let's get started with the Random Forest algorithm.

5.3.1 Random Forests: Beyond Basic Bagging

Random Forests are an extension of the Bagging algorithm, specifically tailored for decision trees. Imagine a magical forest where each tree is trained on a random subset of the data (**not just records, features are chosen randomly as well!**) and makes its own predictions. The forest then combines these predictions to arrive at a consensus, just like a wise council of wizards (similar to bagging).

| Figure 5.8 | Random Forests Simplified! |

Random Forest (In a Nutshell)

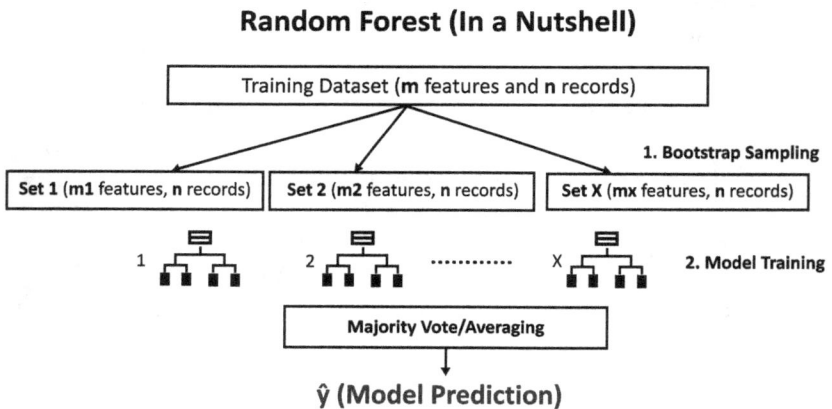

Now, let's understand how the algorithm actually works in practice.

How Does Random Forest Work?

Here are the steps involved in the algorithm:

1. **Bootstrap Sampling:** Just like in Bagging, Random Forests use bootstrap sampling to create multiple subsets of the training data, each with replacement.

2. **Random Feature Selection:** Instead of considering all features while splitting a node, Random Forests randomly select a subset of features. This randomness helps in creating diverse trees and reduces correlation among them.

3. **Building Multiple Trees:** Each tree is built independently using the sampled data and selected features.

4. **Aggregation:** For classification tasks, the final prediction is based on the majority vote of all the trees. For regression tasks, it's the average prediction.

This additional layer of randomness in feature selection enhances the model's ability to generalize, making it less likely to overfit and more robust in its predictions. This helps us draw a very important observation: "More Randomness in a system results in better and more robust performance". Hence, this is the premise on which the concept of Random Forests was built.

Let's cover Light GBM next and then we will implement both these algorithms together in Python.

5.3.2 LightGBM: Speed and Performance in Boosting

Figure 5.9 **The Core Idea of LightGBM**

LightGBM leaf-wise

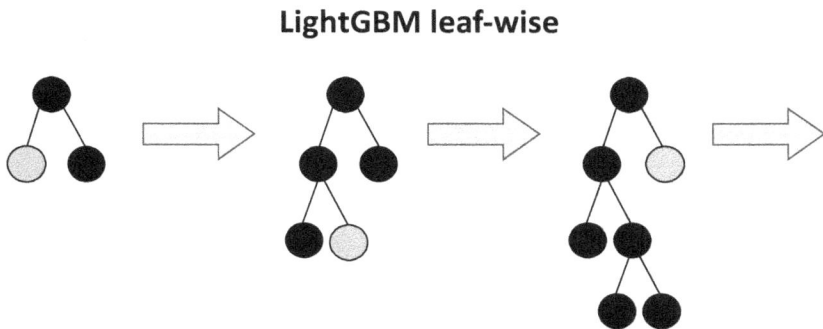

Pushkar Mandot, What is LightGBM, How to implement it? How to fine tune the parameters?, Medium, Accessed December 12, 2024. https://medium.com/@ pushkarmandot/https-medium-com-pushkarmandot-what-is-lightgbm-how-to-implement-it-how-to-fine-tune-the-parameters-60347819b7fc

LightGBM (Light Gradient Boosting Machine) is an advanced implementation of the Gradient Boosting algorithm, designed to be faster and more efficient, especially with large datasets. More particularly, it uses a Leaf wise growth approach to train the individual weak learners. Think of it as a nimble athlete that swiftly navigates through the data, making rapid and precise predictions. Let's understand the inner workings of the algorithm in brief.

Why is LightGBM so effective?

1. **Gradient Boosting Foundation:** LightGBM is based on the Gradient Boosting framework but introduces several optimizations, which are a bit too advanced for this book. Hence, we will just remember that it is an optimized gradient boosting approach.

2. **Leaf-wise Tree Growth:** Unlike traditional Gradient Boosting which grows trees level-wise, LightGBM grows trees leaf-wise. This means it can focus on the most significant splits, resulting in deeper and more accurate trees. This individual model performance improvement translates into a superior boosting model.

3. **Histogram-based Binning:** On top of the above approach, LightGBM uses histogram-based techniques to bucket continuous feature values into discrete bins (based on the frequency of values). This reduces memory usage and speeds up training.

4. **Sparse Feature Support:** Finally, LightGBM is designed to handle sparse features efficiently, making it suitable for high-dimensional datasets.

These innovations make LightGBM exceptionally fast and scalable, often outperforming traditional Gradient Boosting implementations in both speed and accuracy. That is the reason that if you open Kaggle (a machine learning for enthusiasts website), almost all machine learning challenges will have a Light GBM model (with a lot more complex approaches albeit) in some of the top results. I also participated in an old contest and managed to get in the top 5% of the submissions using a LightGBM model.

Now, let's implement both these algorithms in Python.

5.3.3 Implementing Random Forests and LightGBM in Python

In this section, we will walk you through the step-by-step implementation of both the Random Forest and LightGBM algorithms. By following these steps, you'll get hands-on experience with these powerful ensemble techniques and see how they can be applied on the same synthetic dataset we used in the previous sections. Then, we will analyze the results and comment on their performance. So, let's get started.

Before we start, we will need to install the LightGBM package on our systems as it is not part of Scikit Learn. To do this, just open a terminal or command line on your system and type in the following command:

```
pip install lightgbm
```

This will install the package for you. If this does not work, try replacing **pip** with **pip3.** Once you have the package installed, we are ready to get our hands dirty and build some interesting ML algorithms with just a few lines of code.

Importing the Required Libraries and Generating our Dataset

Let's import the necessary libraries and create our benchmark classification dataset with sklearn as we did in the previous sections.

```
from sklearn.datasets import make_classification
from sklearn.ensemble import RandomForestClassifier
from sklearn.model_selection import train_test_split
from sklearn.metrics import accuracy_score
import lightgbm as lgb  # LightGBM Model

# Generate a synthetic dataset
X, y = make_classification(n_samples=2000, n_features=30,
n_informative=20, n_redundant=5, random_state=42)
```

Splitting the Dataset and Training the Classifiers

Next, let's create, train and test datasets from our original set and define and train our Random Forest and LightGBM classifiers.

```
# Split the dataset into training and testing sets
X_train, X_test, y_train, y_test = train_test_split(X, y,
test_size=0.3, random_state=42)

# Create and train the Random Forest model
rf_model = RandomForestClassifier(n_estimators=50,
random_state=42)
rf_model.fit(X_train, y_train)

# Create and train the LightGBM model
lgb_model = lgb.LGBMClassifier(n_estimators=50, random_
state=42)
lgb_model.fit(X_train, y_train)
```

Perfect, we now have our two trained classifiers. Let's make predictions now!

Performance Analysis of Trained Classifiers

Now, let's check how our classifiers perform on the test set and what accuracy scores we get. We will also compare them to the original Boosting and Bagging results. Here are the results for your reference (so you don't have to go back and forth).

Ensemble Technique	Model	Accuracy
	Decision Tree (Stump)	64.50%
Boosting	AdaBoost	82.70%
	Gradient Boosting	87.20%
	Decision Tree	75.30%
	KNN	90.20%
Bagging	Bagging Decision Tree	89.30%
	Bagging KNN	91.20%

```
# Make predictions
y_pred = rf_model.predict(X_test)
y_pred = lgb_model.predict(X_test)

# Calculate and print the accuracy
accuracy_rf = accuracy_score(y_test, y_pred)
accuracy_lgm = accuracy_score(y_test, y_pred)

print(f"Random Forest Accuracy: {accuracy_rf:.3f}")
print(f"LightGBM Accuracy: {accuracy_lgm:.3f}")
```

Running this code will generate the following results (Note that the Info output from LightGBM will be shown when you train your model):

Figure 5.10 **Model Training and Performance Analysis Output**

```
[LightGBM] [Info] Number of positive: 686, number of
negative: 714
[LightGBM] [Info] Auto-choosing col-wise multi-threading,
the overhead of testing was 0.000999 seconds.
You can set 'force_col_wise=true' to remove the overhead.
[LightGBM] [Info] Total Bins 7650
[LightGBM] [Info] Number of data points in the train set:
1400, Number of used features: 30
[LightGBM] [Info] [binary:BoostFromScore]: pavg=0.490000
-> initscore=-0.040005
[LightGBM] [Info] Start training from score -0.040005
Random Forest Accuracy: 0.923
LightGBM Accuracy: 0.923
```

So, it can clearly be seen that both these methods are far more superior then the base and ensemble approaches, resulting in a testing accuracy of over 92% on the test set, which is really impressive. This in turn marks the end of this chapter. Hope you had an informative journey and be more excited, it's still just halfway done! In the next chapter, we will cover a totally untouched topic: **Unsupervised learning**. Simply speaking, it's when we do not have labels associated with our data (which, if you think about it, is the case in most real world problems).

Chapter Summary

We covered a lot of things in this chapter, mainly around Ensembling. We delved into the world of ensemble methods in machine learning, focusing primarily on **Bagging, Boosting, Random Forests, and LightGBM.** Here are the key topics we covered in this chapter:

◆ **Bagging:** We explored how Bagging, short for Bootstrap Aggregating, creates multiple subsets of the original dataset and trains a base model on each subset to reduce variance.

◆ **Boosting:** We learned about Boosting, which sequentially builds models, each correcting the errors of its predecessor, to minimize bias.

◆ **Random Forest:** We learnt about Random Forests and how they use Bagging to combine multiple decision trees trained on different parts of the data and using random subsets of features to enhance performance.

◆ **LightGBM:** We then covered what LightGBM is, which essentially is a fast, distributed, high-performance gradient boosting framework that uses tree-based learning algorithms to further enhance the Boosting process.

◆ **Implementation:** Finally, we went through practical implementations of each of these algorithms in Python, reinforcing the theoretical concepts with hands-on implementations.

Glossary

Term	Meaning
Ensemble Methods	Techniques that combine multiple models to improve the performance and robustness of predictions.
Bagging	Short for Bootstrap Aggregating; a method to reduce variance by training multiple models on subsets of data.
Boosting	A sequential technique where each model corrects the errors of its predecessor to reduce bias.
Random Forest	An ensemble method that uses multiple decision trees trained on different parts of the data and feature subsets.
LightGBM	A high-performance gradient boosting framework that uses tree-based learning algorithms.
Base Model	The underlying model used in ensemble methods, such as a decision tree or linear model.

Quiz

1. **What does Bagging stand for?**
   a. Boosted Aggregation
   b. Bootstrap Aggregating
   c. Bagged Regression
   d. Batch Gradient Descent

2. **What is the main goal of Boosting?**
   a. Increase variance
   b. Reduce variance
   c. Reduce bias
   d. Increase bias

3. **Which algorithm is a type of Bagging?**
   a. AdaBoost
   b. Random Forest
   c. Gradient Boosting
   d. LightGBM

4. **What technique does LightGBM use for improving performance?**
   a. Bagging
   b. Binning
   c. Boosting
   d. Stacking

5. **What type of model does Random Forest primarily use?**
    a. Linear regression
    b. Decision Trees
    c. Neural Networks
    d. Support Vector Machines

6. **How does Random Forest introduce randomness?**
    a. By selecting random samples of data
    b. By using random subsets of features
    c. Both a and b
    d. None of the above

7. **Which library do you need to install for implementing LightGBM in Python?**
    a. scikit-learn
    b. lightgbm
    c. xgboost
    d. tensorflow

8. **What is the key advantage of ensemble methods?**
    a. They are faster
    b. They reduce the risk of overfitting
    c. They require less data
    d. They use fewer computational resources

9. **What is the primary purpose of Cross-Validation?**
    a. To improve the model's performance
    b. To evaluate the model's performance
    c. To tune hyperparameters
    d. To select features

10. Which of the following is a loss function?

a. Accuracy

b. Entropy

c. Precision

d. Recall

Answers	1 – b	2 – c	3 – b	4 – c	5 – b
	6 – c	7 – b	8 – b	9 – b	10 – b

Chapter **6**

Unsupervised Learning: Finding Patterns in Data

KEY LEARNING OBJECTIVES

- Understand Clustering and learn how to group data meaningfully.
- Apply Dimensionality Reduction to eliminate redundant features and retain essential data.
- Explore Market Basket Analysis to enhance decision-making and sales strategies.

So we've covered how ML models handle situations with inputs and their matching labels. But what about the trickier scenario where there aren't any labels? That's where **Unsupervised Learning** comes in - it's a whole branch of machine learning tackling this complex issue. You'll run into plenty of real-world cases where this matters, since getting your hands on neatly labeled data is often a huge pain and often requires hours of manual effort. We'll dive into some key unsupervised learning techniques and see how they're applied to actual problems out there in the wild. It's pretty fascinating stuff once you wrap your head around it!

The chapter will start by covering the basics of clustering in machine learning and why it would be useful to learn these techniques. Next, we will go through a very important and fundamental clustering algorithm: **K-Means Clustering** and take a look at some other clustering techniques like Hierarchical and DBSCAN Clustering to get a better sense of the options that we have at our disposal. After this, we will start with **Dimensionality Reduction** and dive deeper into two of the most popular dimensionality reduction techniques: **Principal Component Analysis (PCA)** and **t-distributed stochastic neighbor embedding (widely known as t-SNE)**. Finally, you will get an overview of what **Market Basket Analysis** is very briefly to get a better idea of how unsupervised learning can be used in real-life applications to get the most out of your data.

6.1 Clustering Basics: K-Means and Other Clustering Techniques

In the last few chapters, our sole focus was on supervised learning, where models learn from input data paired with their corresponding labels. This process allowed us to make predictions on new, unseen data. Now, what if we come across the following scenario: *what if we don't have any labels? What if our data is simply a collection of raw information with no clear structure or pattern?*

This is where **Unsupervised Learning** comes into play. Unlike its alternatives, it *doesn't need labels for the data.* Instead, it tries to find hidden patterns in the data you give it. This is super useful when getting labeled data is a real headache - too expensive, takes forever, or just can't be done. Think about it - what kind of patterns could you spot in your data? Most of you probably thought about grouping similar things together, right? That's exactly what clustering does!

Clustering is a big deal in unsupervised learning. It's all about putting similar data in the same group. People use it for all sorts of things, like sorting customers by how they shop or figuring out what thousands of news stories are about, in turn categorizing them into a few major topics. Pretty neat, huh? Let's take a closer look at how clustering works. Don't worry, it's not as complicated as it sounds!

6.1.1 How does it work?

Clustering is the term given to the process where we separate some data into different groups, or "**clusters**," such that data points within the same group are similar to each other than to those in other clusters. It's like sorting a large pile of mixed items like different rocks into smaller piles based on their similarities by looking at, for instance, their color or shape, which you can think of as features. To get a better understanding of the concept, check out the figure given below of some 2-dimensional data and how can it be divided into 4 distinct clusters just by looking at the data:

Figure 6.1 **Clustering Explained!**

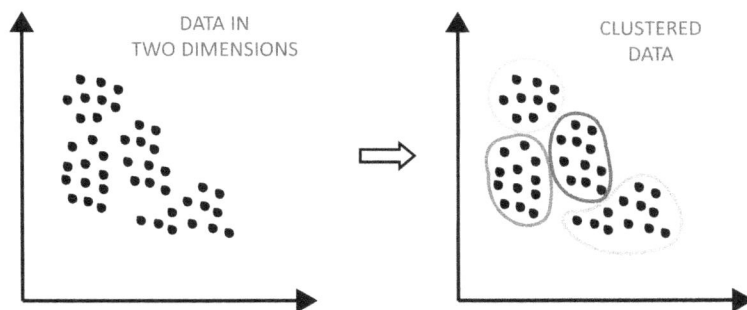

Let's take an example to better understand this. Imagine a study where patients are asked to track how often they experience symptoms and how severe those symptoms are. Researchers could

Machine Learning Essentials You Always Wanted to Know

use clustering to group patients with similar symptom patterns together, allowing them to identify trends or responses to a treatment.

In Figure 6.1, you can see an example where data points have been grouped into four different clusters. Even without labels or specific instructions, you might naturally observe that the data seems to form these clusters. However, in real-world scenarios, we need a defined way to measure how similar or different data points are as there are numerous possible ways to cluster the same data (the figure just shows one possible way to do so). This is often known as a **similarity measure**. When there are only a few features, such as symptom frequency and severity, it's easier to visually check for similarities as we did above. But as datasets grow larger and have more features, it becomes much more challenging to combine and compare them. Selecting the right similarity measure is essential for effective clustering, and later sections will explore how to do this.

Once you have your clusters, each data point will be assigned to a group, or cluster, and often labeled with a unique ID so you can use it to differentiate the data. Clustering, hence, is a really powerful tool because it gives us a way to simplify large datasets by grouping similar examples, reducing the overall complexity and making it easier to understand the various data patterns. Let's take a look at some of the fields where this technique is used for solving different use cases:

- Market segmentation
- Analyzing social networks
- Grouping search results
- Medical image analysis
- Image segmentation
- Detecting anomalies in data

By using clustering, one can uncover hidden patterns and insights which are not possible to do just by looking at the data, which can be especially useful in fields like marketing, healthcare, and technology.

www.vibrantpublishers.com

Let's learn one of the most fundamental clustering algorithms now: **K-Means Clustering.**

6.1.2 The K-Means Algorithm

K-means clustering is an unsupervised machine learning technique that partitions a dataset into clusters based on similarity to something called a **centroid (consider it a reference point).** In this algorithm, first, the data points are assigned to one of "k" clusters based on their proximity to the center of each cluster, known as the **centroid.** So, the algorithm starts by randomly selecting these centroids, which represent the center of each cluster. Each data point is then assigned to the nearest centroid, and once all points have a centroid or group, the centroids are recalculated as the average of the points within each cluster. This process repeats iteratively until the centroids stabilize and no longer change significantly, meaning the clusters have converged (note that there are various other methods for this as well).

Figure 6.2 **How does K-Means Clustering Work?**

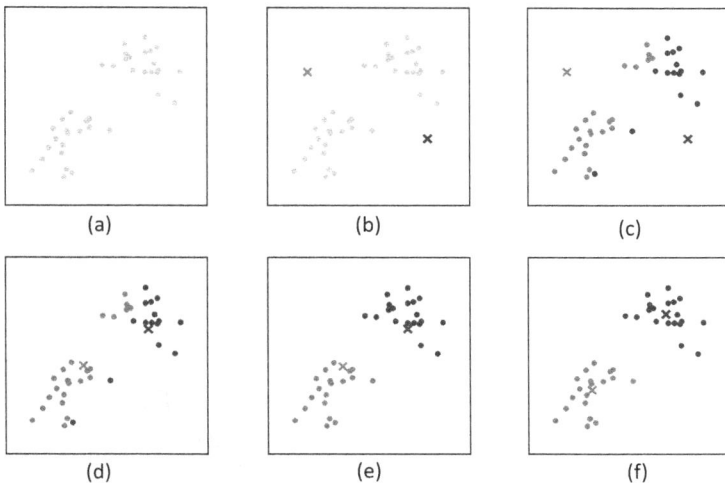

(a) (b) (c)

(d) (e) (f)

Source: Piech, Chris. "K-Means Clustering." CS221: Artificial Intelligence - Handouts. Stanford University. Accessed September 19, 2024. https://stanford.edu/~cpiech/cs221/handouts/kmeans.html.

Based, on our discussion, let's take a look at some key points you should take note about this algorithm:

- **Predefined number of the clusters:** The number of clusters (k) are specified before running the algorithm, making it easier to converge to a solution (albeit not the best one). Otherwise, the value of k might change with every iteration

- **Fast and efficient:** As the method is all about distances, it is computationally efficient and works well even with large datasets, compared to other unsupervised learning techniques.

- **Sensitive to initial centroids:** The initial choice of centroids can lead to different clustering results as they are used to assign the points into their primary clusters So, if you change these initial values, your final results will most probably be quite different

- **Distance metric:** Euclidean distance is a commonly used metric to measure the similarity between data points and centroids. However, we can use any of the distance metrics we covered in the previous chapters based on the problem we are trying to solve and the kind of data we have.

Now, let's see how the algorithm actually works in practice.

1. **Pick how many groups:** First, you gotta decide how many groups (we call 'em "k") you want. You might know this already or just try different numbers until you find the best one.

2. **Put down some middle points:** The computer puts down "k" random spots for your data. These spots are like the reference point of each group.

3. **First Clusters:** Each data point gets put with the closest centroid. This gives us the first set of clusters.

4. **Move the middle spots:** After this, the computer finds the new centroids of each group by recalculating them based on the existing cluster allocations.

5. **Do it again:** The computer keeps doing this until the centroid allocations remain the same after successive iterations.

So, we now have the data points grouped into k distinct clusters, where each cluster contains points that are more similar to each other. This is essentially what is shown in Figure 6.2. Next, let's take a quick detour and try to understand the mathematics behind this algorithm.

Objective of K-Means Clustering: A Math Primer

In this section, we will be covering the math behind this algorithm. As you all know by now, **the primary objective of k-means clustering is to partition the dataset into k distinct groups so that data points within the same group** (or cluster) are more similar to each other than to those in other clusters. This similarity is usually measured in terms of the distance between data points and the cluster's centroid. Hence, minimizing this distance helps form tightly packed clusters, which is what we want (i.e., less space between the points in the same cluster and most space between the different clusters).

The mathematical objective function of k-means clustering can be written as:

$$\text{Objective: } \min \sum_{i=1}^{k} \sum_{x \in C_i} \text{distance}(x, \mu_i)^2$$

Where:

- C_i is the set of data points in the i-th cluster.
- i is the centroid of the i-th cluster.
- Distance is typically calculated using the Euclidean distance.

Now, the question you might have is, how to find what k value would be the best. The truth is, this varies based on a lot of factors like the size and content of the dataset, complexity, etc. In most cases, to determine the best value for k, techniques such as the **Elbow Method** can be used. Let's see what this is.

Elbow method:

The elbow method involves running the k-means algorithm for various values of k and plotting the Sum of Squared Errors (SSE) or inertia for each k. The point at which the SSE starts to decrease more slowly, forming an "elbow," indicates the optimal number of clusters. Take a look at the image given below to see how a sample elbow plot looks like.

Figure 6.3   **A Sample Elbow Plot for K-Means Algorithm**

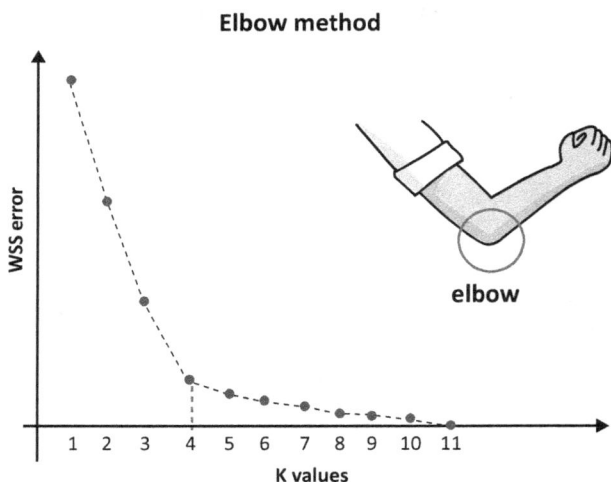

This plot helps determine where increasing the number of clusters no longer significantly improves the clustering performance.

Now that we have a clear understanding of the overall algorithm, let's go through some of its strengths and weaknesses to get a better idea of where it stands compared to the vast variety of ML algorithms available today.

Strengths

- **Simplicity:** K-means is easy to understand and implement.
- **Speed:** It is computationally efficient, especially with large datasets.

- **Works well with distinct clusters:** K-means performs best when the clusters are well separated and spherical in shape.

Limitations

- **Choosing k:** The need to specify the number of clusters (k) beforehand is a challenge.

- **Sensitivity to Initialization:** As we discussed before, different initializations of centroids can lead to different final results, which is not ideal when we want to recreate the same results. For instance, what if your news article groupings keep changing after each refresh.

- **Sensitive to Outliers:** K-means is quite sensitive to noise and outliers, which can significantly affect cluster centroids as they are quite literally the average of all the points in a cluster.

- **Cluster Shape:** K-means assumes that clusters are spherical and equally sized, as we are using centroids and euclidean distances for this which may not be ideal for every use case.

Now, let's do what you all have been waiting for. Let's implement this algorithm in Python and see it in action.

Implementing K-means Clustering in Python

Python makes implementing the k-Means algorithm incredibly straightforward, thanks to **scikit-learn**, which provides a built-in function for k-Means and other algorithms we have already covered. Let's walk through an example using the **Iris dataset**, a well-known dataset that contains measurements of different flower species (remember, we already used it in a number of previous implementation sections). Although generally used for classification problems, it would be interesting to see how clustering can help us understand this dataset better. So, let's start!

Step 1: Import Necessary Libraries

We'll be using **pandas** for data manipulation, **matplotlib** and **seaborn** for visualization, and **scikit-learn** for the k-Means algorithm. If you have come this far, you should already have all these libraries installed in your Python environment.

```
import pandas as pd
import numpy as np
import matplotlib.pyplot as plt
import seaborn as sns
from sklearn.cluster import KMeans
from sklearn.datasets import load_iris
from sklearn.preprocessing import StandardScaler
```

Step 2: Load and Explore the Dataset

We'll use the Iris dataset, which you should already know quite a bi0t about. The target variable is the species of the flower, but since we are applying unsupervised learning, we won't use this information for clustering. As always, let's make it a practice to explore the dataset after importing so we have a better idea of what we are dealing with.

```
# Load the iris dataset
iris = load_iris()

# Convert to a pandas DataFrame for easy manipulation
(not using targets)
df = pd.DataFrame(iris.data, columns=iris.feature_names)

# View the first few rows of the dataset
df.head()
```

You will have the same four columns for petal and sepal width and lengths in the dataset.

Step 3: Preprocess the Data

Before applying k-Means, it's almost always a good idea to standardize the dataset, especially if the features are on different scales. Standardization ensures that each feature contributes equally to the distance calculations. We will use scikit-learn's inbuilt StandardScaler function to do this.

```
# Standardize the data
scaler = StandardScaler()
df_scaled = scaler.fit_transform(df)
```

Step 4: Apply k-Means Clustering

Next, we apply the k-Means algorithm. In this example, we'll assume that there are three clusters (since the Iris dataset contains three species of flowers). However, in a real-world scenario, you would experiment with **different values of k** or use methods like the **elbow method** to find the optimal number of clusters (we will see how to create this plot as well).

```
# Apply k-Means with k=3
kmeans = KMeans(n_clusters=3, random_state=42)
kmeans.fit(df_scaled)

# Add cluster labels to the original DataFrame
df['Cluster'] = kmeans.labels_
```

Step 5: Visualize the Clusters

To visualize the learned clusters, we can plot the first two features (sepal length and sepal width) and color the data points according to the cluster assigned by k-Means. This gives us a rough idea of how well the algorithm has grouped the data.

```
# Visualize the clusters using a scatter plot
plt.figure(figsize=(10, 6))
sns.scatterplot(x=df[iris.feature_names[0]], y=df[iris.
feature_names[1]], hue=df['Cluster'], palette='Set1',
s=100)

plt.title('k-Means Clustering on Iris Dataset (Sepal
Length vs Sepal Width)')
plt.xlabel('Sepal Length (cm)')
plt.ylabel('Sepal Width (cm)')
plt.show()
```

| Figure 6.4 | **Clusters in the Iris Dataset with K-Means Clustering** |

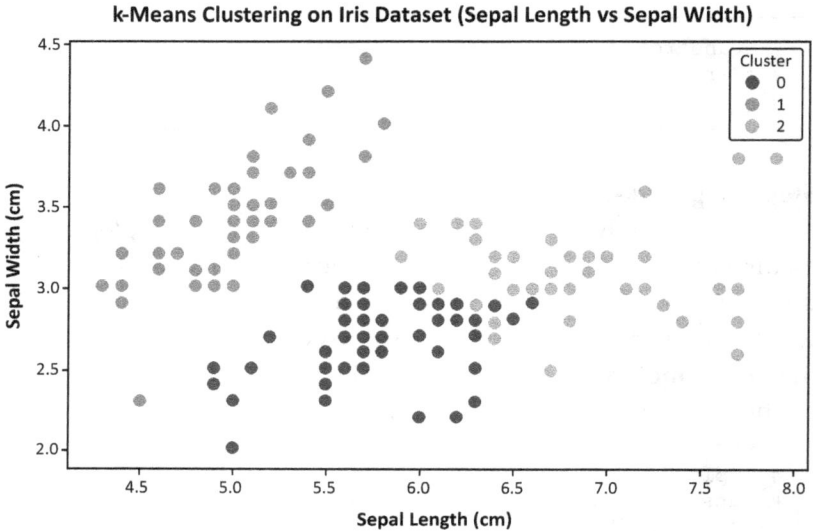

k-Means Clustering on Iris Dataset (Sepal Length vs Sepal Width)

The plot clearly shows that our algorithm did a pretty good job clustering the different flower species (you can see the three distinct clusters clearly). Interestingly, if you as a human were given the task to do the same, the result would most likely be different as from first glance, you cannot see clear clusters in the data.

Now, let's do something a bit more interesting. Let's create an elbow plot for different k values to see how it can help us get the best value for "k".

Step 6: The Elbow Method for Choosing k

Choosing the right number of clusters (k) is one of the challenges of k-Means. The **Elbow Method** is a common technique used to find the optimal value for **k**. It involves running k-Means for different values of **k** and plotting the **inertia** (a measure of how tightly the data points are clustered). The idea is to choose **k** at the point where the inertia starts to decrease more slowly, forming an "elbow" in the plot.

```
# Use the Elbow Method to determine the optimal k
inertia = []
for i in range(1, 11):
    kmeans = KMeans(n_clusters=i, random_state=42)
    kmeans.fit(df_scaled)
    inertia.append(kmeans.inertia_)

# Plot the elbow graph
plt.figure(figsize=(8, 5))
plt.plot(range(1, 11), inertia, marker='o')
plt.title('Elbow Method for Optimal k')
plt.xlabel('Number of clusters (k)')
plt.ylabel('Inertia')
plt.show()
```

Figure 6.5   **Elbow Plot Visualization to get the optimal k value**

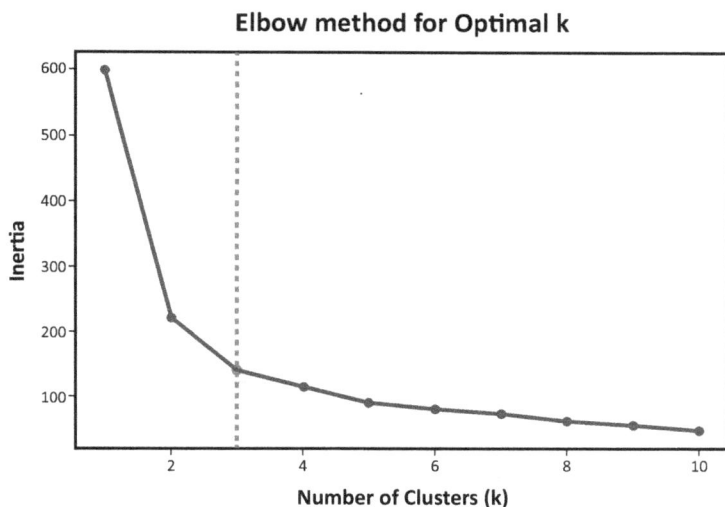

As discussed above, the point where the plot starts to flatten (the step size decreases) is the optimal k value, which is 3 in this case. Hence, you now know a really good method to choose k as well. However, keep in mind that the limitations discussed above still exist: you need to run the algorithm multiple times and for large datasets, it is a big issue. Moreover, the initial centroids play a critical role in the algorithm so a poor choice can lead to a lot of issues.

For this reason, there are a lot of modified K-means algorithms out there which help address these issues. For instance, the **K-Means++ algorithm** addresses the initial centroid problem by employing a strategy for smarter centroid initialization to ensure better clustering results and faster convergence (reaching the (so called) optimal solution).

That was all for K-means, which is a partitioning based clustering technique. However, there are numerous more techniques in which clustering is employed. Let's go through some of these techniques in brief.

6.1.3 Alternative Clustering Methodologies

K-Means Clustering is pretty popular, but it's not always the best way to group the dataset. There are other ways to do it, and some work better for different kinds of data. Let's talk about a few other ways to form data clusters. I will keep it simple and give you some ideas about when you might want to use them.

1. Hierarchical Clustering

Figure 6.6   How does Hierarchical Clustering work?

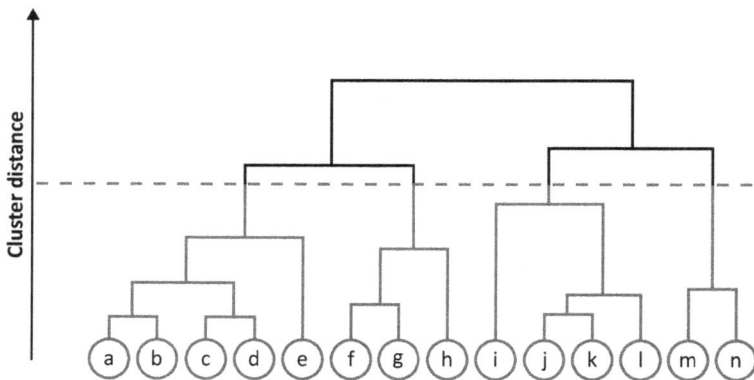

Source: Abrar, Abdullah. "Exploring the Versatility of Hierarchical Clustering: Applications, Working Methods, and Benefits." Medium, June 26, 2023. https://medium. com/@abdullahabrar/exploring-the-versatility-of-hierarchical-clustering-applications-working-methods-and-benefits-5bae54cb9e7b.

Hierarchical Clustering, talking simply, builds a tree-like structure of clusters by either starting with individual data points and merging them (known as **agglomerative**) or instead, starts with a large cluster and splits it down into smaller ones (known as **divisive**). The main advantage of this method is that it does not require you to predefine the number of clusters, which was the case with k-means clustering. Instead, you can decide the number of clusters by cutting the hierarchical tree (called a **dendrogram**) at a certain level, which is like cutting off the last branches to get the perfect looking tree.

This technique is particularly used in **gene expression data analysis**, where the relationships between genes need to be examined at multiple levels and it is quite beneficial to use the tree-like structure. You can explore how genes cluster together at different levels of similarity, providing insight into biological relationships and developing new and innovative solutions.

2. DBSCAN (Density-Based Spatial Clustering of Applications with Noise)

Figure 6.7 DBSCAN Clustering Algorithm

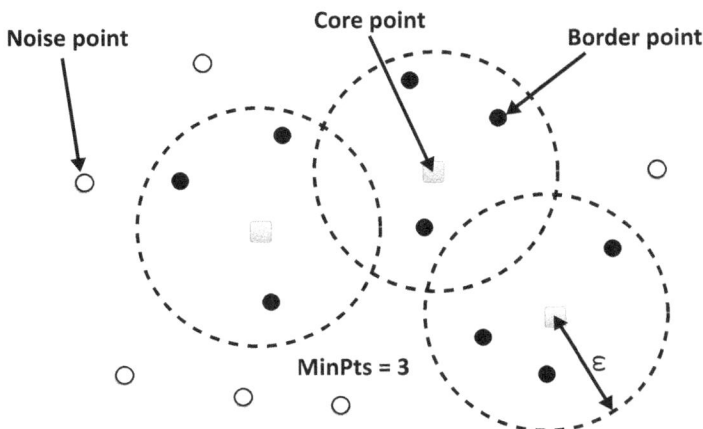

Source: Chauhan, Nagesh. "DBSCAN Clustering Algorithm in Machine Learning." KDnuggets, April 4, 2022. https://www.kdnuggets.com/2020/04/dbscan-clustering-algorithm-machine-learning.html.

DBSCAN is a powerful clustering technique that groups data points based on their density. It does this by discovering clusters of arbitrary shape, making it highly suitable for datasets with complex cluster structures which you might not be able to discern with simple clustering techniques. Unlike K-Means, DBSCAN doesn't require the user to specify the number of clusters and can also detect outliers as noise points.

DBSCAN is highly useful for **spatial data analysis**, which involves grouping different regions in a geographical dataset where clusters are generally not spherical, such as the buildings distribution in a city. Additionally, DBSCAN can detect isolated homes (outliers) that don't belong to any cluster so that they can be dealt with.

3. Mean Shift Clustering

Figure 6.8   **How does Mean Shift Clustering work?**

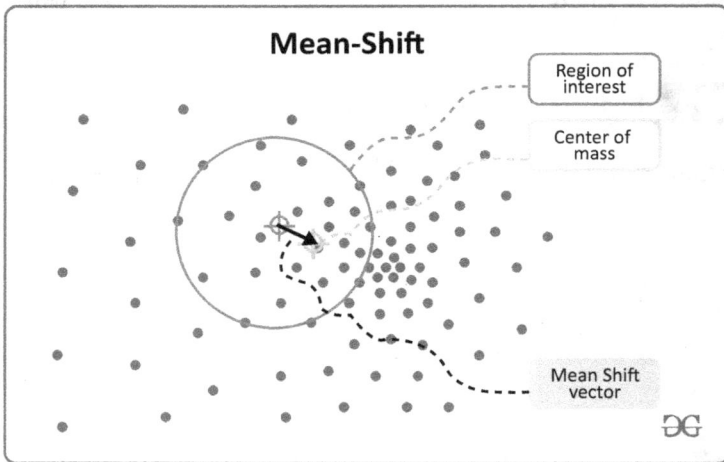

Source: "ML: Mean-Shift Clustering." GeeksforGeeks, January 23, 2023. https://www. geeksforgeeks.org/ml-mean-shift-clustering/.

Mean Shift is a non-parametric (so no parameters to train) clustering technique that seeks to find dense regions in a feature space by iteratively shifting data points towards the mode (i.e. the most dense area). This algorithm does not require specifying the number of clusters beforehand and automatically adapts based on the data's structure.

Mean Shift is often used in **image segmentation to** segment an image into regions of similar pixel intensity without predefining how many segments there should be. This has a lot of applications in the image processing domain.

4. Gaussian Mixture Models (GMM)

A Gaussian Mixture Model works on the primary assumption that our dataset is generated from a mixture of several Gaussian distributions with unknown parameters (at least unknown to us). Unlike K-Means, where each data point belongs to a single cluster, GMM assigns each point with a probability of belonging to a particular cluster (so it may not be a non-zero value for different clusters). This flexibility makes it a probabilistic clustering method.

Figure 6.9   **Showing a Mixture of Gaussians!**

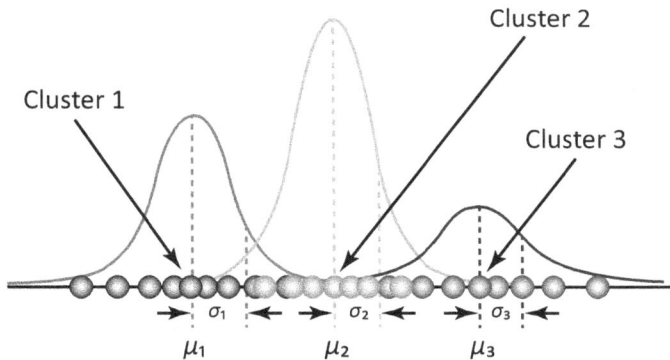

Source: Chadha, Vaibhav. "Gaussian Mixture Models Explained." Towards Data Science, June 3, 2019. https://towardsdatascience.com/gaussian-mixture-models-explained-6986aaf5a95.

GMM is frequently used in **anomaly detection** in domains like finance, where data points (transactions) may belong to multiple clusters (normal vs. suspicious) with some probability. The GMM model can help identify unusual patterns of transactions more accurately.

In conclusion, these alternative clustering methodologies offer different advantages and are useful in specific scenarios. Hence, we can conclude this section by taking note that choosing the right clustering technique depends largely on your data,the number of clusters, the shape of those clusters, and noise or outliers in the data. Each method has its strengths, and the flexibility to choose among them gives us the power to find the best fit for the problem. Next, we will cover another application area for unsupervised learning: **Dimensionality Reduction.**

6.2 Dimensionality Reduction Techniques: PCA and t-SNE

In lots of machine learning tasks, you might have way too much info to deal with, which is particularly true with so much data being collected. Some of this information might not help at all, or even mess things up while learning something. It's like trying to find a needle in a haystack, but the haystack keeps getting bigger! This can make your machine learning work worse, not better. Weird, right? To address this, we can use **dimensionality reduction techniques** to be selective and only choose what's important. This section covers two widely used dimensionality reduction methods: **Principal Component Analysis (PCA)** and **t-Distributed Stochastic Neighbor Embedding (t-SNE).**

| Figure 6.10 | The Concept of Dimensionality Reduction |

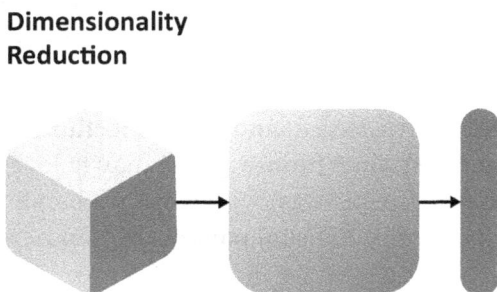

Dimensionality Reduction

6.2.1 Principal Component Analysis (PCA)

Principal Component Analysis (PCA) is a linear dimensionality reduction technique that reduces the dimensions of data by transforming the features into a set of variables called **principal components**. The idea behind this method is to project the data onto a lower-dimensional space such that *most of the variance* in the data is retained in fewer dimensions.

PCA is widely used in applications like **face recognition** systems. Given a dataset with thousands of pixel features per image, PCA can reduce the number of dimensions (i.e. features) by retaining the most informative aspects of the images (like the shape of your forehead, nose, etc). This allows face recognition algorithms to work more efficiently by focusing only on the essential features. Let's see how this algorithm works:

1. **Standardization of the Data:** PCA begins by standardizing the features so that they have a mean of 0 and a variance of 1. This is essential because PCA wants to maximize variance, which is sensitive to the scale of the data.

2. **Covariance Matrix:** Next, it computes the covariance matrix, which measures how the features in the dataset are dependent on each other. If certain features are highly correlated, PCA seeks to combine them into a smaller set of components to capture the most variance.

3. **Eigenvalues and Eigenvectors:** Then, the eigenvalues and eigenvectors of the covariance matrix are then calculated. The eigenvectors represent the directions (principal components) in which the data varies, and the eigenvalues give the magnitude of this variance. We need this for the final projection of this data.

4. **Projecting the Data:** The data is then projected onto the principal components, reducing the number of dimensions while preserving as much variance as possible.

Figure 6.11 | PCA? What is it and How does it work?

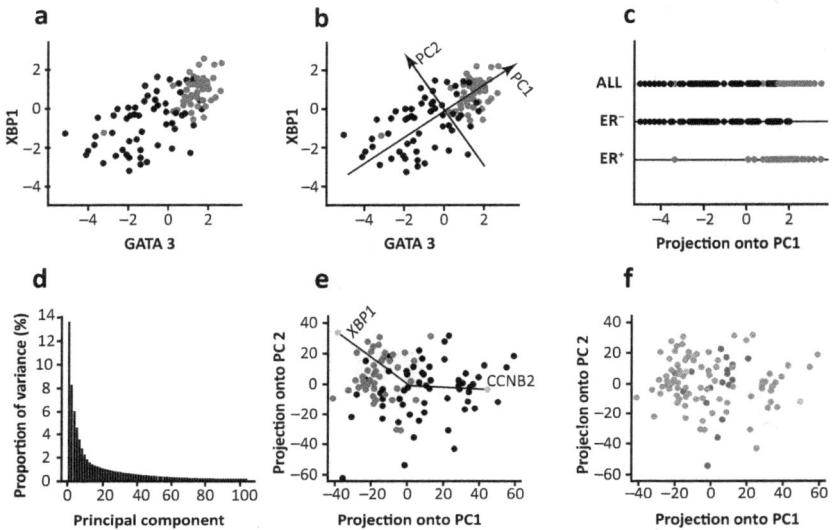

Source: Ringnér, M. What is principal component analysis?. Nat Biotechnol 26, 303–304 (2008). https://doi.org/10.1038/nbt0308-303

Let's dive into the math behind Principal Component Analysis to have a solid understanding about the inner workings of the algorithm.

Math behind PCA

Let's revisit the algorithm but this time from a mathematical standpoint:

Given a dataset XX with nn data points and dd features, the objective of PCA is to find new axes (principal components) such that the variance in the data is maximized in fewer dimensions.

Step 1: Standardization of the Data

The first step in PCA is to **standardize** the dataset to ensure that each feature has a mean of 0 and a variance of 1. This is important because PCA is sensitive to the scale of the data.

$$X_{standardized} = \frac{X - \mu}{\sigma}$$

where:

- X is the original data matrix,
- μ is the mean of each feature, and
- σ is the standard deviation of each feature.

Step 2: Compute the Covariance Matrix

Once the data is standardized, we compute the **covariance matrix** to understand the relationships between the features. The covariance matrix CC is defined as:

$$C = \frac{1}{n-1} X_{standardized}^{T} X_{standardized}$$

where:

- $X_{standardized}$ is the standardized data matrix, $X_{standardized}$ is the standardized data matrix,
- n is the number of data points, n is the number of data points,
- C is a d × dd × d matrix representing the pairwise covariances between features. C is a d × dd × d matrix representing the pairwise covariances between features.

Step 3: Compute the Eigenvalues and Eigenvectors

The next step is to compute the **eigenvalues** and **eigenvectors** of the covariance matrix CC. The eigenvectors represent the directions of the new feature space (i.e., the principal components), and the eigenvalues indicate the amount of variance explained by each component.

To solve for the eigenvalues and eigenvectors, we need to solve the following equation:

$$Cv = \lambda v$$

where:

- C is the covariance matrix,
- v is the eigenvector (principal component), and
- λ is the eigenvalue (variance explained by the component).

This equation can be solved using standard linear algebra techniques. The eigenvectors corresponding to the largest eigenvalues represent the directions in which the data has the most variance.

Step 4: Sort the Eigenvalues and Eigenvectors

After calculating the eigenvalues and eigenvectors, we sort them in decreasing order of the eigenvalues. The eigenvector corresponding to the largest eigenvalue is the first principal component, the second-largest eigenvalue corresponds to the second principal component, and so on.

The amount of variance explained by each principal component can be quantified using the eigenvalues. The **explained variance** for each principal component is given by:

$$\text{Explained variance ratio} = \frac{\lambda_i}{\sum_{j=1}^{d} \lambda_j}$$

where:

- λ_i is the i-th largest eigenvalue, and
- $\sum_{j=1}^{d} \lambda_j$ is the sum of all eigenvalues.

Step 5: Form the Principal Components

Finally, we form the **principal components** by projecting the original data onto the new axes defined by the eigenvectors. This projection transforms the data into a new feature space with reduced dimensions.

The transformation is performed using matrix multiplication:

$$Z = X_{\text{standardized}} W$$

where:

- Z is the transformed data matrix in the new feature space,
- $X_{standardized}$ is the standardized data matrix,
- W is the matrix of eigenvectors (principal components).

If we choose to reduce the data to kk dimensions, we only retain the first k eigenvectors, resulting in a new data matrix Z of size n × k.

Step 6: Reconstructing the Data (Optional)

In some cases, we may want to reconstruct the original data from the reduced dimensions. This can be done by reversing the transformation:

$$X_{reconstructed} = ZW^T + \mu$$

where:

- W^T is the transpose of the eigenvector matrix,
- μ is the original mean of the data.

This reconstruction will approximate the original data but with some loss of information, depending on how many principal components were retained.

Now, you have a pretty solid understanding of how PCA works in practice, let's implement it in Python.

PCA Implementation in Python

In this section, we'll implement Principal Component Analysis (PCA) in Python using readily available libraries. The flow of this section will be as follows: we will import a dataset, preprocess it, perform PCA, and visualize the results.

Import Necessary Libraries

As always, we will start by importing the necessary libraries. The primary libraries are pretty much the same as before with the only change being the PCA library that we import from Scikit Learn.

```
import numpy as np
import matplotlib.pyplot as plt
from sklearn.decomposition import PCA
from sklearn.preprocessing import StandardScaler
from sklearn.datasets import load_iris
```

Load and Inspect the Dataset

As before, we'll use the Iris dataset. In fact, we will skip the explanation part as we already covered that in the previous section. Let's load and take a look at the data once.

```
# Load Iris dataset
iris = load_iris()
X = iris.data
y = iris.target
# Inspect the shape of the dataset
print("Shape of data:", X.shape)
print("First 5 rows:\n", X[:5])
```

Standardize the Data

Since PCA is affected by the scale of the features, it's crucial to standardize the dataset (mean of 0 and standard deviation of 1). We will follow the same procedure we did in the last section of this chapter when we implemented the K-means algorithm.

```
# Standardize the data
scaler = StandardScaler()
X_scaled = scaler.fit_transform(X)

# Check the first 5 rows after standardization
print("First 5 rows (standardized):\n", X_scaled[:5])
```

Applying PCA on Scaled Data

Now that our dataset is ready, we'll apply PCA and reduce the dataset to 2 principal components for visualization purposes (2D visualization is much more interpretable for us). As we learnt from the theory above, PCA will identify the two most important dimensions that capture the most variance in the data.

```
# Apply PCA
pca = PCA(n_components=2)
X_pca = pca.fit_transform(X_scaled)

# Check the shape of the transformed data
print("Shape of transformed data:", X_pca.shape)
```

Once we fit our data with the PCA object as above, our resulting dataset will have only 2 dimensions (as we specified n_components as 2). Now, let's check an interesting metric in PCA: Explained Variance Ratio which allows us to quantify the amount of variance for each new feature.

Explained Variance Ratio

After applying PCA, it's useful to check how much variance is explained by each of the components. This can be easily done with scikit-learn. In fact, it's just a single function call.

```
# Explained variance ratio
explained_variance = pca.explained_variance_ratio_
print("Explained variance ratio of each component:",
explained_variance)
```

For this dataset, the first principal component explains 80% (approx.) of the variance while the other contributes to the remaining 20% variance. Let's visualize the datasets with the corresponding labels to see how this may help in reducing the dimensionality of a dataset when trying to solve a classification problem.

Visualize the Results

Now we'll plot the data in the new 2D space created by the two principal components.

```
# Plot the PCA results
plt.figure(figsize=(8,6))
plt.scatter(X_pca[:, 0], X_pca[:, 1], c=y,
cmap='viridis', edgecolor='k', s=100)
plt.xlabel('Principal Component 1')
plt.ylabel('Principal Component 2')
plt.title('PCA of Iris Dataset')
plt.colorbar(label='Target')
plt.show()
```

The graph shows an almost clear separation between the three classes of flowers in the Iris dataset, indicating that this PCA process works fairly well.

Figure 6.12 | **Iris Dataset PCA Visualization Results**

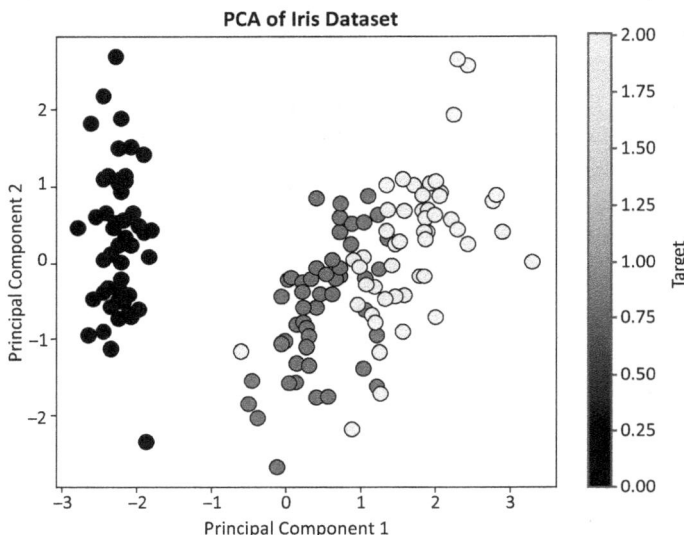

Reconstruct the Original Data (Optional Step!)

Although this step is optional, If you want to reconstruct the original data from the principal components, you can multiply the principal components by the PCA components (loadings) and add the mean back.

```
# Reconstruct the data from the principal components
X_reconstructed = pca.inverse_transform(X_pca)

# Compare original vs reconstructed data (first 5 rows)
print("Original Data (first 5 rows):\n", X_scaled[:5])
print("Reconstructed Data (first 5 rows):\n", X_
reconstructed[:5])
```

The output for this code snippet would be as follows:

```
Original Data (first 5 rows):

 [[-0.90068117  1.01900435 -1.34022653 -1.3154443 ]
  [-1.14301691 -0.13197948 -1.34022653 -1.3154443 ]
  [-1.38535265  0.32841405 -1.39706395 -1.3154443 ]
  [-1.50652052  0.09821729 -1.2833891  -1.3154443 ]
  [-1.02184904  1.24920112 -1.34022653 -1.3154443 ]]

Reconstructed Data (first 5 rows):

 [[-0.99888895  1.05319838 -1.30270654 -1.24709825]
  [-1.33874781 -0.06192302 -1.22432772 -1.22057235]
  [-1.36096129  0.32111685 -1.38060338 -1.35833824]
  [-1.42359795  0.0677615  -1.34922386 -1.33881298]
  [-1.00113823  1.24091818 -1.37125365 -1.30661752]]
```

This will produce a somewhat similar dataset to the original values with some differences.

This marks the end of this section on PCA. In this section, we applied PCA to reduce the dimensionality of the Iris dataset. We went from 4 features to 2, while capturing most of the variance in the data. PCA is a powerful tool for visualizing high-dimensional data and understanding the structure behind it.

Let's cover another popular dimensionality reduction technique now:**t-Distributed Stochastic Neighbor Embedding (t-SNE).**

6.2.2 t-Distributed Stochastic Neighbor Embedding (t-SNE)

Figure 6.13 t-SNE Algorithm - Visualized

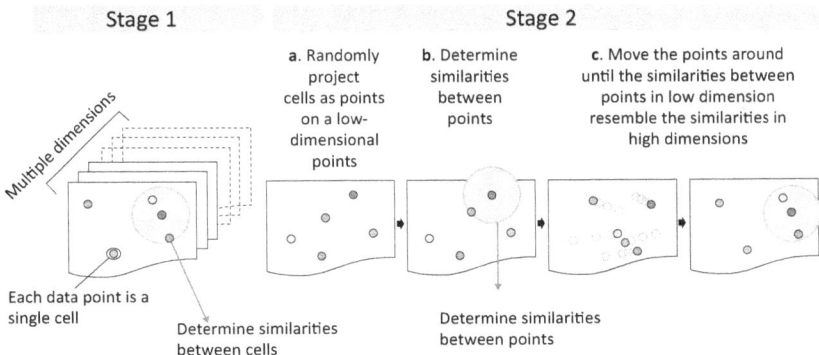

t-Distributed Stochastic Neighbor Embedding (t-SNE) is another popular **non-linear** dimensionality reduction technique used for visualizing high-dimensional datasets in lower dimensions. Unlike PCA, which focuses on maximizing the variance, t-SNE captures the local relations of the data, making it an effective tool for visualizing clusters and finding hidden patterns in more complex datasets, where PCA might struggle. It is especially useful for datasets where clusters are not linearly separable as it is a non-linear method.

One of the primary applications of t-SNE is in **image data analysis**, where high-dimensional data (e.g., pixel intensities or deep learning features) are difficult to interpret directly as at first glance, they are just a bunch of numbers (it is just a matrix with numbers!). For example, in **computer vision**, images of handwritten digits from something like the **MNIST** dataset are often used to train machine learning models. Each image in the dataset is represented as a vector of 784 dimensions (28×28 pixels). Using t-SNE, we can reduce these image vectors down to 2 or 3 dimensions while preserving the local relationships between the images (i.e. the shape and features). t-SNE will capture how similar images (like the same digits) are close together in the low-dimensional space, allowing us to visualize the digits as clusters.

Now that we have a good overview of the algorithm, let's see how this algorithm actually works.

How does the Algorithm work?

t-SNE works by converting the high-dimensional data into a pairwise similarity matrix in both the original high-dimensional space and the lower-dimensional space (usually 2D or 3D). It then minimizes the difference between these two similarity matrices using gradient descent iteratively. The main idea behind t-SNE is to maintain the local structure of the data — i.e., points that are close in the high-dimensional space should also be close in the low-dimensional space as well. But, as always, it's easier said than done.

So, let's see how it achieves this. The t-SNE algorithm works in three major steps:

1. **Pairwise Similarity in High-Dimensional Space:** The first step in t-SNE is to calculate the probability that a point x_i would pick another point x_j as its neighbor based on the distance between them. The probability is modeled as a Gaussian distribution in high-dimensional space.

2. **Pairwise Similarity in Low-Dimensional Space:** Then, t-SNE computes a similar probability distribution for the points in low-dimensional space, but using a **student's t-distribution** with one degree of freedom (which has heavier tails than a Gaussian).

3. **KL-Divergence Optimization:** The difference between the two probability distributions (original and generated) is measured using a metric called **Kullback-Leibler (KL) divergence.** t-SNE tries to minimize this measure by adjusting the positions of the points in the lower-dimensional space to get the optimal solution.

The key parameter in t-SNE is known as **perplexity**, and it determines how many neighboring data points each point is compared to during the analysis. The choice of perplexity can influence the final appearance of the t-SNE plot, like the initial centroids in k-means clustering. Typical, perplexity values range from 5 to 50. Since the best perplexity value depends on the hidden patterns within the data, which are often unknown to the researcher, it is always an experimental process in which different perplexity values are used to find the most suitable one for a given dataset.

These steps enable you to create effective low dimensional results for high dimensional complex datasets. Looking at the content, the mathematics behind this is a bit complex and beyond the scope of this book. So, let's jump straight to its implementation in Python.

Python implementation for t-SNE

Let's walk through a simple Python implementation of t-SNE. As before, we will use the same iris dataset.

Step 1: Import the Necessary Libraries

We will begin by importing the required libraries, including numpy, matplotlib, and sklearn's TSNE for the implementation.

```
import numpy as np
import matplotlib.pyplot as plt
from sklearn.manifold import TSNE
from sklearn.datasets import load_iris
from sklearn.preprocessing import StandardScaler
```

Next, let's load our dataset using the same code we used before.

Step 2: Load and Inspect the Dataset

As before, we'll use the Iris dataset. In fact, we will skip the explanation part as we already covered that in the previous section. Let's load and take a look at the data once.

```
# Load Iris dataset
iris = load_iris()
X = iris.data
y = iris.target
# Inspect the shape of the dataset
print("Shape of data:", X.shape)
print("First 5 rows:\n", X[:5])
```

As before, let's standardize the dataset so that there are no problems even if the data is differently scaled.

```
# Standardize the data
scaler = StandardScaler()
X_scaled = scaler.fit_transform(X)
```

Step 3: Apply t-SNE

Now, we'll apply t-SNE to reduce the dataset from 4 dimensions to 2 dimensions, making it easier to visualize.

```
# Apply t-SNE
tsne = TSNE(n_components=2, random_state=42)
X_tsne = tsne.fit_transform(X_scaled)

# Check the shape of the transformed data
print("Shape of transformed data:", X_tsne.shape)
```

Step 4: Visualizing the resulting dataset

Finally, we can plot the 2D t-SNE embedding, coloring the points based on their respective classes.

```
# Plot the t-SNE results
plt.figure(figsize=(8,6))
plt.scatter(X_tsne[:, 0], X_tsne[:, 1], c=y,
cmap='viridis', edgecolor='k', s=100)
plt.xlabel('t-SNE Component 1')
plt.ylabel('t-SNE Component 2')
plt.title('t-SNE of Iris Dataset')
plt.colorbar(label='Target')
plt.show()
```

Figure 6.14 **2- Dimensional t-SNE Dataset Visualization**

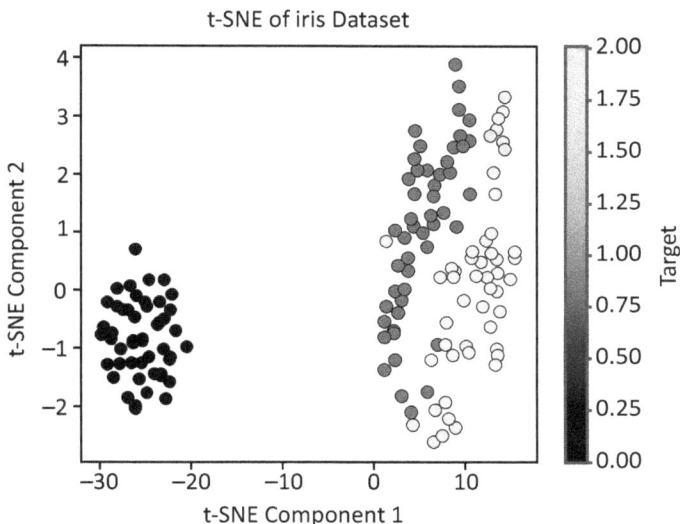

The results clearly show an almost perfect separation between the three flower species. Next, let's play with the perplexity metric for the algorithm and see how our results change to better understand the role of perplexity.

Step 5: Understanding the role of Perplexity

The perplexity parameter controls how t-SNE balances attention between local and global aspects of the data. We can experiment with different perplexity values. Let's change the value of this parameter to see how the output changes.

```
# Apply t-SNE with different perplexity
tsne = TSNE(n_components=2, perplexity=50, random_
state=42)
X_tsne = tsne.fit_transform(X_scaled)

# Plot with different perplexity
plt.figure(figsize=(8,6))
plt.scatter(X_tsne[:, 0], X_tsne[:, 1], c=y,
cmap='viridis', edgecolor='k', s=100)
plt.xlabel('t-SNE Component 1')
plt.ylabel('t-SNE Component 2')
plt.title('t-SNE of Iris Dataset (Perplexity = 50)')
plt.colorbar(label='Target')
plt.show()
```

Figure 6.15 **How perplexity impacts t-SNE**

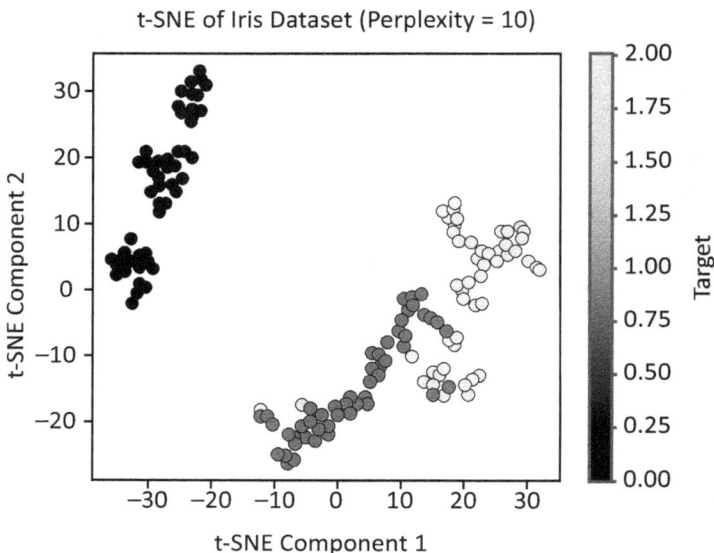

So, intuitively speaking, lower perplexity values tend to cluster points closer together. That was all there was about t-SNE. This marks the end of the Dimensionality Reduction section as well. In the last section, we will cover another very interesting unsupervised learning technique: **Market Basket Analysis.**

6.3 Association Rules: Market Basket Analysis

| Figure 6.16 | Understanding Market Basket Analysis |

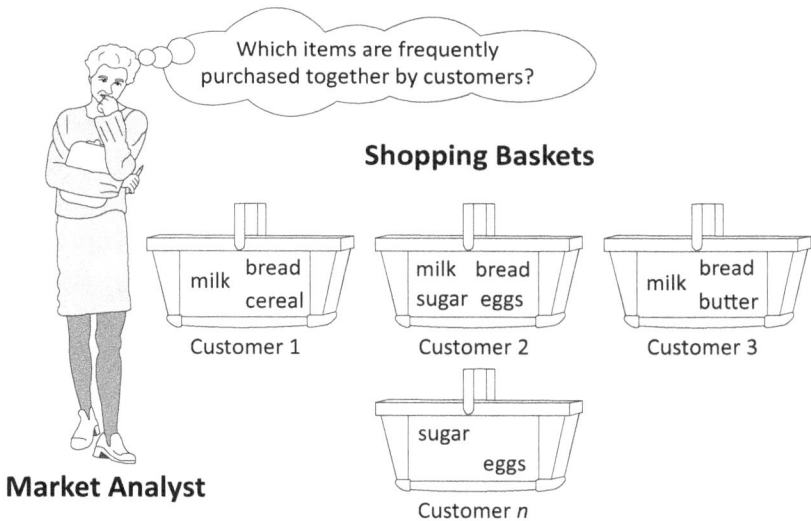

Which items are frequently purchased together by customers?

Shopping Baskets

milk bread cereal — Customer 1

milk bread sugar eggs — Customer 2

milk bread butter — Customer 3

sugar eggs — Customer n

Market Analyst

Market Basket Analysis is a popular data mining (which deals with finding patterns in data) that focuses on discovering relationships between different instances in large datasets. It is most commonly used in the retail industry, where understanding customer purchasing patterns helps businesses identify the products that are frequently bought together and make important decisions like which ones are the most profitable to invest in. These insights are crucial for developing strategies such as product recommendations, store layouts, or cross-promotions that help them grow.

Let's understand the fundamentals of this algorithm. At the core of Market Basket Analysis is the concept of **association rules**. These rules help identify patterns and relationships between items in a dataset. In a retail setting, an association rule might look like this:

- "If a customer buys bread, they are likely to also buy butter." This is called a **rule** because it suggests a relationship between the items in a transaction.

An association rule is typically represented in the form:

A→B

Where A (the antecedent) is the item or set of items that leads to the purchase of B (the consequent). In simple terms, the rule reads: "If A is purchased, then B is likely to be purchased."

To better understand and measure the strength of these relationships, three important metrics are used:

Figure 6.17 **Key Metrics for Market Basket Analysis**

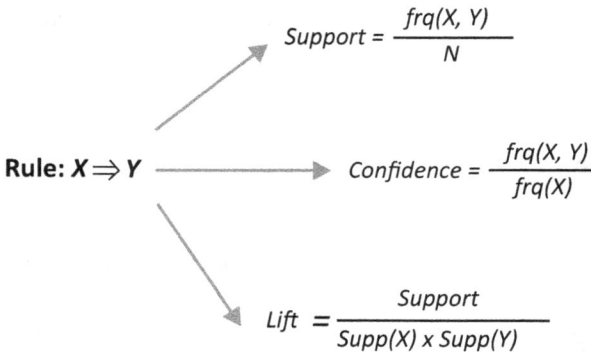

$$Support = \frac{frq(X, Y)}{N}$$

$$\text{Rule: } X \Rightarrow Y$$

$$Confidence = \frac{frq(X, Y)}{frq(X)}$$

$$Lift = \frac{Support}{Supp(X) \times Supp(Y)}$$

1. **Support:** Support measures how frequently an item or set of items occurs in the dataset. For example, if bread appears in 200 out of 1,000 transactions, the support for bread is 20%.

2. **Confidence:** Confidence tells us how often the rule has been found to be true. For the rule "If A, then B," confidence measures the likelihood of buying B after having bought A.

3. **Lift:** Lift measures how much more likely it is to buy B when A has been bought, compared to random chance. It helps evaluate the strength of the association beyond just support and confidence. A lift greater than 1 indicates a strong association.

Let's consider a simple scenario. Imagine you're managing a supermarket and want to understand your customers better. You have transaction data from thousands of customers, and you're interested in discovering which items are frequently bought together. For instance, you may find that customers who buy **coffee** often also purchase **milk**. With this insight, you might decide to place coffee and milk closer together in the store or create a deal to encourage customers to buy both, hereby increasing your revenue and profits.

Now, consider you're running an online store, and you discover that customers who purchase **laptops** frequently add **laptop bags** to their carts. You can use this to recommend laptop bags to customers right after they add a laptop to their cart, increasing the likelihood of the person buying these products. In both cases, Market Basket Analysis allows you to extract meaningful relationships from seemingly unconnected transactions. Businesses can improve marketing strategies, product placement, and customer experience, ultimately boosting sales using this technique.

While Market Basket Analysis is most famous for its use in retail, it has broad applications in various industries:

- **Healthcare:** Identifying which medications or treatments are commonly prescribed together for particular conditions.
- **Telecommunications:** Analyzing customer behavior to find patterns in service usage.
- **Entertainment:** Recommending movies, music, or TV shows based on what similar users have liked or watched.

In essence, Market Basket Analysis helps uncover hidden patterns in large datasets, enabling better decision-making and more effective strategies across a wide range of fields.

This marks the end of this chapter. You should now have a much better grasp on the fundamentals of unsupervised learning and a good grasp on some of the most fundamental techniques. The next chapter will be one of the most interesting things you will ever learn: **Neural Networks**. Interestingly, this field was born when we were trying to understand how our brain actually works!

Chapter Summary

The primary focus of this chapter was Unsupervised Learning, which is a type of machine learning paradigm which does not have associated output labels for the input. So, we learnt that there are various ways to learn more about the data in an **unsupervised manner.** After going through the content of this chapter, you will now know the following:

◆ The first learning technique we learnt was **clustering,** which forms clusters of data points that are similar in some way. We understood the core idea behind this form of learning.

◆ Then, we covered the **K-Means Clustering algorithm** in detail and finally implemented it in Python with a sample dataset.

◆ Additionally, you also have an idea about some alternative clustering methodologies, which provide you with a different way of clustering your data points.

◆ You can now apply various unsupervised dimensionality reduction techniques like **PCA and t-SNE** which can help you select useful features that are for learning.

◆ Apart from this, you now have a pretty good idea on what Market Basket Analysis is and how it works.

Glossary

Term	Definition
Unsupervised Learning	A branch of machine learning that deals with data without labeled responses, aiming to find hidden patterns or structures in the data.
Clustering	A technique in unsupervised learning that groups similar data points together based on their characteristics without predefined labels.
Dimensionality Reduction	The process of reducing the number of features in a dataset while preserving as much information as possible, used to tackle the curse of dimensionality.
K-Means Clustering	A partitioning-based clustering algorithm that groups data into k clusters by minimizing the distance between data points and their respective cluster centroids.
Centroid	The center of a cluster in K-Means clustering, calculated as the mean of all data points within the cluster.
Euclidean Distance	A commonly used distance metric in clustering algorithms, measuring the straight-line distance between two points in space.

Quiz

1. **Which of the following is NOT a type of unsupervised learning?**
   a. Clustering
   b. Classification
   c. Association
   d. Dimensionality Reduction

2. **What is the primary goal of clustering in unsupervised learning?**
   a. Predicting future outcomes
   b. Grouping similar data points together
   c. Determining the target variable
   d. Classifying new data points

3. **Which algorithm is commonly used for clustering?**
   a. Decision Tree
   b. K-Means
   c. Linear Regression
   d. Logistic Regression

4. **Dimensionality reduction helps to:**
   a. Increase the number of features
   b. Reduce overfitting
   c. Simplify data visualization
   d. Increase model accuracy

5. **What does PCA stand for in the context of unsupervised learning?**

    a. Principal Component Analysis

    b. Primary Classification Algorithm

    c. Probabilistic Clustering Approach

    d. Principal Cluster Assignment

6. **Which of the following is an example of an association rule?**

    a. If a customer buys bread, they are likely to buy butter.

    b. Grouping customers based on their buying patterns.

    c. Reducing the number of features in the dataset.

    d. Predicting the stock prices.

7. **What is the K in K-Means algorithm?**

    a. Number of iterations

    b. Number of clusters

    c. Number of features

    d. Number of data points

8. **Which unsupervised learning technique is best suited for market basket analysis?**

    a. Clustering

    b. Association Rule Learning

    c. Regression

    d. Classification

9. **In K-Means clustering, what is the main objective of the algorithm?**

    a. Minimize the number of clusters

    b. Maximize the distance between clusters

    c. Minimize the sum of squared distances within clusters

    d. Maximize the sum of squared distances within clusters

10. What type of problem is t-SNE used for?

a. Regression

b. Clustering

c. Dimensionality Reduction

d. Classification

Answers	1 – b	2 – b	3 – b	4 – c	5 – a
	6 – a	7 – b	8 – b	9 – c	10 – c

This page is intentionally left blank

Chapter **7**

A Gentle Introduction to Neural Networks and Deep Learning

KEY LEARNING OBJECTIVES

- Explore the origins of neural networks and deep learning to understand how these powerful technologies evolved.

- Dive deep into the core building block—a neuron— and learn how it functions as the foundation of deep neural networks (DNNs).

- See how convolutional neural networks (CNNs) revolutionize the way we process and understand multimedia datasets.

- Get a glimpse of recurrent neural networks (RNNs) and understand how they are designed to handle sequences.

We have covered numerous Machine Learning algorithms till now so let's change gears and start on a new path: "Deep Learning." I know that this term looks really scary but trust me on this: once you learn about it, you will not be able to resist yourself to learn more. This is a fascinating field of study which is quite popular right now. Just for context, this provided the foundation for building something like ChatGPT, which most of you would now be using on a daily basis.

So, back to the chapter, we will start with a little bit of history into the origins of neural networks (which is actually related to Biology, of all things!) followed by a brief but comprehensive introduction to what neural networks are. Then, we will know more about the neuron, which is the building block of a neural network (consider it the secret sauce for this framework) and how they can be used to build actual deep learning models. After that, we will again switch paths and get into the realm of image datasets and understand how "Convolutional Neural Networks" address the downsides of traditional NN algorithms to solve this problem in a much better way. Finally, we will then cover the foundational element of LLMs (Large Language Models): Recurrent Neural Networks and conclude with how the concept on which they were built led to the research and finally development of these LLMs.

7.1 Neural Networks - Building Blocks of Deep Learning

Welcome to Deep Learning 101! In this chapter, I will introduce you to a totally new (although branched out) field of artificial intelligence. Before we begin, let's start with a very brief history lesson on how the field of deep learning came into existence.

7.1.1 A Historical Primer on Deep Learning

Figure 7.1 **A brief history of neural network**

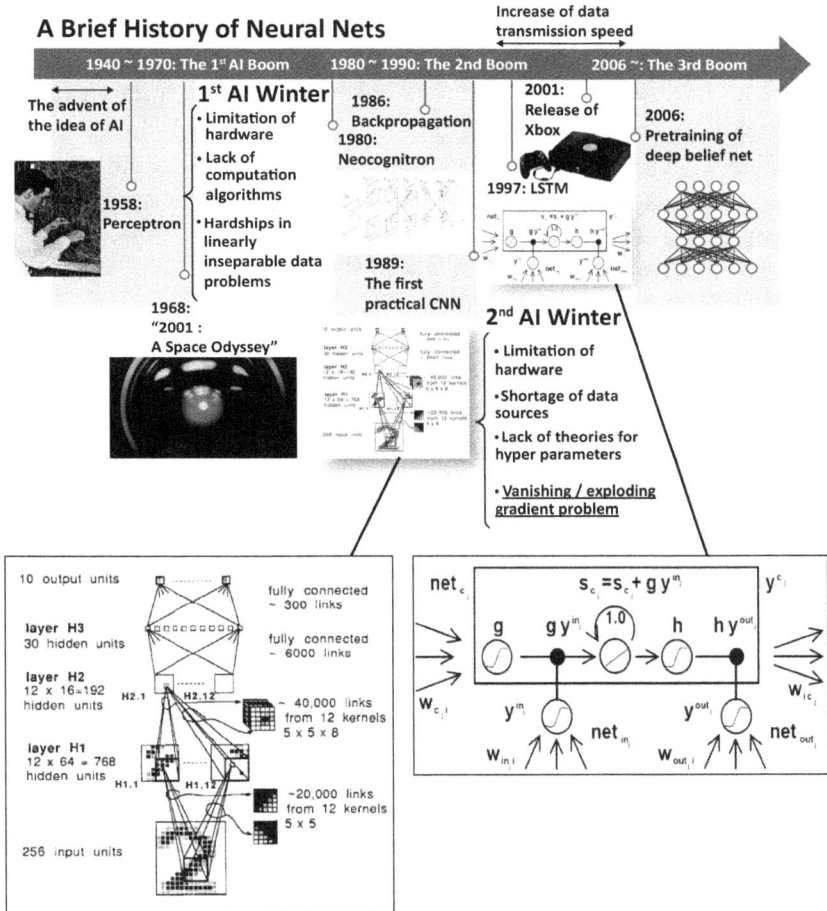

Source: Tamura, Yasuto. "Yasuto Tamura." Data Science Blog, July 17, 2020. http://datasciencehack.com/blog/2020/07/16/a-brief-history-of-neural-nets-everything-you-should-know-before-learning-lstm/.

Let's take a quick journey back in time to see where this whole deep learning adventure began. It all began with researchers being fascinated by the human brain and how it processes information. To learn more about this, they wanted to replicate the same in machines, leading to the birth of the perceptron algorithm in 1958, proposed by Frank Rosenblatt. The perceptron was an early attempt to mimic the brain's neurons and their ability to "fire" based on input signals. But, as groundbreaking as it was, the perceptron hit a wall when it came to solving more complex problems, which was our primary aim, with the human brain being as advanced as it is.

Fast forward to the 1980s, the field started gaining traction again. During this period, Geoffrey Hinton and his team took things to the next level with the idea of multi-layer networks—essentially, stacking layers of neurons to create more complex and powerful models. The real game-changer here was his backpropagation algorithm, which provided a theoretically concrete way to train these models. This concept allowed these deep networks to learn from their mistakes and improve over time, something the perceptron couldn't quite manage with its simplistic learning approach. This breakthrough did not just reignite interest in neural networks; it set the stage for the deep learning revolution we are witnessing today. However, it's important to keep in mind that all this development was separated by two pretty long AI winters (periods where there was a break in research and development), which happened because of several different reasons like the limitations on computer hardware and a knowledge gap. However, we are in an era where this research is at its peak and everyone is talking about AI. Great time to pick up this book, right?

Now that we have a much better idea about the field itself, let's move to the fundamental building block of what we know to be deep learning today: "Neuron."

7.1.2 Neuron: The Fundamental Building Block

As you might know, the name is borrowed from biology, where neurons are the fundamental structures in our human brain. Think of them as tiny messengers that pass signals around, helping us process everything from the simplest reflex to the most complex thought. We've taken this concept and translated it into something that can be coded and is equally powerful: the artificial neuron. Just like its biological counterpart, this artificial neuron is the core unit of a neural network, responsible for processing input(s) and producing an output.

Here's how it works: imagine a neuron as a tiny decision-maker. It receives inputs (which you can think of as pieces of information), processes them by determining how important each part of the input is, and then produces an output. This output is passed on to the next layer of neurons, where the process repeats. By stacking multiple layers of these neurons, we create a (neural) network that can learn and make increasingly complex decisions. It's this simple yet powerful mechanism that forms the backbone of deep learning, enabling them to tackle everything from recognizing images to understanding human language (LLMs are a great application example for this). Let's understand this better by this simple illustration:

Figure 7.2 **A side-by-side comparison of biological and artificial neuron**

Biological Neuron versus Artificial Neural Network

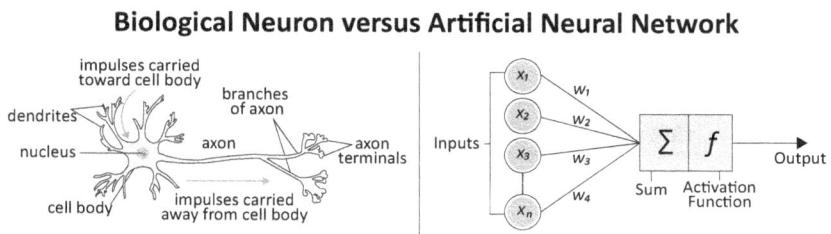

Source: Mwandau, Brian & Nyanchama, Matunda. (2018). Investigating Keystroke Dynamics as a Two-Factor Biometric Security.

Back to artificial neurons. At the heart of an artificial neuron are three key components: weights, biases, and the activation function. Sounds a bit technical, but don't worry—I'll break it down for you. First, let's talk about "weights." Imagine you're trying to decide where to go for dinner, and your friends give you a bunch of suggestions. Not all suggestions are equal, right? Some you will consider more strongly than others. That's exactly what weights do in a neuron—they decide how important each input is. When the neuron receives inputs, it multiplies each by its corresponding weight, giving more influence to some inputs over others.

Next up is the "bias." Think of it as a little push in one direction or another. Even if all the inputs and their weights sum up to zero, the bias can tilt the decision-making process, allowing the neuron to fire (or not) under specific conditions. It's like having a preference for your favourite food—no matter the suggestions, you are just a bit more likely to choose that. Finally, we have the "activation" function, which is the secret sauce that determines whether the neuron should be activated or not (i.e. calculation of the output). After the inputs are weighted and the bias is added, the result is passed through this function. The activation function could be something as simple as a threshold (if the output is above a certain value, return a value else other), or something more complex like a sigmoid or ReLU function (we will cover what they do later). The activation function introduces a very important aspect, "non-linearity", which is crucial because it allows the network to learn and model complex data. Without it, the entire network would just be one big linear equation (remember linear regression?), which would not be very useful for solving real-world problems, where there is no linear relation in most cases, thanks to the noise and outliers.

Figure 7.3   **How does an artificial neuron look and work?**

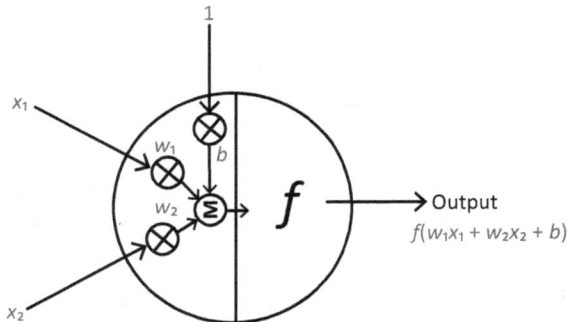

Replicate this for millions of neurons, and you've got a deep learning model that can recognize faces, translate languages, or even beat humans at chess! Now, let's consider the example in Figure 7.3 and understand how things work from a mathematical point of view.

We have two inputs, x_1 and x_2, each with its own weight, w_1 and w_2, respectively. The neuron also has a bias term, b. The neuron processes these inputs using the following formula:

$$z = w_1 x_1 + w_2 x_2 + b$$

In this formula, z represents the neuron's net input. It's like the total score that gets computed before making a decision. Once we have this net input, the neuron uses an activation function f to determine the final output. The output is computed as:

$$\text{output} = f(z)$$

The activation function f introduces non-linearity into the process, allowing the neuron to handle more complex patterns. Different activation functions will shape z in different ways. For instance, if we use the Sigmoid function $f(z)$, it would look like this:

$$f(z) = \frac{1}{1 + e^{-z}}$$

For ReLU, the function is:

$$f(z) = \max(0, z)$$

And for Tanh, it's:

$$f(z) = \frac{e^z - e^{-z}}{e^z + e^{-z}}$$

So, to sum it up: the neuron takes inputs x_1 and x_2, weights them with w_1 and w_2, adds a bias b, and then applies an activation function f to produce the final output. This simple formula is the core of how neural networks make decisions and learn from data. This is all there is to know about an artificial neuron. Now, let's go deeper and learn two fundamental concepts: building and training a neural network.

7.1.3 Building and Training a Neural Network

Let's dive into building a simple neural network and see how we train it using backpropagation. For our example, we will create a network that decides whether to send a promotional email based on two features: age (x_1) and income (x_2). Our network will have two input neurons, one hidden layer with two neurons, and one output neuron as shown below.

Figure 7.4	Our first neural network

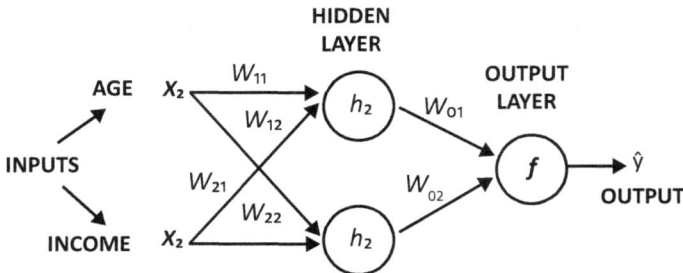

Now, let's try to see how we train this network.

Forward Pass

This is when we move from left to right (i.e. from the input side to the output side) and compute all the required things along the way. Note that before this starts, the weights and biases are given some arbitrary values (which depends on how they are initialized).

1. **Input Layer:** We start with inputs x_1 and x_2. These inputs are fed into the hidden layer neurons. Each input is multiplied by its corresponding weight and summed up with a bias term.

2. **Hidden Layer:** Suppose our hidden layer has two neurons. For the first neuron, the weighted sum can be expressed as:

$$z_1 = w_{11}x_1 + w_{12}x_2 + b_1$$

   and for the second neuron:

$$z_2 = w_{21}x_1 + w_{22}x_2 + b_2$$

   Each of these sums is then passed through an activation function f (e.g., ReLU or Sigmoid). The outputs of the hidden layer neurons are:

$$h_1 = f(z_1)$$
$$h_2 = f(z_2)$$

3. **Output Layer:** The outputs from the hidden layer are then used to calculate the final output of the network. If the

output neuron has weights w_{o1} and w_{o2} and a bias b_o, the net input to the output neuron is:

$$z_o = w_{o1}h_1 + w_{o2}h_2 + b_o$$

The final output $\hat{y}$ is obtained by applying the activation function f to z_o:

$$\hat{y} = f(z_o)v$$

We will choose Sigmoid activation function for this as we want to predict an output which has just two possibilities.

Backward Pass (Backpropagation)

This is where we learn about the true power of neural networks. The main goal of backpropagation is to update the weights and biases to minimize the error in the network's predictions (in other words, learning from the data!). Here's a step-by-step look at the process:

1. **Calculate Error:** First, we need to compute the error between the prediction $\hat{y}$ and the actual target value y using a loss function (how different they are). For example, if we use Mean Squared Error (MSE), the loss L is:

$$L = \frac{1}{2}(\hat{y} - y)^2$$

2. **Compute Gradients:** We need to find out how each weight and bias value contributed to the error, for which we calculate the gradients of the loss with respect to each of them. This involves two main steps:

   - **Output Layer Gradients:** Compute the gradient of the loss with respect to the output layer's weights and bias using the chain rule of differentiation.

$$\frac{\partial L}{\partial w_{o1}} = \frac{\partial L}{\partial \hat{y}} \cdot \frac{\partial \hat{y}}{\partial z_o} \cdot \frac{\partial z_o}{\partial w_{o1}}$$

   where:

$$\frac{\partial L}{\partial \hat{y}} = \hat{y} - y$$

$$\frac{\partial \hat{y}}{\partial z_o} = f'(z_o)$$

$$\frac{\partial z_o}{\partial w_{o1}} = h_1$$

– **Hidden Layer Gradients:** For the hidden layer, compute the gradients with respect to the weights and biases. For each hidden neuron, calculate:

$$\frac{\partial L}{\partial w_{11}} = \frac{\partial L}{\partial \hat{y}} \cdot \frac{\partial \hat{y}}{\partial z_o} \cdot \frac{\partial z_o}{\partial h_1} \cdot \frac{\partial h_1}{\partial z_1} \cdot \frac{\partial z_1}{\partial w_{11}}$$

where:

$$\frac{\partial z_o}{\partial h_1} = w_{o1}$$

$$\frac{\partial h_1}{\partial z_1} = f'(z_1)$$

$$\frac{\partial z_1}{\partial w_{11}} = x_1$$

3. **Update Weights and Biases:** Finally, adjust the weights and biases using the gradients calculated. This is done by subtracting a fraction of the gradient (determined by the learning rate η) from each weight and bias:

$$w_{ij} \leftarrow w_{ij} - \eta \cdot \frac{\partial L}{\partial w_{ij}}$$

$$b_i \leftarrow b_i - \eta \cdot \frac{\partial L}{\partial b_i}$$

By repeating this process with many data examples, the network's weights and biases are learnt, to improve the model and its ability to make accurate predictions. This training process helps the network learn from its mistakes and get better at deciding when to send that promotional email based on the conditions presented before it.

Note that this is just the beginning. You can build much more complex networks using these neurons (adding more neurons, adding more hidden layers, using a different activation function, etc). The possibilities are limitless and there are a lot of resources available online (for free) you can use to learn more about neural networks. For now, we will move onto the next topic of our chapter: "Convolutional Neural Networks."

7.2 Convolutional Neural Networks: A Smarter Approach for Image Data

Alright, let's see what convolutional neural networks (CNNs) are and how they are designed to handle the specific challenges of image and audio data, which normal networks cannot handle. Imagine you're working with deep neural networks (DNNs) to classify images of cats and dogs. If you use a traditional DNN for this task, you might run into a few problems. Let's see what those problems could be.

7.2.1 The Need for Convolution in Neural Networks

Figure 7.5 DNNs and CNNs: A Visual Representation

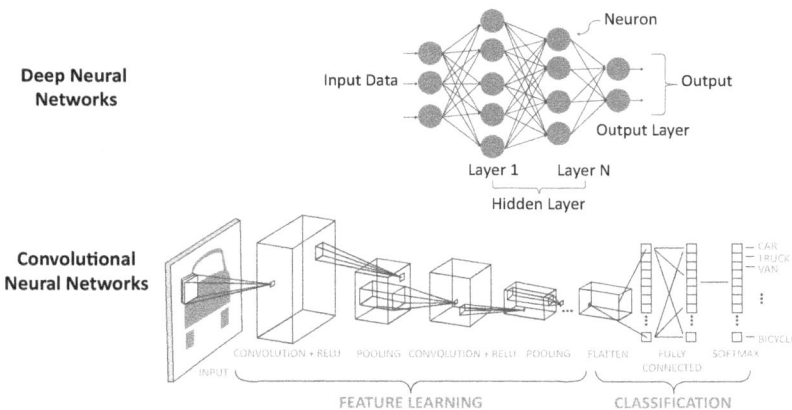

Downsides of Traditional DNNs with Image Data

Traditional DNNs can struggle with images because they require a huge number of weights. Why? Because each pixel in an image is treated as an individual input, and in a fully connected network, each pixel would connect to every neuron in the next layer. For a high-resolution image, this results in an astronomical number of weights, which makes the network very slow to train and prone to overfitting. Imagine trying to solve a puzzle with thousands of pieces, where each piece needs to be considered individually. It quickly becomes overwhelming!

So, what can be the solution? Let's see how CNNs can solve this problem.

How CNNs Solve the Problem

CNNs come to the rescue by reducing the number of parameters while still being able to capture important patterns in the data. The magic lies in two key ideas: convolution and pooling.

Figure 7.6 **How does convolution actually work?**

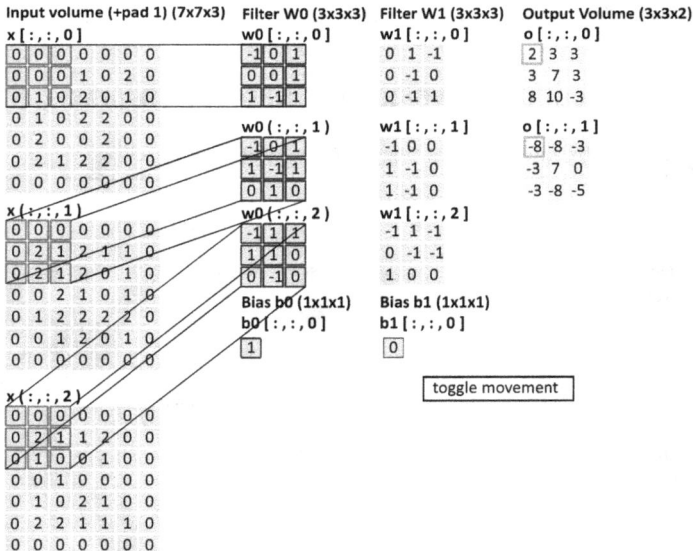

Source: Cornelisse, Daphne. "An Intuitive Guide to Convolutional Neural Networks." freeCodeCamp.org, April 24, 2018. https://www.freecodecamp.org.

1. **Convolutional Layers:** Instead of connecting every pixel to every neuron, CNNs use convolutional layers. These layers apply a small filter (or kernel) that moves across the image. This filter is typically much smaller than the image itself, say

3×3 or 5×5 pixels, and it's used to scan the image, detecting patterns such as edges or textures. Mathematically, the convolution operation can be expressed as:

$$(I * F)(x, y) = \sum_{m}\sum_{n} I(x + m, y + n) \cdot F(m, n)$$

Here, I is the input image, F is the filter, and x, y represents the position of the filter on the image. The result is a feature map that shows where specific features (like edges) are detected in the image.

2. **Pooling Layers:** After convolution, CNNs use pooling layers to downsample the feature maps. The most common type is max pooling, which takes the maximum value from a small patch of the feature map (e.g., 2×2) and reduces its size while preserving important features. This reduces the computational load and helps make the network more resistant to small changes in the input, like slight rotations or shifts in the image.

Figure 7.7 **How does pooling work?**

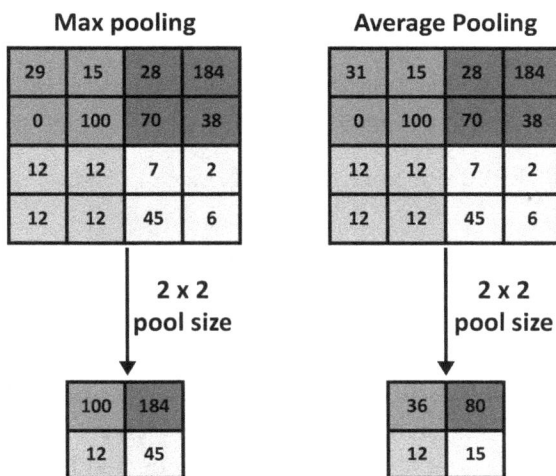

Source: Yani, Muhamad & Irawan, S, & Setianingsih, Casi. (2019). *Application of Transfer Learning Using Convolutional Neural Network Method for Early Detection of Terry's Nail. Journal of Physics: Conference Series. 1201. 012052. 10.1088/1742-6596/1201/1/012052.*

Now, by stacking multiple convolutional and pooling layers, CNNs build a hierarchy of features (you can say a collection of features). Early layers might detect simple features like edges, while deeper layers can capture more complex patterns, such as shapes or even entire objects. This is hence called Hierarchical Learning. This learning makes CNNs incredibly effective for image classification tasks.

Figure 7.8 **An illustration of hierarchical learning**

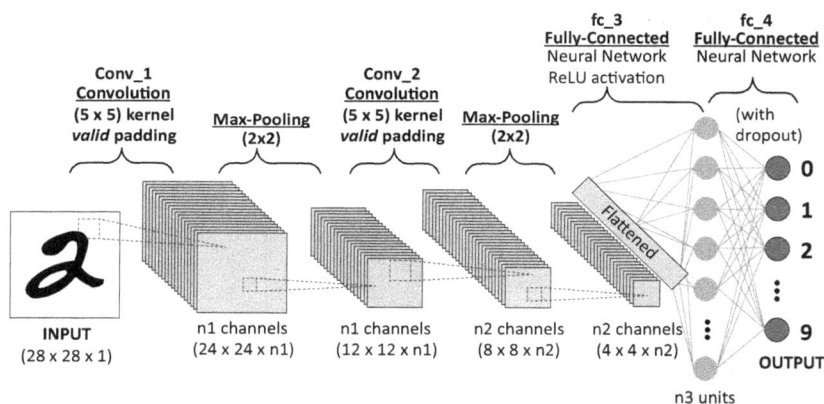

Source: *An Introduction to Convolutional Neural Networks: A Comprehensive Guide to CNNs in Deep Learning, DataCamp, https://www.datacamp.com/tutorial/introduction-to-convolutional-neural-networks-cnns*

Now, let's build our very first CNN with Python.

7.2.2 How to Implement CNNs in Python

Now, let's see how this works in practice with a simple Python example. We will build a basic CNN using the **Tensorflow Keras library** (*this is a dedicated library created for deep learning*) to classify images. We will keep it simple with just one convolutional layer followed by a pooling layer and a fully connected layer.

```
import tensorflow as tf
from tensorflow.keras.models import Sequential
from tensorflow.keras.layers import Conv2D, MaxPooling2D,
Flatten, Dense

# Initialize the CNN
model = Sequential()

# Add a convolutional layer
model.add(Conv2D(32, (3, 3), activation='relu', input_
shape=(64, 64, 3)))

# Add a max pooling layer
model.add(MaxPooling2D(pool_size=(2, 2)))

# Flatten the pooled feature maps into a single vector
model.add(Flatten())

# Add a fully connected layer
model.add(Dense(128, activation='relu'))

# Add the output layer for binary classification
model.add(Dense(1, activation='sigmoid'))

# Compile the model
model.compile(optimizer='adam', loss='binary_
crossentropy', metrics=['accuracy'])

# Summary of the model
model.summary()
```

The output for this code will be as follows:

```
Model: ''sequential"
```

Layer (type)	Output Shape	Param #
conv2d (Conv2D)	(None, 62, 62, 32)	896
max_pooling2d (Maxpooling2 D)	(None, 31, 31, 32)	0
flatten (Flatten)	(None, 30752)	0
dense (Dense)	(None, 128)	3936384
dense_1 (Dense)	(None, 1)	129

```
Total params: 3937409 (15.02 MB)
Trainable params: 3937409 (15.02 KB)
Non-trainable params: 0 (0.00 Byte)
```

One important thing to note from the above output is: the number of parameters for the Dense layer compared to the Convolution layer (see the difference!).

Here is a detailed breakdown of what we did in the above code snippet (I kept it a single snippet so that you don't have to break your flow while understanding the code):

- We start by adding a convolutional layer to our model with 32 filters, each of size 3 × 3, which in turn will scan the 64 × 64 input image.

- Next, we apply max pooling to reduce the size of the feature maps by selecting only the max values from a particular group and retain the most important information.

- Then, the output of this layer is flattened (single dimensional array) and then fed into a fully connected layer with 128 neurons, followed by an output layer with a single neuron to predict the class (e.g., cat or dog).

- Finally, we compile the model using the Adam optimizer (which defines the way in which the weights and biases will be updated) and binary cross-entropy loss (loss function), which is standard for binary classification problems.

And there you have it—a simple yet powerful CNN that's suited for image data rather than a traditional DNN. CNNs not only make training more efficient by reusing parameters but also allow the network to focus on the most relevant features in the images, making them the go-to choice for tasks involving image data.

Now, one thing to note here is that the learning process for the Neural Network remains the same: through back propagation where the gradients are computed and then based on them the parameter values are updated. The network simply learns the weights of each kernel in the convolution layer to facilitate the overall goal: reducing the overall model loss.

Now that we know how to effectively deal with image data in Deep Learning, let's explore yet another challenging deep learning task: **Natural Language Processing (NLP).**

7.3 Recurrent Neural Networks: Sequences and Predictions

Let's complete our deep learning journey with Recurrent Neural Networks (RNNs), a fascinating concept that's built to handle data that follows a particular sequence. If you've ever wondered how machines can understand and generate text, predict stock prices, or even compose music, RNNs are a big part of this answer. But before we dive into the details, let's look at why traditional neural networks struggle with sequences as we did with images in the previous section.

7.3.1 The Need for RNNs

The Limitation of DNNs with Sequential Data

Deep Neural Networks (DNNs) are excellent at handling static data, where each input is independent of the others, like simple tabular data. But what happens when the order of inputs matters? Think about text: the meaning of a sentence depends on the order of words. "The cat sat on the mat" and "On the mat sat the cat" might convey similar ideas, but they're not the same. The field that deals with these textual inputs is called NLP (Natural Language Processing, which literally means processing language data). This is where DNNs fall short—they treat each input independently, ignoring the sequential nature of the data. Without considering the context provided by previous inputs, DNNs can't capture the dependencies that are crucial for understanding sequences. So, to solve this problem, a new type of neuron was introduced: **"A Recurrent Unit"**.

How RNNs Solve the Problem

Recurrent Neural Networks (RNNs) are designed to address this very issue. The key innovation of RNNs is their ability to maintain a "memory" of previous inputs by looping information back into the network. This allows RNNs to process sequences of data, where each step depends on the previous ones.

Figure 7.9   **A Visual Representation of RNN Unit**

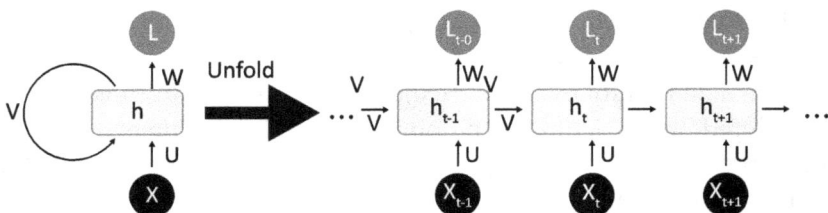

Source: GeeksforGeeks. "Introduction to Recurrent Neural Networks." Accessed December 18, 2024. https://www.geeksforgeeks.org/introduction-to-recurrent-neural-network/.

1. **Recurrent Layers:** In an RNN, instead of just passing the input through the network, each neuron also passes its output back into itself. This feedback loop creates a memory of what's happened before. Mathematically, if we have an input x_t at time step t, the hidden state h_t (which contains the memory) is updated as follows:

$$h_t = \sigma\left(W_{xh} \cdot x_t + W_{hh} \cdot h_{t-1} + b_h\right)$$

Here, W_{xh} is the weight matrix for the input, W_{hh} is the weight matrix for the hidden state (memory), and b_h is the bias. The function σ is typically a non-linear activation function like tanh or ReLU. This equation shows how the current input x_t and the previous hidden state h_{t-1} combine to produce the new hidden state h_t, effectively capturing the sequence information.

2. **Handling Long Sequences:** While basic RNNs can capture sequences, they often struggle with maintaining a record of these long-term dependencies (previous data)—when the relevant information is far back in the sequence. This

is where variants like Long Short-Term Memory (LSTM) and Gated Recurrent Units (GRU) come into play. These architectures include mechanisms that control the flow of information, allowing the network to remember or forget information over longer periods. We will discuss them later in the chapter.

Right now, let's understand how they actually work in practice.

7.3.2 How RNNs Work in Practice

The core processing unit in an RNN is often referred to as a "recurrent unit" rather than a "recurrent neuron." This unit maintains a hidden state, which gets updated at each time step. The hidden state is crucial as it carries information from previous time steps, enabling the network to capture temporal dependencies (like sequence order!). Over time, as the network unfolds, these recurrent units can capture patterns in sequences, whether they span short or long time intervals.

RNNs have similar architecture with other deep neural networks in terms of input and output layers. However, the key difference is how information flows through the network. In an RNN, the same set of weights is applied at each time step (meaning that the information is dead one after the other depending on the sequence), allowing the network to process sequences of varying lengths. The hidden state at each time step is computed using the formula:

$$h_t = \sigma\left(U \cdot X_t + W \cdot h_{t-1} + B\right)$$

Here, h_t represents the hidden state at time step t, X_t is the input at time step t, W and U are weight matrices, B is the bias, and σ is the activation function. The output is then computed as:

$$Y_t = O\left(V \cdot h_t + C\right)$$

This formula above shows the recurrent nature of RNNs, where the hidden state depends on both the current input and the previous hidden state. Now, let's understand their actual learning process.

RNNs operate on this hidden state that evolves over time, capturing the sequential nature of the input data. After each time step, the network updates its hidden state using the current input and the hidden state from the previous time step. This process allows the network to accumulate knowledge over time, making it well-suited for tasks where understanding the context or the order of the data is crucial.

The hidden state is updated as follows:

$$h_t = \tanh\left(W_{hh} \cdot h_{t-1} + W_{xh} \cdot x_t\right)$$

Where:

- h_t is the current hidden state,
- h_{t-1} ht-1 is the previous hidden state,
- x_t is the current input,
- W_{hh} and W_{xh} are the weight matrices for the recurrent and input connections, respectively.

Backpropagation Through Time (BPTT)

Training an RNN involves a process called Backpropagation Through Time (BPTT), which is an extension of the standard backpropagation algorithm. In BPTT, the error is propagated back not only through the layers of the network but also through time steps, adjusting the weights to minimize the loss function. This process allows the network to learn from sequences and adjust its parameters based on both current and past inputs.

The primary challenge in BPTT is the "vanishing gradient" problem, where gradients can become exceedingly small, making it difficult for the network to learn long-range dependencies. Alternatively, the "exploding gradient" problem occurs when gradients grow exponentially, leading to instability in the learning process.

So, training an RNN involves feeding the network with sequences of input data and comparing the predicted outputs with the actual targets. The error is then back propagated through the network to update the weights, using techniques like BPTT. The training process is iterative, with the network gradually learning to capture the dependencies in the input data over multiple time steps.

Now that we have a much deeper understanding of the workings of RNN, let's see their strengths, weaknesses and where this framework is actually used.

Advantages and Disadvantages of RNNs

Advantages:

- RNNs are great at modeling sequential data, making them ideal for tasks where previous context is very important.

- They can remember information from previous inputs, which is beneficial for tasks like time series forecasting and natural language processing where you need previous information to make decisions.

Disadvantages:

- RNNs are prone to vanishing and exploding gradients, making training challenging.

- They struggle with long sequences when using certain activation functions like tanh or ReLU.

- Training RNNs is computationally expensive and can be slow due to the sequential nature of the data processing.

Applications of RNNs

RNNs have found applications in various domains, including:

- **Language Modeling and Text Generation:** RNNs are used to predict the next word in a sequence or generate new text based on a given input, making them the building blocks for Large Language models.

- **Speech Recognition:** They can process audio data, which is sequential in nature to recognize spoken words or phrases.

- **Machine Translation:** RNNs can translate text from one language to another by understanding the context of the input sequence. This is because they support varied input and output lengths (a 10 word sentence may have a 5 word translation).

- **Image Recognition and Face Detection:** RNNs can be combined with convolutional layers to analyze sequences of images or detect faces, providing extra capabilities to the model.

- **Time Series Forecasting:** They can also be used to predict future values in a sequence based on historical data. (for example, predicting stock prices)

However, as discussed above, the primary disadvantage of RNN is its inability to handle longer sequences because of the **vanishing and exploding gradients**, which hamper the learning process. To solve this, there are numerous variations built on top of the traditional RNNs. Let's explore two popular options.

Figure 7.10	Variations of Traditional RNNs

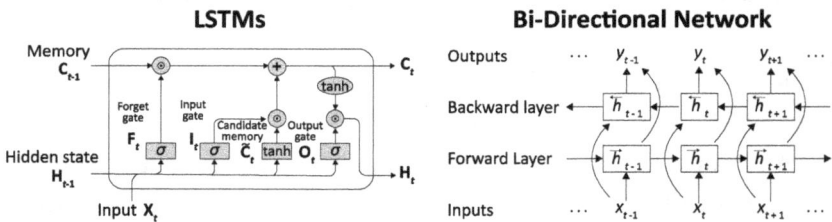

1. **Bidirectional Neural Networks (BiNN):** In BiNNs, the input data is processed in both forward and backward directions, which allows the network to capture context from both past and future inputs (as we have future content for the sake of the learning process). This is particularly useful for tasks like natural language processing and time series analysis where this information is crucial.

2. **Long Short-Term Memory (LSTM):** LSTMs introduce mechanisms for remembering and forgetting certain information, which helps in maintaining and learning long-term dependencies. They use something called **gates** (input, forget, and output gates) to control the flow of information, making them more effective for tasks involving long sequences.

That is all there is to know about RNNs. Now, let's implement a simple LSTM network in Python to see just how easy it is to design very complex and powerful networks in this programming language.

7.3.3 RNN Python Implementation

To see RNNs in action, let's build a simple model to predict the next character in a sequence of text. We'll use Keras to create an RNN with an LSTM layer, which is a popular choice for handling sequence data.

```python
import tensorflow as tf
from tensorflow.keras.models import Sequential
from tensorflow.keras.layers import LSTM, Dense

# Initialize the RNN
model = Sequential()

# Add an LSTM layer with 50 units
model.add(LSTM(50, input_shape=(10, 1)))

# Add a dense output layer with a softmax activation for
multi-class classification
model.add(Dense(26, activation='softmax'))   # Assuming
we're predicting one of 26 letters

# Compile the model
model.compile(optimizer='adam', loss='categorical_
crossentropy', metrics=['accuracy'])

# Summary of the model
model.summary()
```

The output for this code will be:

```
Model: ''sequential_1"

Layer (type)              Output Shape           Param #

lstm (LSTM)               (None, 50)             10400
dense_2 (Dense)           (None, 26)             1326

Total params: 11726 (45.80 KB)
Trainable params: 11726 (45.80 KB)
Non-trainable params: 0 (0.00 Byte)
```

Same as we did above, let's break down this code to understand what we are actually doing.

- We first add a LSTM layer with 50 units. This layer will process sequences of 10 feature values at once, with each time step having one feature (e.g., a character in a sequence of text).

- The output is then passed through a dense layer with a softmax activation function, which will give us an output probability value over the 26 possible characters (we're working with the English alphabet here).

- Finally, we compile the model with the Adam optimizer as before (I use this as this optimizer offers great performance and fast convergence) and categorical cross-entropy loss, which is used for multi-class classification tasks.

This simple example showcases what RNNs are and their ability to handle sequential data, even with long term dependencies. By maintaining a memory of past inputs, RNNs can make informed decisions based on the previous context of the sequence in addition to the current input.

This marks the end of this section and this chapter. With that, we've covered the core components of Deep Learning along with advanced concepts like **Convolutional Neural Networks (CNNs)** for image data and **Recurrent Neural Networks (RNNs)** for sequential data. These are the building blocks that are responsible for countless breakthroughs, from image recognition to natural language processing. With a solid understanding of these concepts, you're well on your way to mastering the fascinating world of deep learning (or at least, have taken your first step).

In the next chapter, we will end by discussing some real-world applications of machine learning and the role that ethics plays in the mix.

Chapter Summary

In this chapter, we went through the fundamental concepts and architectures that form the backbone of deep learning, providing a solid foundation for you to dive into more complex subjects. Here are the key points covered:

◆ **Introduction to Neural Networks:** We began with a historical journey of neural networks.

◆ **Understanding the Neuron:** Next, we delved into the structure and function of the artificial neuron, the building block of modern neural networks. This included a discussion on its key components such as weights, biases, and activation functions, explaining how they work together to process inputs and generate outputs.

◆ **Building and Training Neural Networks:** Then we explored how to construct and train neural networks using the backpropagation algorithm, which allows models to learn from errors and improve over time by updating its parameters based on the loss at each step. Then we went through a practical example to learn about the process of forward and backward passes in a simple neural network.

◆ **Convolutional Neural Networks (CNNs):** The chapter then introduced CNNs, highlighting their efficiency in handling image data and overcoming the problems that traditional networks have. We discussed the convolutional and pooling layers that reduce the number of parameters while capturing essential patterns, making CNNs ideal for tasks like image classification.

◆ **Recurrent Neural Networks (RNNs):** Finally, we covered RNNs, designed to handle sequential data by maintaining a memory of previous data (called context). We examined the limitations of traditional neural networks with sequential data and how RNNs, along with their variants like LSTM and GRU, which were developed to overcome the initial limitations, overcome these challenges by capturing long-term dependencies in sequences.

Glossary

Term	Definition
Neural Networks	Computational models inspired by the human brain, consisting of layers of interconnected nodes (neurons) that can learn patterns from data.
Deep Learning	A subset of machine learning that uses neural networks with many layers (deep neural networks) to model complex patterns in data.
Neuron	The fundamental unit of a neural network that processes inputs, applies weights, adds biases, and passes the result through an activation function to produce an output.
Perceptron	An early type of artificial neuron used in binary classifiers.
Backpropagation	A method used to train neural networks by calculating the gradient of the loss function with respect to each weight and updating the weights to minimize the error.
Weights	Parameters within a neural network that determine the importance of different inputs.
Bias	A parameter that allows the neuron to adjust the output independently of the input, adding flexibility to the model.

Quiz

1. What is the Perceptron algorithm known for?

a. Mimicking the brain's neurons

b. Solving complex problems

c. Performing convolution operations

d. Introducing backpropagation

2. Who played a key role in reviving neural networks in the 1980s?

a. Frank Rosenblatt

b. Geoffrey Hinton

c. Yann LeCun

d. Andrew Ng

3. What is the fundamental building block of a neural network?

a. Layer

b. Node

c. Neuron

d. Activation Function

4. What is the primary function of weights in a neuron?

a. Adding bias

b. Assigning importance to inputs

c. Deciding activation function

d. Connecting layers

5. **What does the activation function in a neuron introduce?**

    a. Non-linearity

    b. Linearity

    c. Data normalization

    d. Weight adjustment

6. **Which algorithm allows deep networks to learn from their mistakes?**

    a. Forward propagation

    b. Backpropagation

    c. Stochastic Gradient Descent

    d. Activation function

7. **What is the main challenge traditional DNNs face with image data?**

    a. Overfitting

    b. Lack of layers

    c. Too few weights

    d. High computational cost

8. **How do CNNs reduce the number of parameters?**

    a. Using fully connected layers

    b. By performing pooling operations

    c. By using convolutional layers

    d. By using ReLU activation

9. **What does a pooling layer in CNNs do?**

    a. Increases image size

    b. Decreases the number of channels

    c. Reduces the size of feature maps

    d. Adds more layers to the network

10. What type of tasks are CNNs especially well-suited for?

   a. Text processing

   b. Time-series prediction

   c. Image classification

   d. Numerical regression

Answers	1 – a	2 – b	3 – c	4 – b	5 – a
	6 – b	7 – d	8 – c	9 – c	10 – c

This page is intentionally left blank

Chapter **8**

Machine Learning in Real-World Scenarios

KEY LEARNING OBJECTIVES

- Understand machine learning applications across industries like healthcare, finance, and hardware.
- Learn about the lifecycle of a typical machine learning project.
- Discover the future trends and emerging technologies in ML.
- Discuss the ethical impact of ML, especially with the rise of Large Language Models.

What an interesting journey it has been into the world of machine learning! But, as always, all good things come to an end as we are at the end of this book. I know that most of you would have questions like "what next now?" and "how can I apply everything I learnt". Don't worry, I will guide you through that as well. In this chapter, we will cover some real world solutions which use machine learning in a bit more detail (remember how a typical ML project looks? [Hint: Chapter 1]).

8.1 Exploring Machine Learning Use Cases across Domains

Figure 8.1 **Machine learning in various Industries**

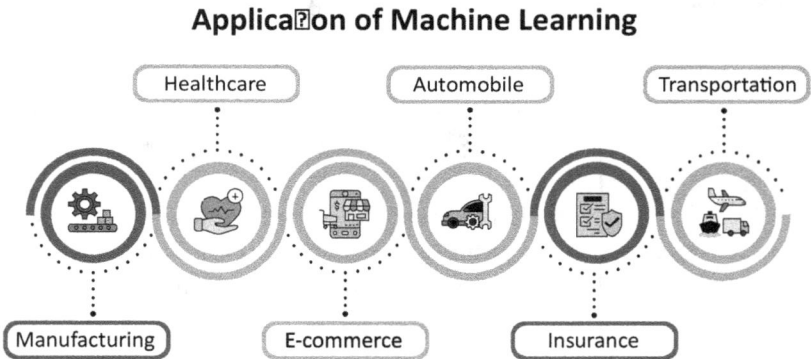

Application of Machine Learning

Source: Alagar. "Machine Learning Applications and Examples." IABAC®, October 31, 2024. https://iabac.org/blog/machine-learning-applications-and-examples.

There is no shortage of machine learning applications in the industry in the last decade, when *data became the oil of the 21st century*. Almost every sector you can think of uses machine learning in one way or the other. In this section, we will take a look at two different domains in which machine learning is used and explore how it actually helps them use their data most effectively.

Let's start with the **Healthcare domain.**

8.1.1 Machine Learning in Healthcare

Machine learning has rapidly become one of the most impactful technological fields in the 21st century when it comes to healthcare. It not only helps healthcare professionals make faster and more accurate decisions, but also enables them to manage massive amounts of data, and improve their overall patient outcomes and experiences using innovative solutions. In this section, we will break down how ML is being used in healthcare and why it's crucial for the future of medicine.

How ML is Used in Healthcare

One of the biggest impacts ML has on healthcare is its ability to analyze and process large datasets to support clinical decisions (it is a kind of Learning mechanism in a sense, right?). Medical data is often vast and complex—think about electronic health records (EHRs), lab results, imaging data, and genetic information.

Figure 8.2 **How ML is used in the Healthcare Domain**

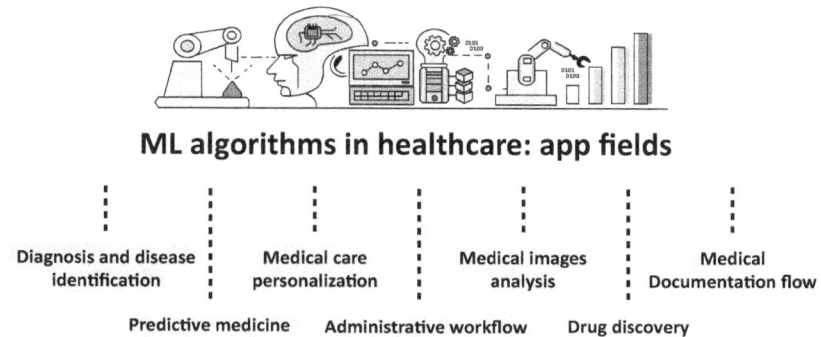

ML algorithms in healthcare: app fields

Diagnosis and disease identification	Medical care personalization	Medical images analysis	Medical Documentation flow

Predictive medicine   Administrative workflow   Drug discovery

Source: Riseapps. "Machine Learning in Healthcare: Applications and Benefits." Accessed December 18, 2024. https://riseapps.co/machine-learning-in-healthcare/.

Traditionally, processing this data manually to identify patterns, trends, or risks was time-consuming. ML algorithms can now sift through this information quickly, thanks to the almost unlimited compute capabilities we have providing clinicians with insights that improve diagnosis and treatment plans. On top of that, they often identify some really complex relations which people or doctors tend to miss as they aren't obvious. Let's see how iot helps in various applications:

1. **Medical Scans:** Just like doctors, ML models can analyze medical pictures such as MRIs and X-rays to identify issues. Trained on a vast amount of photos, these intelligent algorithms can sometimes detect early indicators of diseases such as cancer more accurately than human physicians. This aids in early problem detection, which is critical to providing patients with quality care.

2. **Guessing Patient Outcomes:** Machine learning also aids in forecasting potential patient outcomes. These algorithms use historical data to identify patients who may have complications following surgery or who are at higher risk of developing more serious conditions. This keeps patients from returning to the hospital too soon and enables doctors to provide better treatment.

3. **Virtual Assistants:** Finally, with the introduction of Large Language Models, Virtual health assistants powered by ML have greatly helped in managing and providing enhanced patient care. For instance, they remind patients to take medication, schedule appointments, or provide them with answers to common health-related questions (this has a very serious ethical implication as people might ask life-or-death questions to the model), improving patient engagement and to make sure they stick to their treatment plans. However, ethical considerations like data privacy are a big thing to consider in this case (more on this later).

Apart from this, another major advantage of ML is its ability to automate routine tasks, which until now took a lot of manual labour and time. Healthcare professionals often deal with time-consuming administrative tasks like documentation, billing, and appointment scheduling. These models can take over much of this administrative burden with advanced algorithms based on Neural Networks and Large Language

Models, allowing doctors and nurses to spend more time on direct patient care.

A Review of Real World Applications of ML in Healthcare

Based on what we discussed about the potential of ML in this domain, it shouldn't be surprising to know that it is actually used in quite a lot of applications already. In this short section, we will take a look at few of these applications:

- **Robot-Assisted Surgery:** Robotic surgery is one of the most complex yet a very fruitful use case where machine learning can be used. The most recent version of **Intuitive Surgical's Da Vinci Surgical System** is one such robotic instrument powered by machine learning to help surgeons execute minimally invasive surgeries more accurately. This greatly lowers the risk of surgical problems both during and after the procedure.

- **Drug Discovery:** The pharmaceutical sector is also utilizing machine learning (ML) for a variety of purposes like drug testing and discovery. ML algorithms are being used by businesses such as **Deep Genomics** to go through enormous genetic datasets and find the most viable candidates for drug trials. The time it takes to introduce new medications to the market can be greatly reduced by using machine learning to simulate how a drug interacts with particular genes or proteins. This has been particularly helpful in treating complex illnesses like cancer or uncommon genetic problems, and it also helps patients who would otherwise die very soon.

- Predicting disease epidemics with machine learning is an intriguing use of the technology. For instance, **ProMED** is a company that evaluates numerous data sources, including weather reports, satellite imagery data, and medical histories to predict possible disease outbreaks in real time. For example, temperature variations and rainfall patterns can be used to forecast malaria epidemics and in turn take proactive precautions to avoid them. This makes it possible for authorities and medical institutions to act quickly, thereby saving lives, particularly in third world countries where there is inadequate access to proper healthcare. Imagine if we had sophisticated machine learning algorithms in place to anticipate another COVID-level outbreak before it even occurs!

- **Enhancing Cancer therapy:** A healthcare firm called **Oncora Medical** is utilizing machine learning to improve cancer therapy. Their software lets physicians decide on treatment options and evaluate the efficacy of medicines by analyzing data from EHRs and cancer registries. Patients receive more individualized care thanks to this data-driven strategy, which raises survival rates and enhances quality of life.

These are just some ways in which ML is revolutionizing the Healthcare domain. As always, it isn't without its challenges. So, let's cover some of them next.

Challenges Faced while using ML in Healthcare

While ML has tremendous potential, there are a lot of things to be considered before they can be used to their full potential for healthcare applications. Here are a few of them:

Data Availability and Quality: For the final model to be effective, it requires large amounts of **high-quality and** structured data. Unfortunately, many healthcare systems still struggle with data, both in terms of collection and quality: it is often fragmented or unclean, making it difficult to train good ML models. Additionally, **privacy concerns** around patient data can limit access to the datasets needed for ML algorithms to be effective. Take an example of determining an outbreak; releasing patient addresses is a big privacy breach but the information can actually help the model in predicting a more accurate location.

Bias in Algorithms: ML models can inadvertently reflect the biases present in the data used to train them. In healthcare, this could lead to unequal treatment of patients from different demographic groups as the models are trained on this very biased dataset. For example, if a model is trained mostly on data from one ethnic group, it may not perform as well for other populations as the conditions and scenarios will more often than now be quite different. Hence, it is critical to ensure that ML models are trained on diverse datasets to avoid bias and improve fairness in healthcare (same treatment for all).

Limited Expertise: Implementing ML in healthcare requires collaboration between technical experts from both fields, i.e. data scientists, ML engineers and medical professionals. Many healthcare organizations lack the in-house expertise or the funds needed to build and integrate ML solutions effectively, which in turns makes them skeptical in implementing this solution

That being said, all the above three limitations are the prominent research areas right now in the field of healthcare. As things continue to evolve, we can expect that machine learning will play an even greater role in making healthcare more efficient, personalized, and accessible to all.

8.1.2 Machine Learning in Education

Education is another prominent field where ML has had a really great impact, specifically after the advent of Large Language models. Fun fact, I even used AI and ML in various ways for this book. It's used in a wealth of applications, offering everything from personalized learning experiences to streamlining administrative tasks, and providing educators with valuable insights to improve their existing learning process. So, Let's explore how ML is reshaping education and learn about its impact on both students and teachers, and help in the building of **Education 4.0.**

We will do the same as before and start by going through some areas in this domain where ML can prove to be effective.

Figure 8.3   **ML powering the Education 4.0 Era**

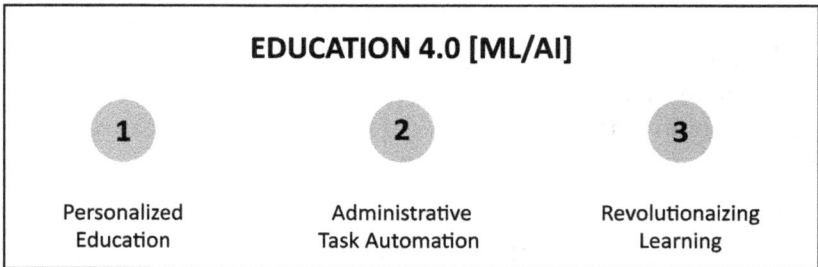

EDUCATION 4.0 [ML/AI]

1	2	3
Personalized Education	Administrative Task Automation	Revolutionaizing Learning

Potential Applications of ML in this field

One of the most significant ways ML is changing education is by enabling personalized learning. Every student learns differently, and this helps cater to these individual learning styles by analyzing data such as student performance, behavior, and engagement. Based on this data, ML algorithms can tailor content, suggest resources, and adjust the pace of lessons to fit the unique needs of each student. This personalized approach ensures that students who need extra help can get it, while those who excel can move ahead more quickly, making the overall experience for everyone more seamless and effective.

We already covered the ways in which ML can help provide a tailored learning experience for each student. Let's see how it can actually enable this:

Adaptive Learning Platforms: ML can help provide an adaptive learning experience, like vary the question difficulties based on the student's performance or create questions based on some provided content (Thanks to LLMs, this is really easy to do now). If a student struggles with a particular concept, the system can use recommendation system based algorithms to provide additional resources, explanations, or simpler exercises. Conversely, if the student grasps the material quickly, the platform may offer more advanced problems or new topics. It can even help students transform their existing textbook content into interactive materials like images and videos using the current state-of-the-art models. This helps create a more individualized learning experience compared to traditional one-size-fits-all education.

Predicting Student Performance: Additionally, we can use traditional ML techniques to analyze historical data to predict how a student is likely to perform in future assessments based on his previous performances. This capability allows teachers to identify students at risk of failing and intervene in advance by providing them the extra lessons they need to cope with the coursework.. Additionally, it can allow a teacher to better understand which concepts are difficult in general (for all students), and focus on those topics more by, let's say using a different approach to teaching it (like using visual content to supplement the theory).

Apart from these, another critical application of ML in education is **automating administrative tasks**. Teachers often spend a significant amount of time grading assignments, creating tests, managing schedules, and handling paperwork. With the help of ML, many of these routine tasks can be automated, like creating a simple program that can take some content as input and create a weekly quiz with that (LLMs can do this in seconds!), freeing up educators' time for more meaningful interactions with students and focusing more on the quality of their learning material.

Now, let's check out some real world applications of ML in the field of study.

Real-World Applications of ML in Education

Due to its limitless potential, ML is already being used in a variety of educational tools and platforms:

- **Smart Tutors:** ML-powered virtual tutors, such as **Socratic by Google** and even more general LLM-based chatbots like ChatGPT, help students with homework by providing them with step-by-step explanations on different concepts or explaining something in a really simple manner. These tutors use natural language processing to understand student questions and provide relevant answers (which is what LLMs do). Virtual tutors can offer instant feedback, helping students learn at their own pace without waiting for teacher input.

- **Automated Grading Systems:** Grading assignments, especially essays and open-ended responses, can be time-consuming for teachers. ML algorithms can now grade papers automatically by analyzing student submissions for content accuracy, grammar, and even writing style based on specific criteria defined by the faculty. This allows educators to focus on providing constructive feedback rather than spending hours on grading, which can help the students improve. Companies like **Gradescope** use ML to assist in grading, particularly in subjects like math, where structured answers are easier to evaluate.

- **Learning Analytics:** Apart from this, ML can be used to analyze student engagement and performance on various topics using various metrics, providing teachers and administrators with better insights into what is working and what isn't with the present system. For example, by tracking which topics students spend the most time on, educators can identify areas of improvement for their existing curriculum. Learning analytics tools such as **Knewton** use ML to collect and interpret data about student interactions with learning materials, enabling better decision-making and curriculum design.

- **Course Recommendations:** Just as streaming platforms recommend movies based on history, ML-powered systems in education recommend courses or learning materials based on a student's past performance, interests, and goals. For example, if a student performs well in mathematics but struggles with science, an ML based system can look at his previous records and suggest additional resources regarding the weaker concepts to strengthen their understanding and thereby helping them improve.

Let's take a look at the challenges faced in this sector and trust me there are quite a lot of them.

Challenges in Implementing ML in Education

While ML holds tremendous promise in education based on our discussion so far, there are also challenges that educators and institutions need to address to get the :

1. **Privacy is a critical concern in education**, especially when it comes to using machine learning. We're talking about kids' personal information here, so schools and ed-tech companies need to be super careful. It's not just about following rules - it's about making sure the data is used in a way that doesn't result in any serious breaches. We need solid plans to keep student info safe while still using ML to make learning better.

2. Not everyone's got the same access to technology, and that's a problem. In some parts of the world, kids don't even have reliable internet or computers. It's creating this big gap in who can benefit from ML in education. If they want these new tools to help all students, they've got to figure out how to get everyone connected, no matter where they're from or how much money they have, which is a major challenge the government's all around the world are trying to solve.

3. There's a tricky thing about ML - it can accidentally favor some groups over others if people aren't careful. If the data used to train these models doesn't represent everyone equally, they could end up with a system that gives better advice to some students and worse advice to others. That's not at all ideal for real word use cases. Hence, it is crucial to make sure that data used to train these models is diverse, so everyone gets a fair shot at learning.

4. **Training the Faculty:** For ML to be effective, teachers need to be comfortable using these tools and interpreting the data they generate. This requires ongoing training and support to help educators integrate ML technologies into their teaching strategies. For instance, taking the case we discussed before, if a teacher wants to use a tool to grade assignments, they

need to learn how to define the grading criteria as it will be different for different scenarios.

That is all for this section. We went through two very important industries and how ML is used to create an overall positive impact. Now, let's see how these industries work on creating these innovative ML applications and what is involved in terms of planning, research, implementation and deployment.

8.2 How to Develop a Machine Learning Application

In the last section, we covered how machine learning is used in various industries and just how impactful it is for everyone, including the businesses and the end-users. However, developing these applications is in no way an easy task. It involves a lot of different steps and in this section, we will take a deeper dive into how we can develop such an advanced application, from scratch. This will not only help you gain information about the process but also provide you with the knowledge you need to start developing your own ML application.

So, let's start with the process. As with everything else, everything starts with a *"great idea"*!

8.2.1 The Idea: Defining the Problem Statement

Although this may look obvious, it is quite difficult to determine which problem will be most beneficial using ML and most importantly, **what are the tradeoffs in doing so**. While it might seem obvious that machine learning could be used to solve many issues, not every problem is an ideal fit for ML. So, how do you determine whether ML is the right approach? Here's how you can define your problem statement:

Identify a Pain Point: The first step is to look for a specific challenge that needs improvement. This could be anything from automating a repetitive task to analyzing vast amounts of data, which a person might be doing manually presently. Then, the next step is to ask yourself, "Can this problem be solved with existing tools or would predictive, data-driven insights make a real difference (in simple terms, machine learning!)?"

Evaluate the Need for ML: Not all problems require ML. For instance, if the task involves rule-based decisions or small datasets, simpler algorithms might work just fine and even provide an upper hand in terms of speed. Machine learning shines when there's a need to recognize patterns in large datasets, predict future outcomes, or make decisions with minimal human input. If your problem fits these characteristics, ML might be the right solution for this problem.

Define Success: You must establish a "**clear success criteria**". What exactly do you want your ML application to achieve? This could be something measurable, like reducing error rates or improving response times. Having a concrete goal will definitely be helpful for the rest of the development process.

Now that we have the idea, and the problem, the next step is to start on the solution. For machine learning, the most important thing that you need is Data, lots of it! So, let's figure out how we can get that.

8.2.2 Gathering and Preparing Data: Fuel for Your Model

Once you've defined the problem, it's time to gather the data that will be used to train your ML model. Data is the fuel that drives the complex ML model vehicles, and having the right data is crucial for building a successful application (imagine powering a petrol engine with diesel, the consequences won't be good). In my opinion, this will be the easiest for you now that you have gone through this book. You already have all the tools and knowledge you need to define a successful and most importantly, a working solution for your problem (I bet those Python implementations will come in clutch now). Anyways, let's go through some points you should focus on during this step.

1. **Collecting Relevant Data:** As always, the first step involves gathering as much relevant data as possible from various sources to create a diverse and informative dataset. For example, if you're building an ML model to predict how likely a customer is to return to your platform, you'll need a lot of data on customer behavior, transaction histories, demographics, and much more. This data can come from a variety of sources like databases, APIs, sensors, or even manual human entries. In some cases, you may need to generate synthetic data to supplement your dataset for certain very rarely occurring cases which are still important to capture (for instance, fraud transactions).

2. **Data Processing:** Raw data is often messy, incomplete, and inconsistent as it isn't collected keeping machine learning models in mind. Hence, Data Preprocessing is crucial and it involves removing or fixing errors, dealing with missing values, and standardizing certain data formats. This step is time-consuming but essential to ensure your model learns from reliable, high-quality, and accurate data.

3. **Feature Engineering:** This is where you transform your raw data into the features that will be fed into your ML model. For example, you might extract key metrics like average purchase value, customer interaction frequency, or time spent on a website. Feature engineering helps highlight the most relevant patterns and relationships in the data, improving model accuracy. This is the step where the majority of the brain storming happens. However, we now have Neural Network based models that have this Feature Engineering baked into the model itself! So, model selection is also crucial, which will be covered in the later section.

4. **Splitting the Data:** Finally, once you have the final data, you'll need to split your data into training, validation, and test sets. The training data is used to train the model, the validation set is used to tune the model's parameters and choose the best ones, and the test data is used to evaluate its

performance to obtain the best model. Ensuring that your data is properly split prevents the model from overfitting (i.e., becoming too tailored to your training data) and gives us a model that is generalized and can work well in all the scenarios we throw at it (some we wouldn't even have thought of).

Perfect, we now have the data we need for our application's model training. The next part is obvious, right? Choosing the right model!

8.2.3 Model Development: Choosing and Training the Model

Now comes the core of the development process—choosing the right machine learning model and training it on your dataset. This is a very important step in this entire lifecycle as once you finalize on a model architecture, it is very difficult, time consuming and expensive to change the model later on as choosing to do so would mean that the entire process needs to be repeated.

1. **Model Selection:** There are many types of ML models, from linear regression to neural networks. The type of model you choose greatly depends on the nature of the problem you're solving and the data you have. For example, decision trees or random forests might be suitable for classification problems, while convolutional neural networks (CNNs) are great for image recognition and classification as we saw in the previous chapters. Moreover, it also depends on factors like how critical the application is. If it is a time sensitive transaction, using a mix of accurate and simpler but faster models would be preferred over a complex and slower model. Hence, as I said before, it's all about managing tradeoffs.

2. **Training the Model:** During training, your model learns from the data by finding patterns and relationships and training to generalize over them by setting its parameters. So, this is done by feeding the model a set of inputs and

adjusting its parameters (weights) to minimize errors in its predictions. This can take anywhere from a few minutes to several hours (or even days) of compute resources depending on the type of model you have chosen and the training process. So, it's imperative to ensure the data is of high quality and useful so this process doesn't have to be repeated.

3. **Model Fine Tuning:** During training, you'll use your validation set to evaluate the model's performance with different hyperparameter values. This can be done through various metrics. Some common metrics include the ones we have already explored in the previous chapters, namely accuracy, precision, recall, and F1-score, depending on the type of task (classification, regression, etc.).

4. **Avoiding Overfitting:** One common challenge is ensuring that your model generalizes well to new data. Overfitting occurs when the model learns the training data too well, capturing noise rather than underlying patterns. This is done by using the test data, which is not used during the training phase, which gives us a better idea on how our model performs on previously unseen data. Additionally, techniques like cross-validation, regularization, and dropout (for neural networks) help prevent overfitting.

Perfect, now we have our final ML model for the application. This is where you can stop when doing a proof of concept to verify that you can indeed use ML to solve a problem. However, when working in the industry, there is one very important step which is still remaining: Deployment.

8.2.4 Implementation and Integration: Bringing Your Model to Life

Once you're satisfied with your model's performance, it's time to implement it and add it into an actual application. This step involves embedding the ML model into a larger system that end-users can interact with. Deployment is the primary and a very important step.

1. **Model Deployment:** Deployment refers to making your model accessible through an application, website, or other platforms. This might involve creating an API that other software systems can call to get predictions from your model. Services like AWS SageMaker, Google Cloud AI, or Microsoft Azure make it easier to deploy ML models into production environments as you don't have to worry about the infrastructure management and monitoring, the cloud platform does that for you. Hence, you can focus on your model.

2. **Integration with Existing Systems:** This is a crucial consideration that ensures that your ML model can integrate smoothly with your existing systems, whether it's a website, a mobile app, or a backend service. This integration often involves software development teams working together to ensure seamless communication between the model and other components of the application with minimal changes in the existing systems.

3. **Monitoring and Maintenance:** Once deployed, it's important to continuously monitor the model's performance in the actual application. Data often changes over time in most cases, meaning that a model that works well presently might not perform as well tomorrow. Regularly retraining (or rather fine-tuning) your model with fresh data helps it stay accurate and relevant. This basically means that we tweak our existing parameters a bit to accommodate these data changes.

Perfect, now we have a deployed machine learning application. However, there should be a way to test just how effective it is and what impact it has on the existing system. This is where testing comes in for the clutch.

8.2.5 Testing and Refining: Improving the User Experience

Before launching your ML application to the public, thorough testing is critical to ensure it functions properly for real-world users, which can be done through various testing techniques.

- **User Testing:** Gather feedback from real users to understand how well the ML model integrates into the user experience. Does it provide accurate predictions? Is it easy to use? Does it improve the user's workflow? Early user feedback can help you catch any issues and refine the application before a full release. *We can do this by exposing our new application to a fixed set of users and gathering information about their experience from them.*

- **A/B Testing:** In many cases, you might want to compare the performance of your ML-driven solution against a non-ML version (or an older version) through something called A/B testing. This allows you to see if the ML model is genuinely improving outcomes and delivering value.

Hence, we saw that developing an ML application, from idea to deployment, involves several critical steps. It begins with a clear problem definition and the collection of high-quality data, followed by building, training, and evaluating your model. Finally, integrating this model into real-world applications and continuously improving it ensures that the solution remains relevant and valuable. With the right approach and tools, you can successfully develop an ML application that solves real-world problems and drives meaningful impact. This marks the end of this section. Now, let's move to a very important and sensitive topic: **"Ethics in Machine Learning"**.

8.3 Ethics in Machine Learning

With the rise of powerful Large Language Models (LLMs) such as **OpenAI's ChatGPT, Google's Gemini**, and other advanced natural language processing systems, ethical considerations in machine learning (ML) have taken on new urgency. LLMs, capable of generating human-like text, have been widely adopted in applications ranging from chatbots and content creation to legal drafting and customer service automation (I bet most of you will be using ChatGPT at least once a day). This has given rise to a wealth of startups aiming to solve various problems using this very technology. However, the widespread use of these models has raised new ethical challenges, especially around issues of bias, misinformation, transparency, and privacy. In this section, we will briefly touch on the ethical concerns specific to this recent boom in LLM-based applications.

8.3.1 Why Ethics Matter in this Scenario?

LLMs are trained on vast amounts of data, including text from books, websites, social media, and more. Basically, they are trained on a huge chunk of the Internet. Hence, they have the ability to generate coherent, contextually appropriate language responses for questions on various industries like education, healthcare, and entertainment. However, their growing influence raises significant ethical questions. The decisions made by LLMs—whether generating responses in a customer service bot or assisting in medical diagnoses—can have real-world consequences, and these systems are often opaque and difficult to interpret.

LLMs, like other ML models, are not inherently neutral. They learn patterns from data that often reflects societal biases of humans, and without careful regulation, they can perpetuate harmful stereotypes, misinformation, or even amplify malicious content. In fact, there have been several incidents regarding this, which should be considered a well intentioned warning. In addition to this, privacy is a major concern given the increasing amount of data breaches in recent times. It's entirely possible that an LLM is trained using some really personal and private datasets. As these models become more ingrained in our daily lives, ensuring that they behave ethically is crucial to prevent unintended hate. On top of that, these models have the capability to learn from what is fed to them as questions and as its use increases, so does the data fed to it. Without proper technical literacy, people tend to provide their personal information to these systems, which is a major concern. Let's now discuss some key ethical concerns.

8.3.2 Key Ethical Issues in LLM-Based Machine Learning

1. **Bias and Fairness:** One of the most critical ethical concerns in LLMs is bias, which can manifest in their outputs based on the data they are trained on. Since LLMs are fed with vast datasets from the internet and other sources, they often absorb biases present in that data. On top of that, they also learn from the questions they are asked, which comes with their own set of challenges. This could result in outputs that reflect or even reinforce harmful stereotypes related to race, gender, or socioeconomic status. For example, an LLM used in an automated hiring system might unfairly favor certain demographic groups over others if the data used to train the model was biased.

2. Addressing fairness in LLMs requires a lot of effort from some really big governments and organizations, such as defining guidelines for curating balanced, and ethically viable datasets, applying fairness constraints during model training, and regularly auditing the systems for biased behavior.

3. **Misinformation and Hallucination:** One of the most problematic issues with LLMs is their tendency to produce outputs that sound confident but are factually incorrect or completely fabricated—commonly known as "**hallucinations**". This is primarily because LLMs are ideally new word predictors so they can generate very, should I say, "real sounding) content which is actually non-existent. This can lead to the spread of misinformation, especially in contexts where users trust the model's output without verifying its accuracy.

- **Impact on Trust and Safety:** When LLMs generate inaccurate information in sensitive domains like healthcare or finance, the consequences can be devastating and can have life and death implications. For instance, a medical assistant powered by an LLM might suggest a treatment plan based on incorrect data, leading to dangerous outcomes. So, choosing where to use LLMs is also a very important consideration.

- **Combatting Hallucinations:** While LLMs are not yet perfect at filtering out incorrect information, efforts are being made to fine-tune models, increase fact-checking capabilities, and reduce the likelihood of hallucinations in critical applications. This can be done by training LLMs to provide verifiable sources on the web from where it has generated a particular piece of information.

4. **Transparency and Explainability:** LLMs are often seen as **"black boxes"** because their decision-making processes are complex and not easily interpretable. They essentially use the Internet to predict the next word based on the content provided to it. Users and developers may not fully understand how an LLM arrives at a particular output, making it difficult to explain decisions in high-stakes areas such as legal advice or loan approvals. This lack of transparency can undermine accountability and trust in LLM-powered systems.

5. **Privacy and Data Security:** LLMs require large datasets for training, often containing sensitive personal information which needs special attention, which are often overlooked. This raises concerns about privacy, especially when LLMs are used in industries handling confidential data, like healthcare or finance. If personal information is unintentionally leaked through generated text or if data is mishandled during training, it could lead to serious privacy violations. This is particularly true for today's conversational chatbots like ChatGPT, which are becoming

an essential part of a person's life (with their integration coming to our cell phones now).

- **Data Anonymization:** LLM developers must ensure that the training data is properly anonymized so that no personal details are ever revealed in the model's responses.

- **Handling Sensitive Data:** Special care is required when LLMs are used in applications that process a lot of sensitive information like a person's medical or financial records. For example, an AI-driven customer service bot must avoid revealing or misusing particular customer data during interactions with other customers.

Now that we know about the concerns when it comes to the use of LLM-based ML applications, let's see some solutions that are being implemented as of now to address these challenges.

8.3.3 Ensuring Fairness in LLM Applications

Ensuring fairness in LLMs essentially involves designing these systems to avoid discriminating against individuals or groups based on characteristics such as race, gender, or age. In applications like automated customer support, educational tools, or personalized content recommendations, fairness is crucial to ensure that all users are treated equally and that the algorithms do not favor one group over another in any scenario. However, with the inherent bias present in the data, this is quite a challenging task to solve.

However, LLMs often reflect the biases present in the vast datasets they are trained on, which can lead to unequal treatment. For example, an LLM used for legal document drafting might generate language that is unintentionally biased toward or against certain demographics if trained on skewed historical data.

Mitigating bias in LLMs requires:

- **Diverse and Balanced Datasets:** Ensuring that the training data represents a wide array of voices, perspectives, and experiences can help minimize bias.

- **Bias Testing:** Developers can run regular audits and bias tests to identify and address areas where the LLM may be producing biased or unfair outputs.

8.3.4 Mitigating Bias and Hallucinations in LLMs

Addressing bias in LLMs is a complex task, but it is essential for ensuring that these systems are used ethically. Developers can use a variety of methods to reduce bias and hallucinations in LLMs:

1. **Bias Mitigation Techniques:** Here are some technological supported solutions to address bias:

   - **Data Augmentation:** One way to reduce the bias in the data is by augmenting the training data to include underrepresented groups or viewpoints, thereby creating a more balanced dataset. This can be done using techniques like synthetic data generation and data replication.

   - **Algorithmic Fairness:** Incorporating fairness constraints during the training process like ensuring equal and unbiased performance across all groups helps ensure that the model's predictions do not favor any one group unfairly.

2. **Reducing Hallucinations:** As we already discussed, Hallucinations can greatly impact the effectiveness of LLMs. So, let's take a look at some techniques you can use to reduce their occurrence:

   - **Post-Training Calibration:** After training, LLMs can be fine-tuned or calibrated to reduce the likelihood of generating hallucinations, especially in high-risk applications such as legal or medical advice. For instance, you can train it to respond with a generic message saying it does not have enough information for all the questions it cannot answer.

   - **Fact-Checking Mechanisms:** Integrating real-time fact-checking tools like adding content reference and fact checking algorithms into LLM applications can help ensure that generated content is accurate and reliable, especially in critical areas like journalism or customer support.

In the end, I would just like to say that this rise of LLMs has revolutionized how we interact with technology, offering unprecedented capabilities in language understanding and generation that we didn't have access to until now. However, these advancements come with ethical challenges—such as bias, misinformation, and privacy—that must be addressed to ensure these models are used responsibly. As LLMs continue to evolve and integrate more deeply into various applications, developers, users, and regulators must work together to navigate these ethical complexities and create a more just and transparent future for AI-driven technologies. In fact, there are steps already being taken to create stricter data privacy laws to ensure that LLMs are trained on fair datasets.

Finally, let's conclude this book by taking a look at the future and seeing where machine learning will take us in the next two decades!

8.4 The Future of Machine Learning

Looking at the current pace of development, we can be sure that machine learning (ML) will continue to transform our world in exciting and profound ways. Here are three key developments that, according to me, will shape the next 20 years and will have a profound impact on humanity as a whole.

8.4.1 Advancements in Generative AI and Artificial General Intelligence

One of the most exciting areas of ML is the progress toward **Artificial General Intelligence (AGI),** which is quite a hot topic right now. It essentially means a computer powered human brain with all its abilities. Today's generative AI models, like the large language models we use for chatbot applications, are already impressive, but they are just the beginning. They don't have a reasoning capability as of now, limiting them to just specific cases. AGI will take this a step further by enabling machines to learn and perform a wide range of tasks without human intervention at all. This could lead to major breakthroughs in everything from healthcare to automation, making machines smarter and more capable of solving complex problems on their own. Although getting to this point in 20 years is not as likely, we will definitely get a lot closer than we are today. However, the flip side of it is that with computers that can think, there is always a chance of a machine doing something which could be a threat to humans (as it comes to a conclusion that it would solve the problem). So, ethics and privacy are also important factors to consider to balance this explosive innovation.

8.4.2 The Growing Importance of Ethical Machine Learning

As ML becomes a bigger part of our everyday lives, ethical concerns are becoming more important than ever. Issues like **bias, fairness, privacy**, and **transparency** will be major focuses in the years to come. In fact, there are Governments and companies are already working on new rules and frameworks to make sure ML is used responsibly and fairly. There are organizations being set up for this that will be key to building trust in AI and ensuring that its benefits are shared by everyone, without causing harm or discrimination.

8.4.3 Tackling Global Challenges with Machine Learning

Machine learning will be a crucial tool in addressing some of the biggest challenges our planet is facing right now, like climate change, healthcare, and fossil fuel shortage. ML can help us develop better climate models, optimize energy use, improve agricultural practices to ensure a sustainable future and even help us develop alternative energy sources at a much faster rate. In healthcare, it will drive innovations in disease prevention, personalized medicine, and global health systems. As we confront these global challenges, ML will be at the forefront, helping to find smarter, more efficient solutions.

In summary, the future of machine learning is full of possibilities. With advancements in AGI, a stronger focus on ethics, and its potential to tackle global issues, ML will continue to shape a smarter, fairer, and more sustainable world.